For Arlen +

Every good Jewish
Home should have!.
this book - Read it!
Live it! + only good can
come from practicing it.

Happy New Year 9/80

Love
Mom + Dad

THE GLORY
OF THE
JEWISH HOLIDAYS

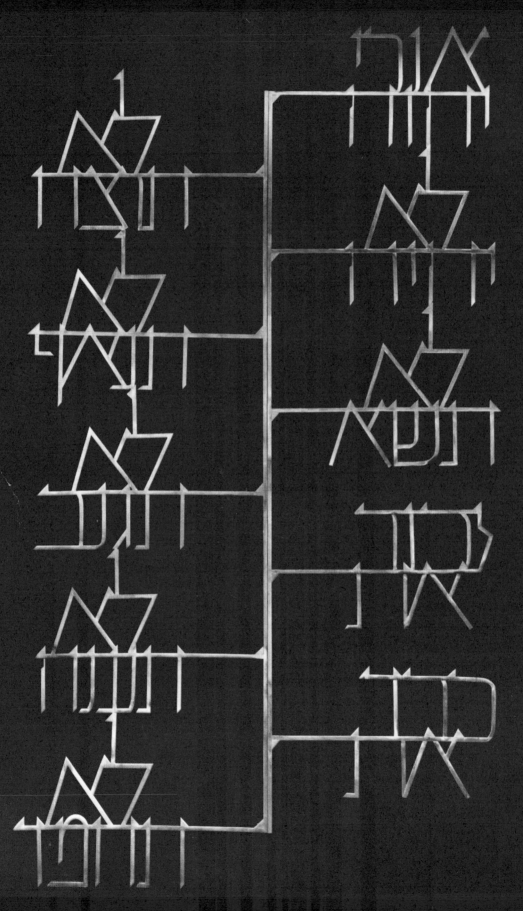

The Ten Commandments, cast in bronze, eight feet high, by Ludwig Y. Wolpert, for Mizrach (eastern) wall of a synagogue.

THE GLORY
OF THE
JEWISH HOLIDAYS

by

HILLEL SEIDMAN

Edited by Moses Zalesky

SHENGOLD PUBLISHERS, INC.

New York City

Library of Congress Catalog Card Number: 68-58504

Published by Shengold Publishers, Inc., New York

Copyright © 1968 by Shengold Publishers, Inc.

First Edition, 1969

Contents

JERUSALEM 1875

To Sarah and our children: Ruchama, Miriam, Abraham-Moshe and Naomi — the Sabbath of my life

INTRODUCTION

THE HOLIDAYS ARE EXTERNAL manifestations of internal turbulences. When we look at a tall, majestic mountain, we are awed by its magnificence, but are totally oblivious to the agitations beneath that have lifted it above the surrounding plain. Nor do we stop to consider the multiform layers that have folded and piled up, one atop the other, to raise that mountain.

So it is with the holidays. They do not represent an ordinary organic process of growth. They are, rather, the product of upheavals, the result of revolutionary events that have radically shaken the pre-existing, "normal" world order. They came into being as a consequence of happenings that had brought about a turning-point, created an epoch, given direction to a people's history for hundreds, even thousands of years, changing and shaping the character of that people.

Every holiday has its nature, its meaning and its effect. Each festival was created for its appointed time as a result of a "volcanic eruption," as it were, in the history of the people and, once emerged, each festival helped mold that people's essence and image.

Therefore, the inner character of the nation is not revealed during uneventful week-days. It is the holiday and the festival that provide a most reliable criterion to him who would evaluate the spirit of the House of Israel and of every man within it. The true strength of group and individual alike can be gauged only by their finest hour. The true common denominator is neither the lowest nor the mean—but only the highest.

It follows then that in order to assess the spiritual qualities of the Jewish people, we must delve into the nature of its holidays and festivals which faithfully reflect the very soul of the Jew and Judaism. This requires probing below the surface, penetration into the deeper layers of history, investigation of the forces and factors underlying the turbulences and upheavals whose external manifestation the holidays and festivals represent. It is necessary to scrutinize the origin of every festival and to determine how it became rooted in the people's national and religious consciousness and how it permeated every aspect of the people's way of life.

Such is the object of the survey contained in the following pages in which an attempt will be made to examine in depth the historical background, specific content, meaning, laws and customs pertaining to each festival of the Jewish year. For just as one cannot enter into the holiday without physical or spiritual preparation, so, too, one cannot comprehend its significance without an understanding of how it came to be, and how it evolved into what it is today.

This book is an attempt to prepare the reader for the experience of the Jewish holidays. Its aim is to help maintain and strengthen the continuity of the sacred traditions of Judaism and of Jewish awareness in the face of the corrosive influence of a religiously indifferent environment.

Of late, a glimmer of hope has appeared on a horizon which until quite recently seemed bleak indeed. The secularist and materialistic orientation which for decades crowded out Jewish ways of living and thinking has proven disenchanting, and our "moderns," particularly our younger generation, are seeking a new philosophy to fill the vacuum in their hearts and minds.

If this book will encourage the reader to delve further into the teachings of Judaism, I will feel that my efforts have been rewarded.

I respectfully acknowledge my gratitude to H. E. Zalman Shazar, President of the State of Israel, for the personal encouragement he gave to me and for his gracious permission to use an excerpt from his memoirs, *Morning Stars,* published in the United States by the Jewish Publication Society of America.

My deepest appreciation goes to Moshe Sheinbaum, President of Shengold Publishers, who conceived the idea of this book. He gathered the many illustrations that enhance the text, and spared no effort to make THE GLORY OF THE JEWISH HOLIDAYS a work truly worthy of its title.

H. S.

March, 1969
Nisan, 5729

LIST OF ILLUSTRATIONS

LIST OF ILLUSTRATIONS (con't)

ACKNOWLEDGMENTS

I am happy to join the author, Dr. Hillel Seidman, in expressing profound gratitude to Dr. Moses Zalesky who, in addition to his skillful, meticulous editing, has contributed writings of his own to the present volume and has greatly helped us with his invaluable counsel.

Thanks go to Miss Gertrude Hirschler for helpful advice and constructive suggestions.

The following noted artists have most kindly consented to have their work reproduced in this book: Chaim Gross—paintings and *menora;* Sol Nodel—illuminations; Ludwig Y. Wolpert and Moshe Zabari—ceremonial objects; Mrs. Sidney L. Quitman—tapestry and hand-woven *tallit.* To them, my heartfelt appreciation.

I am deeply indebted to Mr. Felix Kraus for his expertise on art, and to Mr. Alexander Bistritzky, Dr. A. Kanof and Mr. Isadore M. Marder for illustrations from their collections of ceremonial objects.

I am profoundly thankful to the staff of The Israel Museum in Jerusalem for affording me the opportunity of choosing illustrations from the Museum's treasures of Jewish art.

The outstanding illustrations placed at my disposal by Mr. Y. L. Bialer, Curator of the Museum of Hechal Shlomo in Jerusalem, are greatly appreciated.

The Jewish Museum of New York very kindly opened its photographic files to us for study and picture selection, and the Museum of the Hebrew Union College, Cincinnati, Ohio, made available to us reproductions from its collection of ceremonial objects.

I am particularly indebted to the Israel Office of Information in New York and to Consul Malka Ben Yosef for their help in enriching this volume with illustrations of life in Israel.

Finally, I thank Mrs. Reene Kreincses for the infinite care and patience which she devoted to the technical preparation of the manuscript for publication.

The Publisher

Menora. Modern by Chaim Gross, Temple Adath Jeshurun, Elkins Park, Pa. It may be used either as a seven-branch candelabrum or, with the additional lights, as a Hanukka menora.

THE GLORY OF THE JEWISH HOLIDAYS

ON THE SURFACE, it seems that *Halakha** governs the Jewish holidays, and law, by its very nature, is cold and impersonal. In reality, however, the Jewish holidays are a rare blend of *Halakha and Aggada,* of law and legend, of prose and poetry. Strange as it may seem, even sober, prosaic *Halakha* has contributed to the splendor of thé Jewish holidays. Just as there is law in poetry, so, at least in the Jewish way of life, there is poetry in law. No wonder, then, that the recapitulation of the Law of

---

* The legal teachings of the Oral Tradition as distinct from *Aggada.*

11

Torah crown. This keter of Eastern European origin features a pressed design, birds, and the little bells found on many such ornaments. (The Jewish Museum, New York City).

Moses in the Book of Deuteronomy ends with the statement: "So Moses recited the words of *this song* . . ." (Deut. 31:30).

Without a doubt, there is beauty in the observance of command ments involving spiritual obligations. This is all the more true of the Jewish festivals which, in essence, represent an expression of esthetic ideas in symbolic terms. A case in point is the elaborate ceremonial that is part of the celebration of Passover. Slavery debases the spirit while freedom ennobles the soul. Freedom, holiness and beauty are all aspects of the harmony of Jewish life and thought. It is written in the Holy Scriptures: "You shall *hallow* the fiftieth year " (Lev. 25:10). And how is this to be done? "Proclaim liberty throughout the land to all its inhabitants" (ibid.). Holiness, *ipso facto*, implies human dignity; human dignity is inconceivable without liberty. And liberty, in turn, endows life with beauty. Only when the Israelites emerged from the crucible of enslavement and were purified by the miracle of their redemption could they become worthy of receiving the Divine Commandments. Thus was molded a nation responsive to lofty ideals; a nation that could appreciate the true glory of the "ways of pleasantness" contained in the Law of God. And so, too, it is with all the other holy days of Israel, as though a master educator had succeeded in creating a people whose true spiritual nature is most strikingly revealed on its festive occasions.

While the artists of ancient Greece carved statues of granite and chiseled away at cold marble, the Sages of Israel fashioned a Jewish personality in the flesh—alive, and capable of thought and action. *Halakha* created a people steeped in Torah and steadfast in its faith—a phenomenal people indeed. Verse 11 in Chapter 30 of the Book of Deuteronomy should be interpreted: "For this commandment (the Torah) is no more marvelous than you," meaning that although the Torah is indeed a wondrous creation, you, the Jew, are no less extraordinary than your Law.

Prayerbook cover. This silver repoussé prayerbook cover was made in Italy in the 17th century. The decoration on the right-hand cover depicts the sacrifice of Isaac (Gen. 22:1-18). (The Israel Museum, Jerusalem).

Illustrated chapter heading from an edition of the Hebrew Bible by Daniel Bomberg, Venice, 1517. This is the opening section of the Book of Psalms: "Happy is the man that walks not in the counsel of the ungodly . . ." (Psalm 1).

How, then, did the Jew manage to make his way through the jungle of nations and to overcome the obstacles forever piled upon his path by cruel foes? No doubt it was his Sabbaths and festivals, the shining moments in his life, that raised his morale, elevated his spirit, and so enabled him to overcome the vicissitudes of his struggle for survival. It is the Sabbaths and the festivals that kept the beauty of Jewish life from withering, that guarded human dignity from debasement and decay in the misery of exile.

While other nations reared imposing structures of stone and steel, the Jew has built fortresses of the spirit. He continued to evolve more laws and customs for his Sabbaths and festivals, integrating these commandments and practices into his way of life and absorbing them into his very heart and soul, until there shone forth the wonder that found expression in the Jewish holidays.

Take, for instance, the Sabbath. Here an abstract concept of time was transformed into an inspiring image, that of the "Sabbath Queen"— a vision of splendor and magnificence, raising individual and community alike to new spiritual heights. At the concluding verse of the familiar hymn *Lekhah Dodi* ("Go forth, My Beloved"), the worshipers turn to the door of the synagogue to welcome the Queen with reverence and affection, chanting, "Come O Bride, come O Bride, Sabbath Queen . . ." The disciples of the saintly Ari* went even further. Not

* Rabbi Isaac Luria   (1534-1572)), leader of religious mystics (Cabalists) in Safed, Palestine.

14

Wall carpet from synagogue. Turkish, 17th century. Hebrew inscription is from Psalm 118: "This is the gate of the Lord; the righteous may enter into it."

satisfied with merely welcoming the royal visitor on the threshold of the sanctuary, they went beyond the walls of the city, out into the fields and mountains, toward the setting sun, to usher her in with love, longing and joy.

Thus the Sabbaths and festivals were imbued with a living soul so that they became a transcendent, inspiring reality.

In oral as well as in written tradition, the esthetic factor ranks high in the observance of Sabbaths and festivals. The Psalms consistently refer to the intimate association between beauty and holiness: "Bow down to the Lord in the beauty of holiness" (29:2); "The voice of the Lord resounds with majesty" (29:4); "Out of Zion, the perfection of

The etching on this glass goblet (Germany, 19th century) represents the synagogue of Bad Karlsruhe. (The Jewish Museum, New York City).

beauty, the Lord shines forth" (50:2) ; and "Strength and beauty are in His sanctuary." (96:6) .

In every generation, poets of Israel, from Shlomo Alkabetz* and Yehuda Halevi** of bygone centuries down to our own day, have exalted the beauty of the Sabbath and of the festivals. The Jewish people as a whole, from men of wisdom, learning and vision down to the common masses, beautified these occasions with lovely settings and fine utensils, as well as with dignified conduct and distinctive mores which reflected glory not only upon the celebrations but also upon the celebrants.

Our sages, of blessed memory, have instituted benedictions not merely over acts of physical pleasure, but also over esthetic joys. "Whosoever says: 'How goodly is this morsel, blessed be He Who has brought it forth'; whosoever says: 'How lovely are these figs, blessed be He Who has created them'—therein lies their blessedness. Moreover, when beholding handsome people and beautiful trees, one should recite the benediction: 'Blessed be He Who has dealt thus with his world.'" (Tosefta) .

  * Cabalistic poet of the sixteenth century, author of the Sabbath hymn *"Lekhah Dodi"* mentioned above.
** Celebrated Hebrew poet (1086-1145) of the Golden Age in Spain.

Ark of the Law. This modern-style Ark of the Law with the Ten Commandments on the doors and the Eternal Light (above) decorated with the signs of the Zodiac is the work of Ludwig Y. Wolpert. (YWHA Chapel, New York City).

Truly, here is appreciation for both beauty and religious values. The gratification of our senses by the beauties of man and nature, or by a sublime work of art obligates us to perform a religious act: the recitation of a blessing of thanks to the Almighty. Now if this is so in the case of secular objects, it is all the more relevant in things holy—Sabbaths and festivals where esthetic enjoyment and fulfillment of Divine law blend into one harmonious whole.

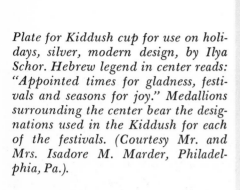

Plate for Kiddush cup for use on holidays, silver, modern design, by Ilya Schor. Hebrew legend in center reads: "Appointed times for gladness, festivals and seasons for joy." Medallions surrounding the center bear the designations used in the Kiddush for each of the festivals. (Courtesy Mr. and Mrs. Isadore M. Marder, Philadelphia, Pa.).

The festivals are closely bound up with the appreciation of beauty in nature, for they are based primarily upon natural phenomena hallowed by seasons of rejoicing and thanksgiving. Pesah is the festival of spring, **Shavuot** is the feast of the first fruits, and Sukkot marks the late harvest. The fragrance of the good earth, the exhilerating miracle of growth, flowering and fruition which emanate from them all serve to bring the Jew, who is basically a city-dweller, close to tree, meadow, field and orchard; to grain and fruit of earth and tree, from the time of sprouting to the season of ingathering. Each festival bears the fragrance of garden and vineyard, the joy of planting, harvesting, and idyllic tranquility: "Each man under his grape-vine and his fig tree" (I Kings 5:5 and elsewhere).

The green branches and brightly colored flowers adorning Jewish homes and sanctuaries on Shavuot; the leaves and fruits that decorate the *sukka;* the symbols of spring incorporated into the Pesah *seder* service —all these are visible manifestations of the beauty which has become an integral part of these festivities.

The spirit of growth and vitality keeps Jewish festival observance from degenerating into dead formalism. Like life itself, they undergo continuous change and rejuvenation. The annual cycle of nature is reflected in the annual round of the festivals whose anticipation from year to year is, in itself, an exciting experience.

The *Mahzor,* or the High Holiday prayer-book, is a structure of singular harmony. Its poetry is magnificent; the traditional melodies for the various prayers are moving and inspiring. Even the physical aspect

18

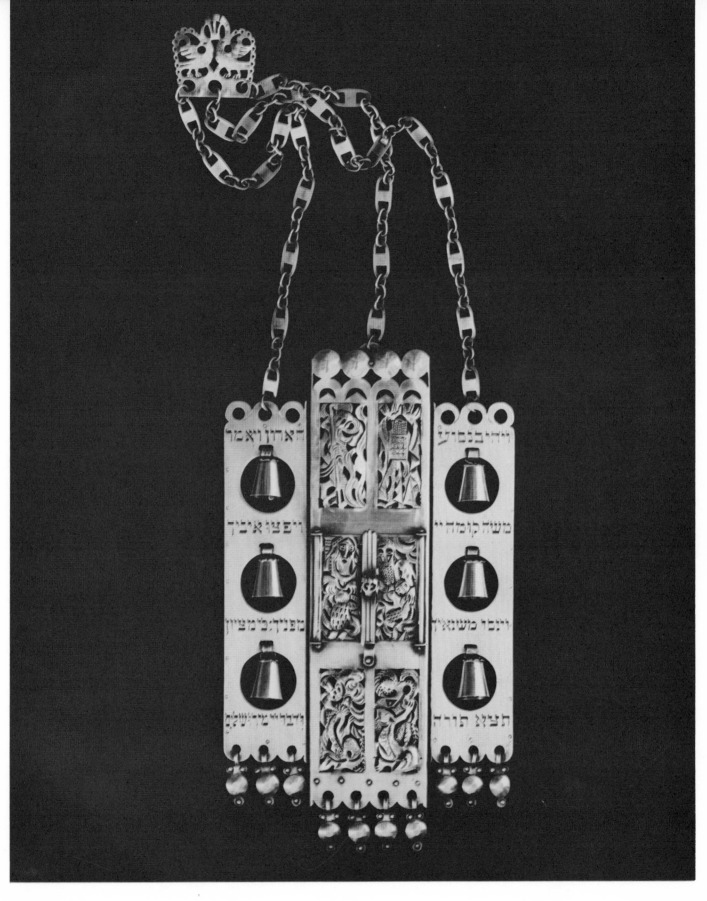

Torah breastplate. Modern silver by Ilya Schor. Hebrew inscription is the prayer recited when the Scrolls of the Law are removed from the Ark: "And it came to pass, when the Ark set forward, that Moses said: 'Rise up, O Lord, and Thine enemies shall be scattered, and they that hate Thee shall flee before Thee. For out of Zion shall go forth the Law, and the Word of the Lord from Jerusalem.'" (Collection of Temple Beth-El of Great Neck, N. Y.)

Tallit (prayer shawl), contemporary design, all silk, narrow, and gracefully shaped attara woven with gold thread into the tallit. Design by Mrs. Sidney L. Quitman, Philadelphia, Pa.

of the synagogue with its special holiday decor of white, the color of purity, contributes to the beauty and solemnity of the occasion.

Our sages repeatedly stressed the importance of external appearance and esthetic atmosphere at religious services. They went so far as to prohibit a scholar from meditating on the Law amid improper surroundings. The attainment of the high esthetic standards which characterize the Jewish holidays necessitates complete coordination between form and content, between matter and spirit.

Harmony must reign also between the inherent values of the festivals and their manifestations in actual observance. Many details go into the creation of an architectural entity. But lest sight be lost of its total composition, such a structure must be viewed in its overall perspective. At the same time, however, it must also be examined with close attention to its details the more to appreciate their place and function in the artist's overall scheme. Similarly, in the proper evaluation of any Jewish holiday, we should not only view it in its harmonious whole but also delve deeply into its laws and customs—the colorful pieces that fit so admirably into the complete mosaic of that festive occasion.

The beauty of the Sabbath and the festivals serves a dual function—it sets the Jewish community apart from its non-Jewish environment, while at the same time serving as the link that has united Jews the world over through four thousand years.

ESSENCE AND FORM

THE JEWISH HOLIDAYS and festivals were not created for external effect. Their chief object is not *decoration*, but *consecration*. Essentially they are intended to appeal to the Jew's inner soul, to stir his mind and heart with the exaltation of holiness.

Nonetheless, the festive observances of the Jew, like all else, have both content and form. Admittedly, form *is* important. The beauty of the Jewish holidays and festivals is a highly significant factor in Jewish living. It is manifest in colorful symbols and activities, each intended to appeal to the personality and to the mental and spiritual sensibilities of those who observe these days of celebration.

It should be understood—as it is realized by every Jew who considers each holiday an integral part of his world—that the preparation for the festival may be a major experience in itself. One cannot be instantaneously transported from the lowliness of the profane to the loftiness of the sacred. One enters holy ground by slow degrees, in fear and trepidation, and only after considerable self-conditioning.

Technical and physical preparations are obviously insufficient. Spiritual readiness is also required.

What with today's electrically-equipped kitchens, refrigeration and efficient methods of food preservation, it no longer takes extraordinary

Synagogue, Holland. This etching of Rembrandt (1648) depicts worshippers at a synagogue in Amsterdam. (The Jewish Museum, New York City).

Torah pointer, silver, Poland, 18th century. A pointer (yad) of precious metal is used to indicate the place during the reading from the Scroll of the Law. In Sephardic congregations the yad is kept in the Ark; in Ashkenazic congregations it is hung over the Scroll by a chain.

efforts or tedious labors to "bring" the holiday into the home; and yet, even today, we find ourselves caught up in a tension on the eve of the Sabbath or of a holiday, even on long summer days when evening comes late and there really is no rush to "get ready" in time. Why should this be so? Because the state to which we aspire is *spiritual readiness* which cannot be conjured up at will or on the spur of the moment. There are times where no amount of effort will invoke the desired mood. When a Jew enters into the holiday while his soul is hollow and irreverent, will the spirit of the holiday enter into him? Will he reflect its radiance and will he glory in its splendor? One man might be blinded by its brilliance; another might be dazzled by its splendor. He may be likened to a wayfarer who travels through magnificent scenery, amidst primeval mountains, rippling streams and blossoming gardens, and keeps his soul's eyes closed to the enchantment of the beauty around him. Still another man might be keenly responsive to the colorful setting and joyful atmosphere of the holiday. The determining factor, then, is perceptive capacity and esthetic sense, as well as desire to apply these qualities to a given situation.

Individuals may even differ in the manner in which they savor the holidays, depending on their personal characteristics and predilections. Some prefer solitary tranquility and silent spiritual exultation while others prefer to celebrate the festival amidst loudly jubilant crowds. Actually, the benediction praising the Lord "Who hallows Israel and the festivals" contains an element of sanctity which, in turn, implies *separation*. But this is in no sense *isolation*; it is separation in the sense of "setting apart" for a special function and purpose. In this instance, "hallowing" signifies the apportionment of a specific amount of time for a sublime objective. Within this time span, the Jew does not isolate himself from the world, but passes from one world into another—from the sphere of the profane to that of the sacred. Only then does the holiday unfold before him in all its shining splendor and heart-warming charm.

The beauty of the holiday is the result of the creativity of generations. In every age, ever since remote antiquity, people have been adorning the holiday with various embellishments whose lines and colors differed in accordance with the taste of each generation and with the spirit of each period. But over and above these time-bound differences, there have stood out basic similarities which have been common to the beauty of holiday observance throughout the ages. Consequently, there has gradually emerged a blend of unity and diversification.

One of the aspects of beauty in Jewish tradition is the extreme contrast between the workday on the one hand, and the Sabbath and festival on the other. The degradation of the daily struggle for existence, its terrors and frustrations, the misery of *galut* life under the heel of tyrants and oppressors—all these vanished completely with the approach of the Sabbath or of the festival. They gave way to beauty—in decorations in homes and synagogues, holiday attire, illuminated sacred books, inspirational song permeated with emotion and ecstasy and echoing the bliss of higher spheres, the yearning for redemption and the elevation of the spirit to the realm of pristine radiance.

The festive decoration of home and synagogue, the creation of religious poetry, the illumination of prayer books, the craftsmanship of ritual objects, the composition of liturgical music and other forms of expression developed through the ages, in consonance with the specific nature and content of each holiday. The resulting beauty was even more unique and admirable when viewed against the background of privation, humiliation and indignity to which the Jew was exposed in the reality of everyday living.

Torah pointer, silver, Poland, 18th century.

There was *originality*, too, in the beauty of the Jewish holidays. Throughout history, even during the more recent era of so-called "emancipation," the Jew had scrupulously observed the precept: "In *their* statutes ye shall not walk." Therefore, he had to be *different*, *original*, unaffected by the "statutes" and customs that had prevailed in the non-Jewish world. Various styles of ritual observance—*nusach Ashkenaz, nusach Sepharad, nusach Polin*—have been evolved among the Jews. But the rituals that developed among the Jews of Germany, Spain or Poland, different though they were, all had in common the fact that each was totally unrelated to the surrounding non-Jewish culture.

Save for these external influences which no people, group, or individual can escape, the beauty of the Jewish holidays has remained inherently original, mainly because it came from within; it was eminently spiritual, derived from the cultural treasure of Judaism. Thus, the Jew persisted in his originality despite his alien environment. Whatever elements Judaism had borrowed from alien cultures were modified and adapted to the Jewish way of life.

The commandment, "Thou shalt not make unto thyself any graven image," has led some non-Jewish observers to the erroneous conclusion that the Jewish people had no sense for beauty. Nothing can be farther from the truth. On the contrary, the Jew has attained a high degree of esthetic development, but it was entirely distinct from that which prevailed in the non-Jewish milieu. Together with luster and splendor, and perhaps at their very core, the Jew has accentuated the qualities of nobility and tenderness which were rooted in his ancient and glorious tradition.

כיור נחושת מזבח העולה לחם הפנים

Ark canopy (Kapporet). This canopy cloth for the Ark of the Law, made in Eastern Europe in the 19th century, depicts the copper laver, the sacrificial altar and the golden table with the twelve loaves of shewbread kept in the Temple in Jerusalem. (The Israel Museum, Jerusalem).

This tradition has found expression in numerous physical manifestations such as synagogue architecture and decoration, the graphic arts and, particularly, in the celebration of holidays and festivals which reflect the majesty and splendor of Judaism.

The distinctiveness of the beauty of Jewish holidays stems from a singular outlook. While Hellenism elevated the beautiful above the good, Judaism stressed the good over the beautiful. Hence, to the Jew, content is more basic than form. It does not follow, however, that Jewish tradition considers external appearances unimportant. On the contrary, form plays a valuable part in every important facet of Jewish living. For example, the numerous laws pertaining to places of worship, as set forth in the *Talmud*, tractate *Berachot*, in the *Shulchan Aruch* and in other codes of religious law attest to the highly-developed esthetic sense among the Jews. Here external beauty constitutes a necessary requisite for worship through prayer. Indeed, our fathers were extremely punctilious regarding the beauty of synagogues and unconditional adherence to the concept: "This is my God and I will glorify Him," since true glorification cannot be achieved without beauty. No wonder, then, that synagogue art was so prominent in Jewish history.

Thus, Jewish tradition has consecrated the element of beauty and raised it from the level of personal choice or taste to the pinnacle of divine worship. It is this transcendental beauty that has been distilled in the observance of our Sabbath and holidays.

24

Italian synagogue. This synagogue of Vittoria Veneto (1702) was brought to Israel and reconstructed in The Israel Museum, Jerusalem. Note the hanging lamps and elaborately carved Ark. (Gift of Jakob Michael in memory of his wife, Erna Sondheimer Michael).

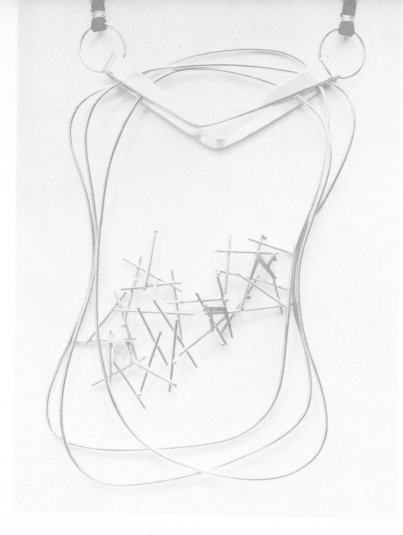

Torah breastplate, silver and gold, contemporary design, by Moshe Zabari.

THE JEWISH HOLIDAYS—A FAMILY CELEBRATION

THE ROLE OF THE FAMILY in Jewish life is particularly evident on Sabbaths and holidays.

We read in Scripture: "And thou shalt rejoice before the Lord thy God, thou, and thy son, and thy daughter" (Deut. 16:11). The celebration of the holidays cannot be complete without the family. The phrase "before the Lord thy God" implies that the delight of each festival is sanctified by the Divine Presence. "Thou, and thy son, and thy daughter" obviously means that the true festival spirit requires the active participation of the entire family.

Attending synagogue services together, sitting down together to festive meals at home, observing all the commandments that are part of each festival—all these acts lend to the holidays the character of family celebrations.

All week long each member of the family goes his own way, busy with his own pursuit. But on the holidays, when all work ceases, the family is reunited by tradition in good cheer and mutual affection. The holidays are a very real cementing force in Jewish family life.

26

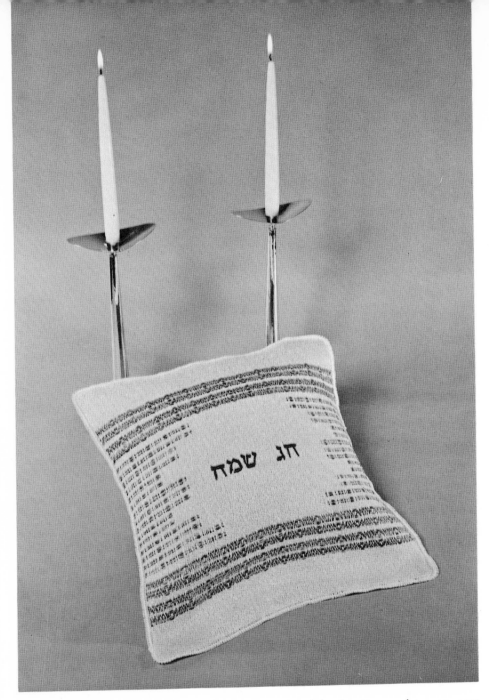

Halla cover for use on holidays, contemporary, hand loomed, tapestry. Hebrew lettering: "Happy Holiday." By Mrs. Sidney L. Quitman, Philadelphia, Pa.

Harmony in family life, so vital to all healthy human existence, was developed to a particularly high degree by the Jews. This tendency was encouraged by two main factors—one environmental and one internal.

The environmental factor was, of course, anti-Semitism. In the lands of oppression, it was from his family that the Jew derived psychological support and found refuge from a hostile environment. His family gave him the strength to cope with the adversities he faced each day. As an individual he felt helpless, isolated in the midst of evil and persecution all around him. It was amidst his near and dear ones that he regained the human dignity which had been trampled by the cruel overlords from whom he was obliged to wrest his daily sustenance.

27

When one member of the family became ill, the entire household joined forces to nurse him back to health. When one member was in distress, all the family would help him in his trouble in true fulfillment of the adage "one for all and all for one."

It was a relationship defined in universal terms by the Roman poet Titus Lucretius:

> "Quo magis in dubiis hominem spectare periclis convenit adversisque in rebus noscere qui sit; nam verae voces tum demum pectore ab imo eliciuntur et eriptur persona, manet res."

("Thus it is more useful to scrutinize a man in danger or peril, and to discern in adversity what manner of a man he is: for only then are the words of truth drawn up from the very heart, the mask is torn off, the man remains.") *

The internal factor was the emphasis which Judaism always placed upon bonds of kinship and the obligations of the individual toward his family. The commandment "honor thy father and thy mother" (Exodus 20:12) not only spells out the duty of children to their parents but also implies the responsibility of parents toward their children. If they are to earn and keep the respect of their children, parents must show respect for their dignity as human beings. The Talmud points out that parents must be careful not to be unduly harsh toward their children, but to exercise the utmost patience and understanding in their relationship with them.

Thus the commandment that bids us honor one's parents also enjoins us to give due respect to our parenthood, or, more accurately, to the responsibilities parenthood entails. Prominent among these responsibilities, incidentally, has been the education of the young. The Biblical precept "and thou shalt teach [the Word of God] diligently to thy children" (Deut. 6:7) has been scrupulously observed in every generation.

Close family ties, hallowed by Torah and tradition, became an integral part of the Jewish way of life. They found their expression in mutual love, trust and responsibility which further strengthened the institution of the Jewish family.

The warm, cordial atmosphere prevailing in the Jewish home was so natural and all-inclusive that demonstrative behavior became utterly unnecessary and was even deemed inconsistent with good taste. The bonds of affection within the Jewish family were so deeply rooted in the consciousness and emotional experience of our people that they were simply taken for granted.

---

* Titus Lucretius Carus, *De Rerum Natura* III, verse 55.

Sabbath lamp. Silver, Poland, 19th century, with eagle decoration.
(The Jewish Museum, New York City).

Of all the social institutions of Judaism, the family was undoubtedly the most vital and fundamental. Its impact upon the individual Jew was incalculable. It has molded his character and determined his way of life. The quality of Jewish family life came to the fore particularly on the holidays, which became milestones in every Jewish household. Certain religious observances, such as the Passover *Seder*, are inconceivable outside the framework of the family. In fact, Sabbaths and festivals are basically family events and have persisted as such among tradition-oriented Jews.

Thus, the Jewish family became the medium through which traditions have been transmitted from generation to generation. This family factor has crossed geographical boundaries, bridged historical epochs and transcended differences of language and culture. Every child born to a Jewish family became a link in the long chain of tradition, an inseparable part of the eternity of Israel, extending beyond time or space. And it was the holidays within the Jewish family circle that became the main channel for this transmission of values, for the historical continuity of Judaism.

Unlike the adherents of other creeds who primarily sense their religious identity through their places of worship, the observant Jew mainly relates to his faith through the home rather than through the synagogue. The genuinely Jewish home, in which the library of sacred books occupied a prominent place and in which the holidays were the spiritual highlights of the year, has therefore had a greater influence on the historical development of our people than the synagogue.

In the song he sang at the Red Sea (Exodus 15), Moses extolled the God *of his father*. It was "my father's God," the God of each family in Israel, Who had enabled the Israelites to walk unharmed through the perilous waves of the sea to dry land.

Through countless generations the Jewish family and home became a very effective extraterritorial enclave, a safe island haven amidst a sea of hostile nations.

It was only at the time of Emancipation, when the walls of the ghetto crumbled, that this extraterritorial enclave threatened to break down. The new winds of Enlightenment swept away time-honored tradition, including the observance of Sabbaths and festivals, and seriously undermined the foundations of home and family. In our own day, this trend assumed sufficiently menacing dimensions to present a grave danger to the basic structure of Judaism.

The "generation gap" has caused a fearsome array of social and psychological problems throughout the world. But its implications for the Jewish people are even more ominous, for they imperil the very survival of the Jews as a distinct group in the Diaspora.

Torah mantle. This richly embroidered Torah mantle was made in Germany in the 18th century. The Hebrew legend near the hem gives the name of the woman in whose honor the mantle was donated. (Hechal Shlomo Museum, Jerusalem).

We have witnessed two manifestations of the disintegration of Jewish traditional values: a rebellion of youth against accepted norms on the one hand, and a moral decline and the pursuit of material pleasures on the other. Amazingly, both these phenomena were envisioned over three thousand years ago by Moses in his farewell oration (Deut. 32) in which he laid down the foundations of Jewish living for all times to come. He referred to the "angry generation" ("the anger of his sons and daughters") and aptly characterized rebellious youth ("for a perverse generation are they") as "children in whom there is no faith." They had revolted against the existing order of things, but having *no faith* and professing no constructive ideals, they could advance no positive values to replace the concepts they considered outworn. Moses castigated them severely: "They have angered Me with their vanities, and I shall incense them with what is *no-nation.*" For their destructive, purposeless rebellion, they were to be punished with a "no-nation" existence—with anarchy, roaming in a no-man's land, without a sense of belonging, without roots, aim or direction.

As to the second category, the snobs and cynics who lapse into a life of empty material pursuits, Moses described them as follows: "Jeshurun grew fat, and he kicked . . . and he forsook the God who made him." (Deut. 32:15) These effete creatures are possessed by a passion for success, status, wealth, luxury, power and physical pleasures, which most of them achieved, thus forfeiting their faith and nation, the spiritual and ethical values of Judaism that give real meaning to the life of the Jew.

It is even more remarkable that in the same last will and testament, Moses should have prescribed the remedy for these ills of society: "Remember the days of old, consider the years of former generations; ask thy father, and he will tell thee; thy elders, and they will say it unto thee." Obviously, the answer lies in a *return to tradition,* a bridging of the gap that could so easily widen into a chasm swallowing up our people. "Ask thy father, thy elder"—this is an unmistakable reference to the *family,* the basic institution in Jewish life which guards our tradition and transmits it from generation to generation. Only such a return can and will reunite and revitalize our people.

The holidays are a potent help in the restoration of the family which, in turn, is the most effective means of bridging the generation gap created by disruptive forces in modern society.

The sanctity with which these observances endow Jewish family life, the joy and harmony they bring to every Jewish household—these are the glory of the Jewish festivals.

Rimonim (Torah headpieces), silver and gold, ca. 1765, Congregation Shearith Israel, New York City. The craftsman, Meyer Myers, was a well-known early American silversmith of Dutch-Sephardic origins.

SABBATH AND FESTIVAL PRAYERS

THERE ARE CONSPICUOUS DIFFERENCES between the weekday liturgy and the Sabbath service, and between Sabbath prayers and the order of worship on festivals. The High Holiday service follows an order completely different from all of these.

One of the main differences between weekday prayers on the one hand, and Sabbath and festival services on the other is that on our Sabbaths and holidays we do not pray for the fulfillment of physical or material wants but solely for spiritual blessings. Thus, the Sages of the Talmud decided to omit from the Sabbath *Amida* the twelve intermediate petitions for bodily vigor and material prosperity that are recited at daily services on weekdays, for "In honor of the Sabbath it is unbecoming to trouble the Almighty [with worldly concerns]" (Berakhot 21) and "One does not plead for one's daily needs on the Sabbath" (Shabbat 15:3). These rulings have been applied to the festival liturgy also.

Festival prayers are not of incidental value: they are part and parcel of the festival itself. Also on the Sabbath, prayer occupies a central position. Maimonides rules: "It is a positive precept to hallow the Sabbath in concrete terms, namely by remembering and sanctifying it "(*Mishne Torah,* Laws of Sabbath, Chapter 29, *Halakha* 1). How can we remember and sanctify the Sabbath in a concrete manner?

On workdays we hustle and bustle to earn our daily sustenance. Making allowance for this fact, the Talmud has kept the weekday liturgy brief. This consideration extends even to the *Minha* (late afternoon) service on the Sabbath. There, fewer men are called to read from the Law than during morning worship, to make sure that the service does not extend beyond the end of the Sabbath but ends early enough to enable the worshippers to prepare for whatever work they may have to do on Saturday night.

But in the observance of the Days of Awe, Rosh HaShana and Yom Kippur, all considerations of time and personal convenience yield place to total concentration on the act of prayer. Prayer is one of the three means by which one can "avert the evil decree" (*Unetane Tokef,* Rosh HaShana Service).

The liturgy of these most solemn days in the Jewish calendar was designed to inspire the worshipper not only by the content of the prayers themselves but through the special, time-honored festival melodies to which the prayers are chanted. *Alenu,* the Hymn of Adoration which

34

Sabbath service in a synagogue. Jews at prayer at a synagogue in 19th century Poland, by Peczely. The men are wearing the traditional shtreimel (fur hat.) (The Jewish Museum, New York City.)

is recited hurriedly, almost perfunctorily, at the conclusion of the week-day service, assumes central prominence in the sequence of the High Holiday ritual and is chanted with particular fervor. The *Kol Nidre,* the highlight of the service on Yom Kippur Eve is, in the reading, a dry, legalistic formula. But the stirring melody to which it is sung the world over endows it with an aura of awe and profound emotion.

Prayer has been characterized as a "service of the heart." In its intensive form, it becomes a deep emotional experience, an expression of yearning for Divine love, grace and protection. In the words of Scripture, "As a deer longs for brooks of water, so does my soul long for Thee, O Lord." The thirst for God stems from an instinctive source, an inborn spark that can be fanned by faith into a burning flame of passionate prayer.

No matter what its style or outer form, prayer can bring peace to a troubled mind and new strength to a suffering soul only if it comes from the heart. Mere lip-service—a "precept of men that is learned by rote" (Isaiah 29:13)—cannot serve that purpose.

The more one's prayer is imbued with these truly religious sentiments, the more difficult it is to restrict by cold formality, artificial decorum or uniform ritualism. The prayer of deeply devout Jews, particularly in the Hasidic *shtibel,* is characterized by spontaneity and ecstasy, by ardor rather than order. As they pray, the truly devout, like a forest of trees swaying in a storm, are tossed by an inner turbulence, shaking in their zeal to serve their Creator with a perfect heart. The Hasidic rabbi does not "conduct a service" *for* his congregation; he prays *with* his flock. There is no cantor to perform works of liturgical music or a choir to uplift a passive "audience." Instead, the entire congregation becomes one in its prayer. Excited voices, of varied pitch and volume, swell in an outpouring of thanksgiving and supplication rising from the depths of hearts overflowing with emotion. Radiant faces and shining eyes reflect profound feeling beyond the power of ordinary words to express. True prayer, then, is not a ceremony, but a deeply personal spiritual experience.

Unlike the reader of secular literature, the worshipper in true prayer does not overly concern himself with the authorship of the texts he reads. The personality of the author of each prayer—whose name is mostly not given—fades into insignificance before the worshipper's awareness of his own relationship with God. The genuinely religious person who reads the Psalms of David chants them as if the tale of David's personal struggles were not David's but his own. In his turn, David himself, in his famous Psalm 90, the "Prayer of Moses, the Man of God," uses the experiences and reflections of the Prophet as the medium for expressing his own emotions. Hence, the real power of prayer lies in its subjectivization. It is not the text, but the devotion with which that text is read, that endows congregational worship with personal significance.

Thus the poignant prayer: "O open for us the Gate at the time of the closing of the Gate" uttered in fear and trepidation at the *Neila* * (closing) service of Yom Kippur could have been recited with equal relevance at the historic moment when the heroic soldiers of Israel, having made Jerusalem one again, clung in silent prayer to the hallowed stones of the Western Wall, and each man experienced an "opening of the Gate" and received his personal glimpse of the *Or HaGanuz,* the hidden Heavenly light of purity and exaltation.

I shall never forget my own experience with yet another classic prayer. As I stood with a group of worshippers at the Western Wall on Tisha B'Av, I heard a sweet melancholy voice chant Judah HaLevi's

* In this prayer the Jew makes his final impassioned plea to God for mercy and forgiveness before the Gates of Heaven are closed at the end of the Day of Atonement.

36

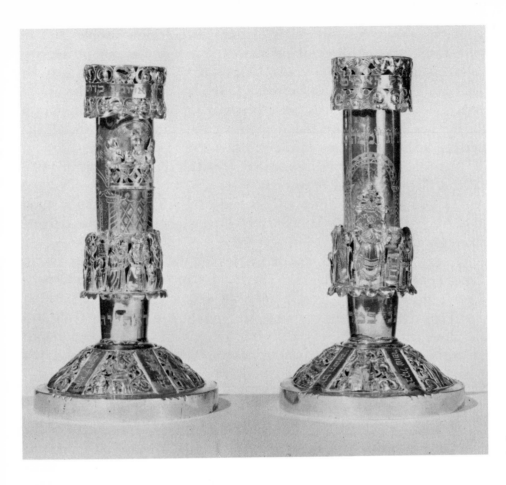

Candlesticks, by Ilya Schor. (Courtesy Mr. and Mrs. Mortimer J. Propp, New York City).

"Zion, Wilt Thou Not Inquire?" As this man of Jerusalem, who had come from far-off Glasgow in Scotland, sang the hauntingly beautiful hymn we felt the anguish of countless generations of Jews in exile who, like the poet of old, yearned for the restoration of our beloved Home-land. But now that our fondest hope had been fulfilled and we stood within the walls of reunited Jerusalem, this elegy assumed a new meaning—a meaning best expressed by the Psalmist (126:1): "When God returned the captivity of Zion, we were like dreamers." We were dazed by the new light that had suddenly and miraculously come to us.

But there were memories of darkness, too. I recalled that Tisha B'Av twenty-five years before, which had marked the beginning of the mass murder of our brethren in the Warsaw Ghetto. Then it was with hearts heavy laden that we recited Judah HaLevi's song of yearning for Zion.

It was one and the same hymn—but what a difference in feeling and emotion!

Prayer in Judaism is the means by which the individual identifies with his community. In addition to personal hopes and wishes, Jewish prayer expresses the aspirations of the entire Jewish people—and in some cases those of all mankind as well. For instance, one of the passages in the daily *Amida* reads: "Heal us, O God, that we may be healed." This prayer must be recited even by individuals who are in perfect health because it is not a personal supplication but an appeal for the sick in the entire House of Israel and, beyond this, for all the stricken and the suffering in the world.

National and universal motifs are particularly prominent in Festival and High Holy Day prayers, such as:

"O God and God of our fathers, merciful King, have mercy upon us . . . return us in the abundance of Thy compassion for the fathers' sake who did Thy will . . ."

"Grant glory, O Lord, unto Thy people, praise to them that revere Thee, hope to them that seek Thee . . . joy to Thy land, gladness to Thy city, a flowering of strength unto David Thy servant . . ."

"Then shall the just see and be glad, and the upright shall exult, and the pious triumphantly rejoice, while iniquity shall close her mouth and all wickedness shall be wholly consumed like smoke, when Thou causest the dominion of arrogance to pass away from the earth."

A number of holiday prayers, while universal in essence, also reflect the history of the Jewish people, for example:

"Because of our sins we were exiled from our land and removed far from our country . . . May it be Thy will . . . that Thou mayest again in Thine abundant compassion have mercy upon us and upon Thy sanctuary, and mayest speedily rebuild it and magnify its glory . . . Our Father, our King, do Thou speedily make the glory of Thy kingdom manifest upon us . . ."

"Thou didst reveal Thyself in a cloud of glory unto Thy people in order to speak with them. Out of heaven Thou didst make them hear Thy voice, and wast revealed unto them in clouds of purity. The whole world trembled at Thy presence, and the works of creation were in awe of Thee, when Thou didst reveal Thyself, O our King, upon Mount Sinai to teach Thy people the Torah and commandments, and didst make them hear Thy majestic voice and Thy holy utterances out of flames of fire . . ."

While prayer demonstrates the unity of the Jewish people, it was never meant to imply strict uniformity. Various communities through the ages have perpetuated their own time-honored customs. There are differences in liturgy, in *nussakh* (style), pronunciation and melody, as well as in details of observance and procedure. The distinctions between *Nussakh S'fard* and *Nussakh Ashkenaz* are well known, but there are variations even within these modes of worship. Each of these forms has its own devoted adherents, and history records incidents of real conflict when followers of two different modes of worship happened to join the same congregation.

For many generations, synagogues have been careful "not to change the customs of our fathers" and to insist upon the preservation of their distinctive styles of liturgy and ritual. For example, in the Greek city of Salonica alone there were, before World War II, approximately fifty synagogues most of which had been founded by the descendants of the exiles from Spain. Each of these houses of worship rigidly followed the ritual of its original community, such as *Nussakh* Toledo, *Nussakh* Cordoba and others. The consistent preservation of each *Nussakh* served to strengthen the Jewish consciousness of these congregations.

The distinctiveness of each community, whether Oriental or Occidental, was especially evident on Sabbaths and festivals. Together, these communities presented a veritable symphony of spiritual exaltation.

Breadplate, silver, modern design by Ilya Schor. Hebrew lettering in center: "For good and for blessing; for gladness and joy; for salvation and consolation." Lettering on edge of plate: "Blessed art Thou, O Lord our God, King of the Universe, Who brings forth bread from the earth. Yitzchak and Hanna Marder." (Courtesy Mr. and Mrs. Isadore M. Marder, Philadelphia, Pa.)

PRAYER AS A SPIRITUAL EXPERIENCE

IN JUDAISM, prayer can be a profound spiritual experience if it is preceded by proper emotional preparation. The Talmud states that the early *Hasidim* would spend an hour putting themselves in the proper frame for prayer (Berakhot 5:1).

Before a Jew can approach his Creator with true reverence, he must transform his very self into *prayer,* in the spirit of total self-immersion implied in the words of the Psalmist "And I am prayer" (Psalms 109:4). How could a mere mortal enter the exalted gates of prayer while engrossed in his daily, frequently degrading, toil for material sustenance? How could a creature of flesh and blood appear in the august presence of the King of Kings with trivial requests? How could man, with his limited mental capacity, presume to address himself to the infinite, incomprehensible, all-embracing Kingdom of Heaven, unless, in fear and trembling, he first undergoes a process of spiritual self-conditioning, as described by the Psalmist: *Tikon Tefilati* (Psalms 141:2)? The Hebrew word *tikon* has two connotations—to "be prepared" and to "be established." These two connotations are mutually complementary: in order to be "established" or "approved," *Tefilati,* my prayer, must be preceded by a thorough preparation of self.

What is the essence of preparation for the service of the heart?

According to Jewish tradition, this preparation consists of two aspects which, on the surface, may appear contradictory. As the Jew prepares for prayer, he is bidden to say to himself, practically in the same breath: "How insignificant is man!" and "How great is man!" On the one hand, he is told to express the nothingness of man as compared to infinity; on the other hand, he is commanded to extol the potential greatness of man who is created in the image of God!

When, in one of the first recorded prayers in Jewish history, our patriarch Abraham said: "I have taken upon myself to speak to the Lord, and I am mere dust and ashes!" (Genesis 18:27), he meant "I have dared to speak to God *although* I am but dust and ashes," and at the same time, *"because* I have reached a sufficient degree of humility and self-negation before the Almighty to realize that I am nothing but dust and ashes."

Only the humble in spirit can rise to the heights of intimate communication with Heaven.

Humility is not only a stepping-stone to the gates of prayer, but also the climax of Divine inspiration. After the Jew, in the *Amidah,* has petitioned God for personal forgiveness, healing and salvation and has then gradually ascended to the level where he can make selfless supplication for the welfare and redemption of his entire people, he concludes with the benediction: "May my soul be lowly as the dust to all."

Another concept basic to the Jewish approach to prayer is that congregational worship supersedes individual devotion. It is the *duty* of the individual to pray with a congregation even when his prayer is one of personal nature.

The Jewish religion places a high value on the individual, his distinctive qualities and his personal needs. Judaism does not favor the submersion of individuality into group uniformity. But no individual may keep aloof from his community and from its joys and sorrows. Maimonides states: "He who sets himself apart from the ways of the community, even if he does not transgress any precept; he who separates himself from his fellow-Jews and does not observe the commandments jointly with them; he who does not participate in their grief or fasts, but follows his own path like a heathen, as if he were not a son of Israel—such a person has no portion in the world-to-come" (*Mishne Torah*).

Thus, the bond between the individual and the community is a basic pillar of Judaism.

Even the *content* of many prayers is communal. The individual prays amongst·the community and for the community. Even numerous personal prayers are worded in the plural form. This is thought to render such prayers more readily acceptable, in accordance with the well-known rabbinic dictum: "He who prays for his fellow-man will have his own prayer answered first."

The final benediction in the *Amidah* service for all occasions is particularly suggestive of this reciprocal relationship between the individual and the community: "Bless us, our Father, *all as one*, with the light of Thy countenance."

While only personal preparation, without communion with others, can set the proper mood for prayer, worship in communion with a congregation is necessary to endow prayer with its full spiritual effectiveness.

Thus the heavens and the earth were finished, and all the host of them. And on the seventh day God ended His work which He had made; and He rested on the seventh day from all His work which He had made. And God blessed the seventh day, and sanctified it because in it He had rested from all His work which God created and made.

GENESIS 2:1-3

Remember the Sabbath day, to keep it holy. Six days shall you labor, and do all your work: but the seventh day is the Sabbath of the Lord your God; in it you shall not do any work, you, nor your son, nor your daughter, your manservant, nor your maidservant, nor your cattle, nor your stranger that is within your gates: for in six days the Lord made heaven and earth, the sea, and all that in them is, and rested on the seventh day; therefore the Lord blessed the Sabbath day, and hallowed it.

EXODUS 20:8-11

See, the Lord has given you the Sabbath (Exodus 17:29). What does "see" mean? Said Rabbi Jose: Behold the gem I have given you.

YALKUT SHIMONI, P. BESHALAH

THE SABBATH

In some communities the Sabbath lights at home were kindled in a special Sabbath lamp that was suspended from the wall or ceiling. This silver Sabbath lamp (17th century, Frankfort-on-the-Main, Germany) has an ornate tower-shaped center stem and oil containers set in a star design. (Hebrew Union College Museum, Cincinnati, Ohio).

THE SABBATH

THE SABBATH IS THE DAY which Almighty God Himself blessed and made holy (Genesis 2:3).

What is true meaning of the Sabbath? What great riches does it hold for those who drink deeply of its refreshing, healing waters? What is there about the Sabbath which prompted Ahad HaAm to declare that "more than Israel kept the Sabbath, the Sabbath has kept Israel?"

A study of the vast Sabbath literature reveals seven elements that make Sabbath observance a uniquely uplifting spiritual experience: 1. Rest; 2. Holiness; 3. Pleasure; 4. Intellectual Growth; 5. Spiritual Elevation; 6. Expression of Jewish Identity; 7. Community Consciousness.

1. REST

Sabbath *rest* involves not merely a cessation of work, or a long list of bans on all manner of weekday pursuits. As we shall see, it is a positive concept closely related to the other six elements mentioned above.

In order to grasp the meaning of this particular kind of rest, let us examine the whole concept of leisure which has become a problem and a burden instead of a source of enjoyment. The progress of science and technology has not only made life more comfortable but has also endowed man with one of his most valuable possessions—time. Man today spends considerably fewer hours and days at work each week than he did fifty years ago. As a result he has more free time. But his *free* time has become *empty* time. And like nature, man dreads a vacuum. People do not know what to do with the added time on their hands because they do not know what to do with themselves. Man knows how to deal with things, with situations, and with other people—but not what to do with himself or, for that matter, with his time, which is an essential part of himself. He "kills time" without realizing that by so doing he destroys part of himself. On week-ends and at vacation time many people yield to an irresistible urge to travel. What drives them? The inner unrest, the desire to "get away from it all"—and "it" being no one else than *themselves*. The Jew who observes the Sabbath knows how to rest. He knows the secret of relaxation, of being at peace with himself. The rabbinical counsel that, on the Sabbath, "all our endeavors and all our plans should be considered as completed," liberates us from work and worry; it frees not only our body but also our mind. On the Sabbath, the Jew is transposed to another world and transformed into another being.

Referring to the verse in the *Song of Songs* (1:5) "I am black and beautiful," the *Midrash* comments: "I am black on weekdays and beautiful on the Sabbath" (*Midrash Rabba*).

Entire text of the Song of Songs written by hand on space 3½" x 4¾", late 19th century. (Courtesy Alexander Bistritzky, New York City).

In this "world which is all Sabbath," as the Talmudic expression goes, there are no worldly worries, no gains or losses, no urgent duties or strenuous tasks, no fears or failures and no conquering ambitions.

On the Sabbath, the Jew finds himself on an island of peace, away from the surging breakers of daily toil. On this day he dwells in a sacred palace, in the House of God—a title which is not the monopoly of the synagogue but which every truly Jewish home can attain. What the Temple is in *space,* the Sabbath is in *time,* as implied in the command:

45

Silver box, contemporary design, by Ilya Schor. Hebrew legend: "The Torah is a Tree of Life to all that live." (Courtesy Mr. and Mrs. Isadore M. Marder, Philadelphia, Pa.).

"My Sabbaths ye shall observe and My Temple ye shall respect." Significantly, in this pronouncement the Sabbath and the Temple are placed in juxtaposition.

2. HOLINESS

Creation was completed with a blessing from the Creator Himself. But unlike the earlier blessings which were part of creation and which concerned physical and material abundance, this benediction was not bestowed on man or beast or on anything else in the world but on a specific segment of *time*, which He blessed and "made holy."

We are accustomed to associate holiness with certain people, places and things. Yet the first time we encounter holiness in the Bible, we find it not in a tangible object, but in time, in the Sabbath. "And God blessed the Seventh Day and made it *holy*" (Genesis 2:3).

The Talmud teaches us that there are several kinds of holiness—ten, to be exact, which occur in various degrees. But the supreme and unalterable sanctity belongs to the Sabbath.

Yet we should not think of this kind of holiness as an abstraction. The sanctity of the Sabbath is very real since it is expressed in the practical observance of specific law, which in turn sanctifies us as a people.

3. PLEASURE

Sabbath observance is a serious thing, but the Sabbath is also a day of joy and pleasure. We are bidden to "call the Sabbath a delight." Sadness and gloom, even mourning over a death in the family, are banned on this day when, in the words of a familiar Sabbath prayer, "the keepers of the Sabbath rejoice in Thy kingdom."

How did the Jew accomplish the abrupt transition from the six days of toil and trouble into the seventh day of rest and pleasure? *By creating a world of his own.*

The common notion is that on the Sabbath the Jew is isolated from the world. This may be so. But what is overlooked is that the Sabbath fashions a new world for him. True, so far as he is concerned, all worldly activity ceases, and he lifts himself beyond the world and its affairs—but he does not become suspended in a vacuum. On the Sabbath he lives a life which, albeit of distinct dimension and different values, is rich in content and purpose.

The opening verse of Psalm 95, Lekhu N'ranana ("O come let us exult before the Lord"), with which the Sabbath service begins, inspired this bronze candleholder by Ludwig Y. Wolpert. (Temple Ohabei Sholom, Nashville, Tenn.)

True, for the pious Jew the outside world stops on the Sabbath. He transcends the world of reality. He does not work or travel, shop or cook. He abstains from writing and smoking. He does not use any mechanical appliances. He neither takes part in games nor does he watch them. He does not go out on picnics or excursions, nor does he spend time on mundane hobbies. He lives in an oasis of quiet.

But the Sabbath is not merely a day of restrictions and abstentions. Nor is it made for letting time slip through our fingers. It is a day of ennobling pleasure, of spiritual delight, enriching the mind and gladdening the soul.

The sudden transition from the six days of work to the seventh day of peace is abrupt enough in our bustling industrial and over-civilized society. But it is nothing compared to the contrast which this weekday change-over implied in days gone by. The change then was from actual poverty and want, compounded by the constant threat of persecution, to the sublime world of Sabbath bliss.

With the blessings over the Sabbath light and over the wine, an all-pervading serenity descended upon the Jewish home. Somehow even the poorest Jew managed to free himself from the shackles of his misery and to pass into the world of peace and tranquility which the Sabbath had created for him. To be sure, he was himself a partner also in this act of re-creation, as he had been in the original Creation that had gone before. According to the Talmudic dictum, "he who does justice becomes a partner in the work of creation."

It is in keeping with this spirit that the *Halakha*, the formal code of Jewish Law, prohibits any form of mourning or even worry on the Sabbath. The "middle thirteen" blessings of the weekday *Sh'mone Esrei* which plead for man's material needs are omitted on the Sabbath because they would tend to call the worshipper's attention to the things he lacks on earth, and cause worry and anxiety to mar his Sabbath rest. Similarly, whenever any one of the five commemorative fast-days, except Yom Kippur, falls on the Sabbath, it is deferred to the next day. In like manner, a person observing *shiva*, the week of mourning for a close relative, must refrain from public expressions of sorrow on the Sabbath. Sabbath and mourning are not only incongruous; they are totally irreconcilable. This thought is aptly expressed in the following prayer from the Sabbath service:

"Let them rejoice in Thy Kingdom, those that keep the Sabbath in pleasantness. The people that sanctify the Sabbath Day, *they* are sated and delight in Thy goodness."

4. INTELLECTUAL GROWTH

The Sabbath is the day when every individual has the chance to grow in mind and spirit. On that day, according to the Talmud, the Jew is given a *Neshama Yetera*—"an additional soul" (Tractate Betza, 16). Through diligent study of Torah and self-immersion in spiritual experience, he grows in wisdom. Ideas which elude his grasp in the turmoil of the six days of work become clearly comprehensible to him on the seventh day, when rest makes for increased mental receptiveness. Free from workday pressures, he can cultivate the inner potential that lies dormant in his soul all week long. An "observant" Jew is not merely "observing" as a passive "onlooker" on the outside looking in. He is an active participant in an extraordinary experience of which he is subject and object at the same time.

His relation to the synagogue, particularly on that day, takes on such dimensions that his own home becomes part of it, as it were, since Judaism makes no distinction between religion in the synagogue and in the home.

On that day of intellectual growth, the *Bet HaMidrash*, the House of Study, is no less important than *Bet HaTefila*, the House of Worship.

Thus the entire structure of religious life in the Diaspora has rested on these two pillars of strength—the Sabbath and the Synagogue. The Jew devoted a good part of the day to the study of Torah in accordance with his abilities and insights and with the spiritual guidance available to him. This Sabbath "learning" was not mere study or acquisition of knowledge. It was nothing less than a formative element for the soul, a molding factor for the mind.

The "additional soul" does not descend upon man of itself—he must earn it by preparing himself to receive and to absorb it. This he can do only by studying and by living the Torah with the special fervor and flavor which only the Sabbath can provide.

5. SPIRITUAL ELEVATION

The Sabbath is a day of spiritual elevation, to be attained by joining with a congregation in dedicated observance and by spending at least part of the Sabbath listening to the words of a teacher of the Law.

The traditional practice of leaving home to spend a Sabbath or holiday with a revered rabbi is rooted in the Bible itself. We read in the Second Book of Kings: "Wherefore wilt thou go to him [the holy man Elisha] today? It is neither the New Moon nor the Sabbath" (4:23) . It is from this passage that the Talmud derives the precept that one should make every effort to be with his spiritual mentor on the holiday, even if it means traveling to another town on the day before.

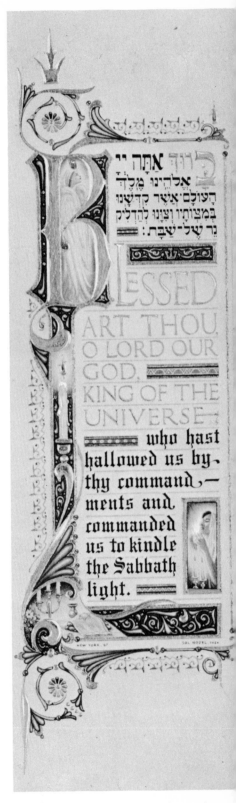

Blessing for the Sabbath candles. Illuminated by Sol Nodel. (From the collection of Mr. and Mrs. Harry Waxman, Milwaukee, Wisc.).

49

Sabbath eve. This Sabbath eve scene is the work of Isidor Kaufmann (1854-1921). Originally a painter of historical compositions, Kaufmann later became a pioneer in the depiction of traditional Eastern European Jewish types and genre scenes. (The Jewish Museum, New York City).

The visits with a rabbi on festive days took on special significance in the *Hassidic* movement where the *Rebbe* became the central figure and chief source of inspiration to the multitude of his loyal adherents.

On the surface, all Sabbaths seem alike. All are governed by the same laws, rules and customs, and by the same spirit. Nonetheless, each Sabbath is unique by virtue of its own *sidra* the Biblical portion that is assigned to it in the annual cycle of Torah readings.

The influence of the weekly *sidra* transcends the bounds of the Sabbath into the six workdays to come. It permeates the secular dealings of the Jew to the extent that he even reckons time by it, heading his letters with the title of the *parsha* read that week.

Rehearsing the weekly Biblical portion on the Sabbath, or listening to it read in the synagogue, the mature Jew who hears it for the one thousandth time is inspired with almost the same refreshing curiosity and genuine interest which animate the child when, for the first time in his life, he reads the events related in the *Humash*. "Every day," we are told, "the Torah should be as new to you as if it were given today." We feel that the events the *sidra* describes are actually happening before our very eyes; great personalities appear, speak, act and pass on—never to vanish from our sight again. We are elated by their joys and sorrows. The exultation as well as the anguish aroused by the Torah readings are very real in our minds even today. The statement in the Passover *Haggadah* that "every man should regard himself as if he himself had been delivered from Egyptian bondage" holds good not only for the *seder* of Passover but for the *sidra* of each Sabbath as well.

Although each Sabbath, by virtue of its *sidra,* is endowed with its own individuality, it does not stand isolated. It is part of a greater entity, of the higher order of the annual cycle regulated by Torah. Like pearls on a string, each shining with its own glow, all the Sabbaths of the year together form a chain of harmonious beauty.

Other events in the history of our people are commemorated only once a year, but the Sabbath is different. It *celebrates the wonder of creation,* a miracle which was manifest only once but which implies a constant process of re-creation at the dawn of each new day by the Most High Who, according to our liturgy, "renews each day the work of primordial creation."

The Sabbath is devoted not only to the study of the Five Books of Moses, but also to the "learning" of Torah in the broadest sense which includes all of our sacred literature. In days gone by even the humblest Jew could recite the Psalms—in fact, each congregation had a special society, the *Hevrat Tehilim,* for this purpose. During the summer months, he would study the *Pirke Avot* ("The Ethics of the Fathers"). We read in *Yalkut Shimoni* (*Vayak'hel*): "Said the Almighty to Moses, 'Form large congregations and publicly teach them the laws of the Sabbath so that they may learn from you and do likewise in future generations, to assemble in their houses of worship each Sabbath to study and to instruct Israel in the statutes of the Torah'."

6. EXPRESSION OF JEWISH IDENTITY

The Sabbath has been defined as the identification mark of the Jew. "It is a sign between Me and the Children of Israel" (Exodus 31:17). Throughout the rest of the week, the distinctive character of the Jew may not be quite so obvious. Sometimes it is submerged altogether in his daily tasks and worldly cares which make him no different from his non-Jewish neighbor in the pursuit of his livelihood. With the coming of the Sabbath, however, the singularity of the Jew comes to the surface. On that day, his inner nature is freed from the fetters that shackle it during his working hours. This day of rest serves as a demonstration of his Jewishness vis-a-vis his environment as well as in relation to himself. The stronger his sense of Jewish identity, the more keenly will his Sabbath express itself through his thoughts and deeds.

The "Jewishness" of a given individual cannot be judged from his everyday affairs but only from his finest hours; therefore the Sabbath, and not the weekday, is the determining factor in Jewish living. In expounding the significance of the Sabbath as a "sign," the Hafetz Hayim*, of sainted memory, related the following parable: "To what can this be likened? To a shopkeeper who left his shop for a brief

---

* Rabbi Israel Meir Kagan (1835-1933), famed Polish religious leader.

51

moment, or for a day, or for a week, to take a vacation or for some other reason. So long as his sign remains above the door, even though the shop is closed, his customers know that the establishment had not been liquidated and that its owner will return and reopen it. If, however, he removes the sign, it is a clear indication that he has gone out of business." A Jew who observes the Sabbath proudly displays the sign of his Jewishness.

Although inner experience and emotional expression are the principal elements in Jewish living, the outer manifestations of "Jewishness" are no less significant. Consequently, the Jew should keep the Sabbath not only for his own sake, but also to demonstrate his Jewish identity. The Sabbath observed in this spirit would be of inestimable influence on the character development of the Jewish child, and on the continued growth of the Jewish adult as well.

7. COMMUNITY CONSCIOUSNESS

Basically, Sabbath observance is not a "communal" affair. Its laws apply to the individual as well as to the congregation. But "this day that is honored," as the Sabbath is called in the well-known *Zemirot* refrain, arouses in the heart of every Jew the desire to enjoy the Sabbath, at least partly, through *togetherness*. On any day of the week, each Jew goes his own way dictated by the realities of his life and work. On the Sabbath, however, he joins his fellow Jews for prayer, study and mutual communion. Well-rounded Sabbath observance must include what modern parlance describes as "group experience."

The community is greater than the sum of the individuals who comprise it. It has a power and an influence that cannot be generated by any individual or even by any number of individuals acting alone. Maimonides ruled that he who separates himself from the community, even if he fulfills all the precepts of the Torah in his personal life, is deficient in his Jewishness. The Sages of the Talmud repeatedly emphasized the obligation of each Jewish individual to be part of the community, to rejoice in its joys and to grieve at its sorrows.

Havdala ceremony. Woodcut from Minhagim Book, Amsterdam, ca. 1662. The youngest child is holding the Havdala candle.

Key casket (coffanetto), silver, partly gilt. Made for a bride in Ferrara, Italy, during the second half of the 15th century, for keeping her keys and valuables over the Sabbath. The Hebrew lettering and pictures describe the housewife's weekly preparation for the Sabbath; (from right to left) baking the halla, making her ablutions and kindling the Sabbath lights. (The Israel Museum, Jerusalem).

The Sabbath and the holidays provide ample opportunity for communal interaction. Solitary prayer cannot compare with communal worship, neither from the viewpoint of *Halakha*, which provides different laws for solitary prayer and congregational worship, nor in terms of emotional stimulation and spiritual elevation to be gained by worship with a congregation. Sabbath worship in the synagogue supplements home observance and endows the day with added content.

Study, an integral part of Sabbath rest and sanctity, is also conducted primarily in groups within the walls of the *Bet HaMidrash*. The value of Torah study is immeasurably enhanced by group participation and discussion. Even the joint reading of the Psalms adds its characteristic note to the Sabbath spirit.

In our modern society, collectivism tends to level down individual values, while at the same time the individual is lonelier than ever before. Sabbath observance affords the Jew an opportunity to identify with his people through joint worship and study, and at the same time to look at his own spiritual growth.

On that day the two most potent forces in Jewish survival, the diversifying and the unifying, come to active expression, and both together form the mortar that binds individual Jews into a community strengthened and elevated by the sublime spiritual experience that is the Sabbath.

SABBATH AND HOLIDAY MELODIES

Ornament of the first verse of Lekhu N'ranana, Psalm 95, by Yoseph Budko.

SONG AND MELODY have always been integral parts of Sabbath and holiday. Melody was woven into the texture of prayers and festivities. It accompanied the Jew every day of the year, but on religious holidays it took on added significance both at home and in the synagogue. Although the character of the people influenced the nature of its music, that music, conversely, determined the character of the people, molding the Jewish way of life from ancient times to our day.

From the Ode of Moses at the Red Sea, to the Victory Song of Deborah and the Psalms of David, to the *Hassidic* tunes of the past two and a half centuries, the Jewish people has expressed itself in melody. When Israel was redeemed from Egyptian bondage, its natural, spontaneous reaction was song: "I will sing unto the Lord, for He is highly exalted" (Exodus 16:1). Even the prosaic laws of the Torah were described in the Bible as "songs": "Thy statutes have been my songs" (Psalms 119:54).

Music played a sublime role in the history of the Jew. It inspired prophecy as in the case of Elisha: "And as the musician played, the inspiration of the Lord came upon him" (II Kings 3:16). Music was also a means of dispelling melancholy moods. When an evil spirit descended upon King Saul, his servants suggested to him that "they seek out a man who is skillful as a player on the harp, so when the evil spirit from God is upon you, he shall play with his hand that you may be well" (I Samuel 16:16).

The melody of a song is often more important, more expressive and more meaningful than its words. A striking example is *Kol Nidre*. Here, the text is but a dry legal formula couched in cold, technical terms. But how moving is the melody to which this prosaic declaration is chanted! How deep, how penetrating are the emotions it evokes! On Yom Kippur, the most solemn day of the year, this melody opens the gates of prayer, calling forth high yearnings for the cleansing and uplifting of our souls. Whatever its origin, it has absorbed into it the sighs and sorrows of generations, and as we listen to its stirring passages, we re-live the anguish and anxiety of our ancestors in ages gone by.

Through the medium of music, generations communicate with each other, speak to each other from heart to heart. True, as in the case of the folk-song, there are differences in the nature of our sacred music due to the influence of the non-Jewish environment in the various communities of the diaspora. Thus, *Hassidic niggunim* (melodies), most of which originated in Eastern Europe, contain readily discernible Slavic elements while Jewish songs of Yemen betray unmistakable Arabic

54

influences. But these alien elements have been thoroughly assimilated and blended into the basic Jewish motifs to the extent that the resulting music is essentially and characteristically Jewish. The expression of the Jewish soul unites the *Hassidic niggunim* and the songs of the Yemenite Jew—the same common longings and echoes of the ancient homeland permeate and dominate both. And even as the bitter cold and violent snowstorms of the severe European winter did not keep us from celebrating Tu Bi'Sh'vat as the holiday that marks the beginning of spring in the Land of our Fathers, so, too, the oppressive spiritual climate of the lands of our dispersion could not silence our Songs of Zion, whether their melodies be *Hassidic* or Yemenite.

An interesting development took place in this area of Jewish creative expression. The harp of our people was apparently silenced by the rivers of Babylon, where the Judean captives mourned: "How can we sing the song of the Lord upon the soil of strangers?" and made the solemn historic vow: "If I forget you, O Jerusalem, may my right hand forget its cunning!" (Psalms 137: 5). Yet paradoxically enough, our people subsequently created beautiful, soulful melodies even for this utterance of woe and for the vow—again, an essentially legal act—which it contained.

No, the harp of our people was never silenced. The first momentary numbness of despair was followed by a long period of renewed musical creativity extending into the present, through all the trials and tribulations that befell our exiles in the various lands of their dispersion. A common motif, like a scarlet thread, passes through the myriads of songs and melodies that have sprung from this uninterrupted activity:

Havdala ceremony. Woodcut from Minhagim Book, Frankfort-on-the-Main, 1717.

liturgical music, particularly for the Days of Awe; cantillations for the reading of the Torah and of the Prophets; the *gemarah* chant to which the Talmud was studied; *Hassidic* tunes and dances, especially for holidays and festivals, and hosts of others. This unifying factor is their characteristic Jewish distinctiveness that can be readily perceived by the sensitive listener.

On the other hand, the diversity of musical expression is determined primarily by the purpose, one might even say the *mission*, of each melody. Liturgical music strives for spiritual elevation, liberation from the shackles of reality, transcendence of the restrictive bounds of daily existence and ascension to the higher realms of infinity. Biblical cantillations serve to facilitate the pronunciation, enunciation and comprehension of sacred text, and to evoke the hidden meanings of words through melodic accentuation. In contrast to the melody of prayer which, as mentioned above, seeks expansion and elevation of the soul, the sing-song chant of Talmudic study sets the mood for total concentration, for immersion into the intricacies of difficult problems; for penetration into the depths of legalistic debate and philosophical or theological discussion; and for mastery and retention of the material studied.

For there is a melody of the heart and there is a melody of the mind. The dominant motifs in both are prayers and praises to God ("I will sing to the Lord") and yearning for Zion. Not only the lyrical poetry of Judah Halevi revealed the emotional discord in a soul torn between two worlds ("My heart is in the East, and I am in the end of the West"), but all *Galut* (diaspora) melodies reflected that dichotomy. Ultimately, it was this very dichotomy that became a potent factor in the Return to Zion.

Most of the *Galut* melodies arose "from the straits" of distress. The cry for redemption ascended "out of the depths." Just as the *Hassidic* dance prominently features narrowness of space as the dancer's arms are raised toward heaven and his feet are stamping on one spot, with an absence of broad, sweeping motions, so, too, the tune accompanying the dance is concentrated within itself, turned inward as it were, restricted in space as though within ghetto walls.

Only in Israel reborn can one sense the breadth of the Divine response "in the wide, open spaces" (Psalms 118:4). Both the dance and the song of modern Israel symbolize the broadening of horizons, the emergence from the bonds of distress into the wide, open spaces. Particularly after the victory of June 1967, the extension of geographic boundaries was paralleled by an increase in song and dance. Now there is plenty of ground underfoot. Voices can ring out openly into the vastness of earth and sky that are ours today.

56

The dominant note in the new song of Israel is not the joy of victory, but the welcome relief of being able to breathe freely after the threat of our enemies to tighten the noose around our necks has been averted, we hope, forever. The songs immediately following the victory were not songs of triumph. They were muted by mourning for the fallen heroes, and even by sadness over the human losses of the enemy, as Rashi comments on the Israelites' song of victory over the ancient Egyptians: "The works of My hands (said the Lord) are drowning in the sea, and you dare to rejoice in song?!" Have we not learned: "Do not rejoice at the fall of your enemy!" (Proverbs 24:17)? Rashi also notes that Jacob feared not only "lest he be slain"—but also "lest he be forced to slay."

This self-restraint reflects the attitude of Judaism toward war and victory, an attitude which seeks peace without bloodshed or destruction rather than one bought by the sacrifice of precious human lives.

Still life of Jewish ceremonial objects, by Werner Philipp, contemporary American. (The Jewish Museum, New York City).

Wine cup for Havdala. This ornate silver repoussé cup was made in Germany about 1900. The Hebrew words on the rim ("I will lift the cup of salvation and call upon the name of the Lord" [Psalm 116]) are part of the Havdala prayer. (The Jewish Museum, New York City).

THE SABBATH—A REVELATION
By Nehemia Anton Nobel

AS THE GREAT REVELATION of Divine freedom, the Sabbath became the manifesto of human liberty. The Ten Commandments, representing solely the fundamental tenets of Judaism, make no other mention of ceremonial law, except the proclamation, in no uncertain terms, that "The Seventh Day is a Sabbath unto the Lord, thy God. On it thou shalt not do any manner of work; thou, nor thy son, nor thy daughter, nor thy man-servant, nor thy maid-servant, nor thy cattle, nor the stranger that dwells within thy gates."

Judaism teaches that work ennobles man. We search in vain for a parallel concept not only in the civilizations of the Biblical era but also among the spokesmen of classic antiquity. Even the great creative minds of ancient Greece considered it quite natural that the burden of work should be placed upon the shoulders of the slave class so that the free man could devote his time to the higher pursuits of the intellect and the field of battle. Slavery was the open sore on the body of antiquity; eventually, too, it caused the economic and moral decline of the Classical Age.

Even as the Sabbath is that great conquering power which, as we have seen in the Biblical account of Creation, overcomes the force of necessity, placing the creative freedom of the Divine at the very roots of world survival so, too, it has prevailed over that spirit of servility which can so easily attach to labor. Again and again the Sabbath restores freedom to the slave by making him an individual endowed with individual human rights. If there is indeed truth in Goethe's proclamation that the preservation of the individual's personality is the supreme bliss of mankind, then the concept of the Sabbath in its infinite depth is an all-conquering force indeed. For the Sabbath teaches us that the right to individuality is not merely a concession grudgingly granted to the slave, but a fundamental human prerogative. Only he truly dwells within the pale of humanity who opens to the man-servant and to the maid-servant the gates to human rights, throwing the portals of personal fulfillment wide open to all that is human. . .

Let him who would wish to know the Sabbath in its entirety listen to the words which were uttered by Moses as he was about to bid farewell to his people and which echo all through the Fifth Book of the Pentateuch. Here again, Moses proclaims the Sabbath in words that will endure through all time. At this point what was merely suggested in the original version of the Fourth Commandment is spelled out as historic fact. Here the role of the Sabbath in. the history of creation recedes into the background, permitting the Day of Rest to become a festival belonging to all mankind.

"And thou shalt remember that thou wast a servant in the land of Egypt, and the Lord thy God brought thee out from there with a mighty hand and an outstretched arm," we read in the Fifth Chapter of the Book of Deuteronomy. "Therefore the Lord thy God commanded thee to keep the Sabbath Day."

In other words, the Sabbath is characterized as a memorial to Israel's liberation from Egypt, an event which the institution of the Sabbath actually antedates and with which, according to the Biblical account, it appears to have no connection at all.

But the deeper relationship between these two historic events does lie open and revealed before the vision of Moses, the father of all prophets. After all, being a prophet implies the ability to discern the innermost essence of things. And the inner essence of the Sabbath, from the very beginning, has centered on earth more than on heaven, stressing the liberation of man from darkness and delusion, from arrogance and self-adulation rather than some mystical quest for the attributes of God, or His creation, or His rest from His labors . . .

It is true that the Rabbis have surrounded the Biblical Sabbath law with numerous hedges and fences. But are the only fences those that are made of rigid grillwork? There are also hedges that are very much alive, sharing in the life of the precious plants entrusted to their protection. Hedges of this sort obtain nourishment themselves from those vital saps which in some mysterious fashion provide the basic conditions for the survival of the plant itself. Such, too, is the nature of the "fence" which the Law has reared around the precious plant that is the Sabbath. It is a living, flowering hedge, richly supplied with the mysterious life-blood of religious living. It has never yet closed off the inner sanctuary of the Sabbath to those who seek it with fervor and devotion.

If we define social ethics as a moral teaching which raises the individual from his state of isolation and which by its very nature can be translated into reality only in and through interaction with a community, but at the same time view it as a form of socialization based on given moral standards, then we can point to the Sabbath as the most felicitous application of social ethics within the religion of Israel.

SABBATH WITH THE JEWS OF BAGHDAD

AT THREE O'CLOCK on Friday afternoon, all business would cease and homes would close their doors. Everyone went home to change into his "Sabbath best" and hurried off to the synagogue to welcome the Sabbath with prayers and hymns of praise. This service lasted until an hour before sunset, when all would return home to sing Sabbath hymns with their families, drinking wine the while to gladden the heart.

As soon as the last rays of the sun disappeared, the head of the family would recite *Sh'ma*, the affirmation of faith that begins, "Hear, O Israel: the Lord our God, the Lord is One" (Deuteronomy 6:4). Then came the Friday evening meal, which sometimes lasted until midnight.

Saturday morning the men would go to the synagogue for prayers, then return home to eat breakfast. That done, they would read the Books of the Prophets, for which purpose several families generally

The end of the Sabbath is marked by the recitation of Havdala (Distinction between Holy and Profane). One of the blessings recited in the Havdala is over spices (besamim) which are used symbolically to cheer the soul after the departure of the Sabbath. The containers for the spices, often in tower form, have been a popular object in Jewish ritual art. This traditional filigree silver container was made in Galicia in the late 18th century. (Hebrew Union College Museum, Cincinnati, Ohio).

59

gathered in one place, and one man would read the text aloud for all the others to follow. The reader would elucidate and explain the text while the others listened intently, in pious concentration.

Then everyone would go off to visit friends, to pay social calls and chat. . . . In the afternoon they went strolling, to enjoy the fresh air. The well-to-do owned lovely summer homes and date orchards on the shores of the Tigris River; and there the Sabbath afternoon strolls were a little like a walk through Paradise. . . .

Israel Joseph Benjamin (1818-1864)

SABBATH CUSTOMS OF THE MARRANOS

THE DREADED INQUISITION that flourished in Spain and Portugal from the 14th to the 16th century, forcing Jews to convert, or else be expelled or killed, produced a vast number of "Marranos." These Jews, and their descendants, though officially baptized, secretly remained loyal to Judaism and observed as much of the faith of their fathers as they could.

At one time all the Marranos in Portugal knew the basic Jewish precept to keep the Sabbath as a day of rest. In our day, however, not many of them are careful to observe it. Yet there was once a time in the past when all faithfully kept the day holy, and many were burned at the stake for it, or were put to torture in an ecclesiastical court of the infernal Inquisition. At present they keep the Sabbath with scrupulous care, especially during the forty days preceding Passover, and again during the forty days from the beginning to the month of Elul (the last month of the Jewish year) until Yom Kippur. But there are also merchants and craftsmen who will do no work on the Sabbath all through the year. . . .

Now, this is what they do to observe the holy seventh day: On Friday they clean and sweep their homes, and they will do no work from the one evening to the next. Before the sun sets, the woman of the house lights a lamp of pure olive oil with a wick of wool made expressly for this purpose. The benediction they recite over the kindling of the lamp is: "Blessed be my God, my Lord, my Master, Who has commanded us and charged us with His holy precept to light this sacred lamp, to illuminate and celebrate this holy night of God, so that God may illumine our spirit and rescue us from our sins, punishments and misdeeds."

In some places in the north this Sabbath light, which is called "the lamp of God," is put inside a kettle like the one used in earlier centuries to hide the light from spies of the Inquisition. They know, too, that it is forbidden to extinguish this light; it had to be left to go out of itself.

On the Sabbath day, the family gathers three times—to hold services for the Morning Prayer and the other devotions that are special for this holy day of the week. The Sabbath meals are prepared on Friday; as a rule they eat only fish and vegetables, so as to avoid, at

Spice container for use in Havdala ceremony, Berditchev, Russia, 1855. Spices are inserted into the flower-shaped container. A dedication inscription at the bottom lists the names of the members of the congregation who had the ritual object made for their synagogue. (The Jewish Museum, New York City).

60

least on the sacred day of rest, those foods which the Torah forbids. Most of them are amazed to learn that Jews are accustomed to having meat on the Sabbath. . . .

SABBATH IN YEMEN

Jewish travelers to distant lands brought back interesting, often fascinating reports of the life of their brethren in distant lands. The following is a description of Sabbath in Yemen :

THE YEMENITE JEWS of the nineteenth century were punctilious in their observance of the Sabbath. Friday afternoon everyone would leave work early to prepare for the day of rest. They would go to rivers or lakes for ritual immersion. But first they had their heads completely shorn. All knew the art of barbering, and everyone gave his neighbor a close haircut before immersion. Dried and dressed, they went to the synagogue for the Afternoon Service. Returning to their homes for a light snack, they would change into their Sabbath clothes. These garments were exactly like their weekday clothes except that they were entirely white, save for the *tallit katan,* the four-cornered garment with fringes (*tzitzith*) at each corner, which they wore over their outer clothing. The darker and coarser that was, the better, or at least so they thought.

While it was yet day, they would gather in the synagogue to chant the *Song of Songs.* Then they read a portion of the *Zohar,* the mystical *Book of Splendor,* in an ancient chant in which everyone joined—until the time came for the prayer service ushering in the Sabbath. Unlike our practice to read Psalms 95 to 99 and Psalm 29, it was their custom to read only Psalm 95 ("O come, let us sing to the Lord") and Psalm 29 ("Give unto the Lord, O Sons of the Mighty"), continuing with *L'cha Dodi* ("Come, my Beloved"). When the stars came out, they would begin the Evening Prayer, returning home afterward for *kiddush* and a festive Friday night dinner.

The next morning three hours before daylight (at least the winter I was there) everyone was awakened by the call of the *shammash,* the synagogue caretaker. The men went to the synagogue to recite portions of the *Zohar,* some night prayers named for the Matriarch Rachel, and several hymns. Each person brought with him an earthenware jug of warm coffee which he had kept in a stove since the day before. This they drank and served one another, for the service was long, continuing until dawn.

Morning Services were held before sunrise. After the *k'dushah* (in which all join in declaring the holiness of the Almighty) the worshipers went off one by one to their homes for a bite of food to sustain them. After reciting *kiddush,* they would partake of a pan-baked stew which had been kept warm from the day before. Then, they would return to the synagogue to hear the reading from the Scroll of the Law. This reading went on for over two hours, as every man who was

Havdala spice container. This engraved container of hammered silver was made in the Near East in the 19th century for rose water used instead of spices for Havdala. (The Israel Museum, Jerusalem).

61

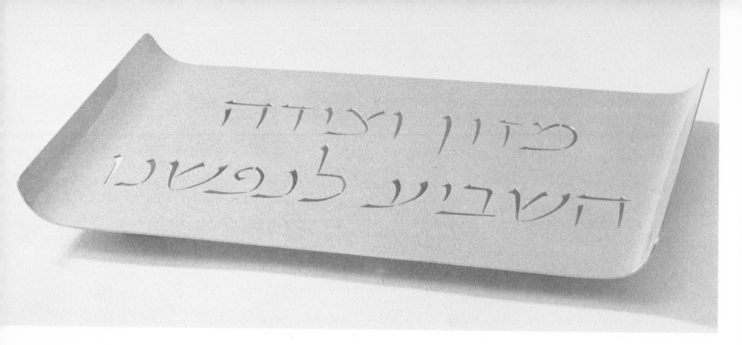

Halla Plate. This modern silver Halla plate designed by Ludwig Y. Wolpert bears a quotation from one of the z'mirot (table hymns) sung during the Sabbath dinner: "Food and nourishment [God] provided for our souls."

called to the Torah chanted his own portion at great length. Moreover, during the entire reading a boy of about nine stood beside the reading desk (it was a different boy's turn each Saturday) and translated every verse, using a manuscript kept for that purpose—also at considerable length and in great detail. The same was done with the *haftarah* (the lesson from the Prophets), the boy following another manuscript of theirs, which mingled the straightforward meaning of the text with elaborate commentary.

Nor was this all. During the entire Torah reading they would listen very critically, expecting each reader to be accurate throughout in pronunciation and chant, and from the lad who translated to acquit himself of his task without errors. For they were so well versed in this that they almost knew the correct reading and translation by heart.

Let me give you a bit of evidence of this. I engaged a lad of about eighteen to be my attendant and guide. By trade he was a cobbler, who made shoes by hand and went about selling them. One Friday in the spring we found ourselves in the town of Hilla. Most of the inhabitants had fled because of ill-treatment from the officers of the new king. It was only with difficulty that we could muster a *minyan*, a quorum of ten, for the Sabbath Morning Service in the synagogue. The portion of the Torah was read and translated in the usual way; but when it came to the *haftara*, the lesson from the Prophets that followed, the worshipers were in a dilemma. Before fleeing from the town, the president of the congregation had hidden all the precious scrolls and manuscripts of the synagogue to keep them safe from the persecutors. The worshipers managed to get a Torah scroll for the Sabbath reading, and read the translation from a printed text. But for the *haftara* they had only had the manuscript translation and that was gone.

As the worshipers stood about sadly not knowing what to do, my young attendant, Saadyah the shoemaker, stepped forward. "*Read the haftara*," he said, "and I will translate from memory." And this he proceeded to do, verse by verse, as the one called last to the Torah read the Hebrew text from a printed Bible. In words and chant he was completely accurate, although the *haftara* about the four lepers (II Kings 7:3-20), was quite long, and their standard translation opened with a long preamble, to expound on who the four lepers were, how they had acquired the disease, and so forth. Had I not seen and heard my attendant with my own eyes and ears, I would not have believed it. . . .

After *Mussaf*, the Additional Prayer that concludes the Sabbath Morning Service, it was the custom in each synagogue for the head of the congregation to deliver a lecture on religious law and ethics. Afterwards, they would all go home, a third of the day being gone by then. Their usual Sabbath meal followed, with fruits, seeds, and warm dishes. Then they would rest a while, and all would gather once more in the synagogue, young and old, to study the Law together. Whoever did not know how to study would listen and ask questions. On occasion the head of the congregation would hold forth on religious matters relevant to that day and time of year.

So they would sit in the synagogue until the day moved to a close. Following the Afternoon Prayer, they would return to their homes to enjoy their third Sabbath meal in their customary way. (Each Sabbath meal, incidentally, began with strong liquor, fruit and seeds.) As night fell, they would recite the Evening Prayer at home.

In the Jewish quarter in Yemen, where our brethren lived apart from the rest of the town, you could see the effect of the Heavenly voice that proclaimed, in the words of the Scripture, "Today is a Sabbath to the Lord! Let every man among you abide in his place; let no man go out of his dwelling!" (Exodus 16:25, 29). The Sabbath was obviously in the air; peace and quiet in the streets, the shops and stalls closed, no one to be seen about. Women and little children remained at home, while the men and boys were at the synagogue. From the House of Study next to the synagogue, however, sounds could be heard half the night and all through the day—the sounds of study and prayer.

It gladdened my heart to watch and see all this. Fortunate indeed were those brethren of our people.

Jacob Saphir

Havdala set, silver, contemporary design, by Ludwig Y. Wolpert. Hebrew lettering cut into spicebox and candleholder is the blessing recited over each; Hebrew lettering on wine cup: "I will lift up the cup of salvation." (The Jewish Museum, New York City).

MY LAST SABBATH WITH GRANDFATHER
by Zalman Shazar

TOWARDS EVENING on the Friday of my brief, last visit I went with Grandfather to the synagogue to welcome the Sabbath. Then I learnt that his *shtiebel*, too, had perished. It had been destroyed during the last fire and now all the remaining Habad *Hasidim* assembled in a *minyan* that met for the time being in the unfinished house belonging to one of the faithful members, a carpenter by trade. In this house that was not yet a house, so workaday in atmosphere, its scaffolding still not removed, bundles of wood scattered everywhere, the worshippers themselves seeming like accidental survivors of some catastrophe, in this casual, unimpressive setting, Grandfather towered over his surroundings, awesome in his dignity and his rare obstinacy of spirit.

Till my last moment I will remember Grandfather standing before the *minyan*, chanting the prayers that welcome the Sabbath. He was thin and tall, and the narrow girdle on his black silk *kaftan* seemed to lend even further length to this figure that was all aspiration to the heavens. He looked as if he were standing on tiptoe; all his movements were directed upwards; even his pointed beard seemed raised. A candle burning in holiness on the eve of Yom Kippur—that was the image he brought to mind.

Sabbath candlesticks. On Friday night the mother of the house kindles the Sabbath lights. The number of lights used varies with local custom but there must be at least two, to symbolize the two synonymous terms "Remember" and "Keep" which introduce the Sabbath commandment in the Bible (Exod. 29:8 and Deut. 5:12 respectively). These silver candlesticks were made in Germany in the 18th century. The bases of the candlesticks show (left) Abraham's sacrifice of Isaac and (right) a woman lighting the Sabbath candles.

Hand-embroidered cloths, like this one dating from 19th century Germany, are used to cover the halla, the loaves of twisted bread traditional to the Sabbath meal at home.

His prayer was a raging fire, kept in check and subdued. It rose from the depths within him to the source of consolation. My eager eyes, with those of all the assembly, were lifted to him. And it was during those flaming moments of prayer that Grandfather and I, his young antagonist, were reconciled. The power of his prayer and my spiritual participation in it bridged the differences between us—there was no discussion nor argument, "no speech nor language," as the Psalmist says.

Actually there had been a perverse occurrence which might have made our reconciliation almost impossible. My Party comrades in the town had learnt of my visit and my forthcoming *aliya*, and arranged a public meeting in my honor. My name leaped out of the advertisements they had posted. The meeting could not be kept secret from Grandfather and his friends, and I was full of fear that, as a result, my visit would only make the chasm between us wider. But when we prayed together, the fear was dissipated and the chasm disappeared. Listening to Grandfather chant, I heard beneath the words his deep lament over the cruel loneliness of his old age and the inexorable decline of the precious world that had been his. I heard his grief over the differences dividing kinsmen and at the same time his proud devotion to the immutable glory. I heard his passionate gratitude for the great bliss he felt in nearness to the source of all blessing; in the

65

eternity of Israel unimpaired from generation to generation; and in the bond—at last—between my soul and his.

I can still hear Grandfather's voice chanting to his Father in Heaven, in the presence of his grandson on earth:

"Sanctuary of the King, city of sovereignty, rise, go forth from thy ruins. Too long hast thou sat in the vale of tears.

"He will lavish His pity upon thee . . . Cease to be ashamed and confused.

"Why art thou cast down and disquieted?

"The afflicted of my people trust in thee—the city shall be built upon its mound."

And then with complete resignation and understanding, Grandfather sang out the Sabbath Psalm in a hearty, rhythmic tune, a mood of purest thanksgiving:

"I will exult in the works of Thy hands.

"How great are Thy works, O Lord! Thy thoughts are very deep.

"A brutish man knoweth not; neither doth a fool understand this. . . ."

That his Sabbath prayer was a gift to last all my years, Grandfather could hardly have known. And in the very last moments before my carriage moved, he gave me still another, utterly precious gift.

Except for set meetings with my comrades, I had spent the whole of the Sabbath and the hours of its departure on Saturday night in Grandfather's company. To the best of my recollection, we spoke very little about the family and not at all about controversial matters. It was scholarly discussion of Torah that occupied almost all the time, and both of us were overjoyed that I could still be somewhat of a match for him, though more as a listener than a talker. Whether he spoke of the mysteries of Hasidism or the rationality of Talmud, with his fellow-worshippers in the *shtiebel* or with the yeshiva students who came to visit him, or even when he sang his prayer melodies before his Creator—it seemed very clear to me that in a sense he was addressing me particularly, in the hope that his words, with all their connotations and all their special flavor, would enter my heart. And my heart was indeed wide open to receive them.

Early Sunday morning when the waggoner came to take my valise, Grandfather put on his summer coat, opened his sunshade, and walked out with me to the end of town.

As he walked, sometimes pausing and standing still, he said something like this:

"My child, you know the melody of the Old Rav very well. There is something special about it that you should be told, something I learned from the old *Hasidim* in the rebbe's house.

"There are times when a man wants to remember a tune familiar to him and he simply cannot recall it no matter how hard he tries. On the other hand, there are times when a tune keeps humming in a man's mind and he does not want it or enjoy it but cannot get rid of it. In both cases it is clear that the tune—however good it may be—does not grow from the same root as the man's soul. He and the tune are two completely separate entities.

66

"But if a man can recall a tune whenever he wants to and it gives him pleasure each time, that is a sign that the tune is really his, deriving from the same source as the man's own soul.

"Thus, my child, the melody of the Old Rav is rooted in the soul of every Habad *Hasid* and his children and children's children until the end of the generations. If a righteous *Hasid* or any one of his descendants wants to remember this holy melody and it escapes him no matter how hard he tries to recall it, this simply proves that at that particular time he has deviated somehow from the true path and must search his soul and repent.

"It cannot be for nothing, my child, that a *Hasid* forgets the Rav's melody—this precious gift and touchstone. Do not lose it, my child!"

Our sages have said that men should part from each other while talking of the Law. Grandfather did just that. When he saw the waggoner hurrying me, he suddenly posed a complicated problem about sacrificial offerings of fruit of the Land and solved it by reference to a passage in Maimonides which he had just noted that week. Then he kissed me on the mouth and the wagon started to move.

Many stormy days have passed since then, but I have never forgotten how Grandfather stood under his sunshade in the middle of the road in the noon heat of a July day, at peace with his grandson and erstwhile antagonist, his lips murmuring the traditional blessing of parting, his moist, shining eyes fixed on the wagon as it moved away towards the Land he and all his people longed for, the Land that was at once his and his grandson's. His radiance will remain in my heart till its last beat, and his wonderful gift, too, is with me till this day.

In all the perplexities of my life whenever I have suddenly wished to remember the melody of the Old Rav and the good tune has responded, I have felt new strength welling up within me each time, evidence that my direction is right. All despair conquered, I have gone on my way in hope and inner peace.

(Zalman Shazar, *Morning Stars, p. 202)*

Havdala Scene, by Chaim Gross.

In the seventh month, in the first day of the month, shall you have a sabbath, a memorial of blowing of trumpets, a holy convocation. You shall do no servile work therein.

LEVITICUS 23

Rabbi Abahu said: Wherefore is the ram's horn blown [on Rosh HaShana]? Said the Holy One, Blessed Be He: "Blow before Me the ram's horn in order that I may consider the binding of Isaac, son of Abraham."

ROSH HaSHANA, 16

Rabbi Abahu said: The Angels of Service said to the Almighty: "Master of the Universe, why does not Israel recite Hallel (Praise) before You on Rosh HaShana and on the Day of Atonement?" He said to them: "Is it possible that the King sit on the Throne of Justice with the Books of the Dead open before Him, while Israel sings praise?"

TRACTATE ROSH HaSHANA 32

ROSH HASHANA

The Sounding of the Ram's Horn. The ram's horn or shofar, the oldest known type of wind instrument, has been sounded to signal important events in the history of the Jewish people. The revelation at Mount Sinai (Exod. 19:16) was introduced by the sound of the shofar, as was the Year of Jubilee (Lev. 25:8). During the High Holiday Season, particularly on Rosh HaShana but also throughout the month of Elul and again at the conclusion of Yom Kippur, the shofar is sounded each day (except on the Sabbath) to call the people to repentance. According to Rabbinic tradition, the ram's horn will also be sounded to herald the coming of the Messiah. (Israel Office Of Information).

ROSH HASHANA

I

THE LITERAL MEANING OF Rosh HaShana is "Head of the Year." According to the teachings of Judaism, it is the "nerve center" of the year. From it flow the decisions which mold our thoughts and determine our actions for the twelve months to come. Therefore, we ought not to let these two days, which the Talmud designates as "the one long day," pass without mustering all our spiritual resources for the lofty task of purifying and ennobling our soul.

Rosh HaShana marks not only a beginning but also an end, for if we are to frame decisions for the future, we must first review the past. Rosh HaShana must be a Day of Remembrance as well as a Day of Judgment; before we can judge, we must go through a process of remembering.

Accordingly, Rosh HaShana is the culmination of the entire year. Life is not a river that glides smoothly by, an endless stream of days following days. There are differences between one day and the next. Each day has its own relationship to the days that follow it. "Day unto day utters speech, and night unto night reveals knowledge " (Psalms 19:3).

If every ordinary day is so meaningful, how much more significant must be the day which is the climax of all time, the "First of the Year," the day that opens and also closes the cycle of the Jewish calendar?

But actually, is it right at all to think of the Jewish year in terms of an annual "cycle"?

Judaism teaches that life is not a cycle. It is, or at least it should be, a consistent and purposeful line of ascent. To be sure, there are steep descents as well, but even these inevitable lapses are meant to be stepping-stones toward ever greater heights. "Why does the soul descend?" the Talmud asks. The answer is, "So that it may ascend again."

Rosh HaShana is a shining spiritual summit beckoning to the Jew, challenging him to reach for it and to attain it. This is what makes Rosh HaShana a day of such momentous significance for the year to come, and even for all the years to follow, a day of decisive import for the formation, and perhaps even for the transformation, of the human personality.

II

Our holidays contain three distinct elements: each is a national festival, observed by the Jewish people as a whole, each is associated with a specific season of the year, and each commemorates a given event in our history. Rosh HaShana is one exception to this rule. It is a day of individual reckoning. Its significance is personal, rather than collective, for it is concerned with the individual and his own relationship with God and with his fellow men.

Rosh HaShana marks no particular season or historic event. And yet, no other holiday has such a profound impact on the Jewish people as a whole. No other prayers are so closely related to creation as a whole as is the liturgy of this holiday. And no other occasion bears quite to this degree the stamp of history—that of Israel and that of the world.

Why these contradictions?

We find the answer in the main units of the Rosh HaShana Service—*Malkhuyot* (The Kingship of God), *Zikhronot* (Remembrance), and *Shofarot* (The Sounding of the Shofar)—which reflect the completeness of Judaism. The *Musaf* liturgy expresses the relation of the individual to God and to his fellow men, the place of the individual in the community, but also the peoplehood of Israel. It reveals the deep roots of current events, thoughts and actions in the work of creation and in the eternal course of nature. At the same time, it marks out the role of the Jewish people and of its history within the context of the story of mankind.

Let us proceed to examine these three main elements of the Rosh HaShana liturgy.

Kiddush cup. This silver cup, partly gilded (Nuremberg, ca. 1680) depicts the story of the sacrifice of Isaac (Genesis 22:1-18). It was meant to be used for Kiddush on Rosh HaShana, when this Biblical portion is read in the synagogue to illustrate man's unquestioning obedience to his God. (The Jewish Museum, New York City).

It is interesting to note that on Rosh HaShana the very portion of liturgy with which we conclude our daily prayers all year round, often casually and in haste, appears as the solemn introduction to the first of the three prayer groups comprising the Rosh HaShana Service—*Malkhuyot,* which proclaims the Kingship of God. This introduction, beginning with *Alenu Leshabeakh* "It is ours to praise," is invocation, proclamation, declaration of faith, and prayer all in one. Its essence is the assertion of God's Kingship over the Universe and of the faith and the obligations of His chosen people.

"And it is said: He has not beheld iniquity in Jacob, neither has He seen perverseness in Israel; the Lord his God is with him and the shout of a King is among them.' And it is said: 'And He was King of Jeshurun when the heads of the people were gathered, the tribes of Israel together. And in Thy Holy Scriptures it is written: 'For Sovereignty is the Lord's; and He is the ruler over the nations'.''

This statement proclaims the unique nature of God and of the Jewish people.

Here the universal character of Rosh HaShana is also expressed. The holiday is set within the context of the cosmos, of its creation and Creator, Ruler and Sovereign.

Nothing of individual nature is contained in this liturgy which reveals the unique character of the Jewish people as well as of the commandments and duties that regulate its life. This invocation reflects that synthesis of universalism and nationalism which is so typical of the teachings of Judaism.

IV

The second unit of the Rosh HaShana *Musaf* liturgy, *Zikhronot,* "Remembrance," begins with the words, "Thou rememberest what was wrought from eternity, and art mindful of all that has been formed from of old..." This is the declaration of the twofold significance of Rosh HaShana: the Day of Remembrance is also the Day of Judgment. On this day the remembrance of man's deeds, of his thoughts and designs comes before the throne of the Almighty. "Thou rememberest every deed that had been done; not a creature is concealed from Thee; all things are manifest and known unto Thee, O Lord, our God..."

However, remembrance and judgment alike are unique in the fact that they are expected not only of the Supreme Judge, but also enjoined on the object of these two processes—man himself. Each individual is bidden to recall his deeds during the year just completed and to pass judgment upon them by himself so that he may repent and mend his ways.

Tashlikh on a Tel Aviv beach. On the first day of Rosh HaShana, following the Minha service, men, women and children go to a body of water, symbolically casting their sins into the sea. This custom, which dates from the 14th century, is referred to as Tashlikh ("Thou wilt cast") from Micah 7:19 ("Thou wilt cast all our sins into the depths of the sea"). (Israel Office of Information).

What is more, each individual is his own record of remembrance. His life is an open book, in which all his deeds are recorded (*Ethics of the Fathers* 2:1). On the Day of Remembrance, it is our duty to open this book and to read it in a spirit of introspection, pondering every step, every decision in our life, and the consequences of each.

Thus, Judaism bids the Jew pass judgment upon himself before he is judged by the Supreme Judge. "Let us search our ways and investigate them—so that we may return to the Lord" (*Lamentations* 3:40). We are commanded to remember our every step, our every act, and our every transgression, so that our repentance will be complete.

Remembrance is therefore an essential preparation for the main act of the Days of Awe—*Teshuva,* repentance. According to Maimonides, remembrance is an absolute condition for reviewing and analyzing our past with the aim of eliminating self-delusion and achieving self-refinement. We are bidden to measure our past against the standards set

73

by the Torah and its principles and by our own conscience. If we do this, then Rosh HaShana may well mark a turning-point in our lives. This day which, as we say in the *Musaf* service, "was the beginning of Thy work," may then also become the beginning of the re-creation of the truly repentant individual in a new world of his own, the opening of a new, brighter chapter in his life.

The Jewish people is essentially a people dedicated to remembrance. We are commanded several times in the Torah to *remember*. In the Fourth Commandment we are told: *"Remember* the Sabbath Day in order to keep it holy" (Exodus 20:8). But in the second enumeration of the Ten Commandments (Deuteronomy 5:12) we read: *"Keep* the Sabbath Day." The Talmud explains this difference as follows: " 'Remember' and 'keep' are actually one and the same commandment." One cannot "keep" Divine commandments without "remembering" them. This admonition of remembrance applies not only to the Sabbath but also to all the teachings of the Torah. For we Jews are an historic people. If we forget our past, we will lose our Jewish identity.

Rosh HaShana is the day on which we are commanded specifically to refresh our individual and collective memories, to become aware of our past in order that we may be able to face our future.

Therefore, Rosh HaShana is known also as *Yom Hazikaron*, the Day of Remembrance, and *Zikhronot*, the Prayers of Remembrance, occupying a central position in the liturgy of the day.

V

The Bible refers to the Jewish New Year as "The Day of the Sounding of the Shofar" (Numbers 23:1), or "The Day of Remembrance of the Sounding of the Shofar" (Leviticus 23:24), but never as Rosh HaShana. That term is found only later, in the Talmud (Rosh HaShana). As for the terms *Day of Remembrance* and *Day of Judgment,* these occur for the first time in the Jewish prayer book.

Thus the Bible itself established the Sounding of the Shofar as the central point of the observance of this holiday.

The sound of the shofar is a clarion call to the slumbering conscience, warning against fixations in personal views and attitudes. It is a call to remember, and review the past, to take stock of the situation into which the individual has been led by his day-to-day conduct.

"Awake, you slumberers," the sound of the shofar proclaims, "and ponder your deeds; remember your Creator and return to Him in penitence. Be not like those who forget the truth in the vanities of the hour; who indulge all year in trifles which cannot profit or save. Look well into your souls and consider your deeds! Forsake your evil ways and return to God that He may have mercy upon you" (Maimonides, *Mishne Torah, Teshuva* 3:4; 5:1-2,4).

Accordingly, the *Musaf* liturgy of the Rosh HaShana, in addition to *Malkhuyot* (the proclamation of God's Kingship) and *Zikhronot* (Remembrance), also includes a part called *Shofarot*, which conveys the manifold symbolism of the call of the ram's horn which, shattering illusions, smashing idols and exploding falsehood and deceit, is meant to bring us back to the eternal values of Judaism.

VI

Unlike New Year's Day of other civilizations, the two days of Rosh HaShana, the Jewish New Year, are not marked by hilarity but by solemn prayer. Rosh HaShana is devoted to serious introspection: every Jew is bidden to review his conduct of the past year toward God and his fellow-men and to resolve to do better in the year to come.

It is interesting to note that Rosh HaShana is known by four different Hebrew names, each signifying another one of its aspects.

1. *Rosh HaShana, literally* "Head of the Year." Rosh HaShana is New Year's Day, as reckoned from the beginning of recorded Biblical history (according to Orthodox belief, from the creation of the world.)

2. *Yom HaDin,* "Day of Judgment." According to tradition Rosh HaShana is the day on which God judges every human being by his deeds during the year just ended and inscribes his fate accordingly in the heavenly record book for the year to come; hence the traditional Jewish New Year greeting: *L'shanah tovah tikatevu,* "May you be inscribed for a good year." Before each Rosh HaShana meal, Jews eat apples dipped in honey to symbolize the wish and hope for a "sweet"

Page from Festival Prayers, Florence, 15th century. This page, showing a man blowing the shofar, is from a richly illuminated manuscript of a book of daily and festival prayers, commissioned by Elijah Dattilo Gallico of Vigevano. The manuscript was presented to the Library of the Jewish Theological Seminary of America, New York City, by Baron Edmond de Rothschild.

year. It is considered within the power of man to avert an unfavorable Divine decree by devoting special effort to penitence, prayer and charity during the ten-day period between Rosh HaShana and Yom Kippur (the *Aseret Y'mei Tshuva*).

3. *Yom HaZikkaron,* "Day of Remembrance." On Rosh HaShana God remembers all the good and evil deeds of man. Accordingly, the Jew pleads with the Almighty to remember the exemplary righteousness of the Patriarchs and other great figures in Jewish history, and, for their sake, to show mercy to the present generation.

4. *Yom T'rua,* the Day of Sounding the *Shofar* (ram's horn). The sounds of the Shofar call upon each Jew to repent of his past sins, to forsake the ways of evil and to pursue goodness and mercy, not only for his own sake but also for the sake of all mankind, because Judaism teaches that only individual morality can bring about universal peace and brotherhood.

Significantly, this universal aspect of the Jewish faith is stressed throughout the Rosh HaShana liturgy, as, for instance, in the following prayer:

"Then shall the righteous see and be glad, the upright shall exult, the pious shall rejoice in song, and inquity shall close her mouth and all wickedness shall be wholly consumed like smoke, when Thou makest the dominion of tyranny to pass away from the earth."

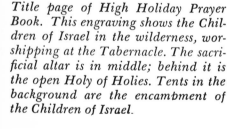

Title page of High Holiday Prayer Book. This engraving shows the Children of Israel in the wilderness, worshipping at the Tabernacle. The sacrificial altar is in middle; behind it is the open Holy of Holies. Tents in the background are the encambment of the Children of Israel.

WHY THE SHOFAR IS SOUNDED

SAADIA GAON (882-942), the celebrated scholar and religious leader of the Babylonian Period, head of the renowned academy of Sura, gave the following ten reasons for the sounding of the Shofar during the Days of Awe.

1. Rosh HaShana marks the beginning of creation. On that day, God created the world and became its Supreme Ruler. Just as trumpets are sounded to announce the coronation of a king of flesh and blood, so do we proclaim the kingship of God each year with the sounding of the ram's horn, as it is written in the Holy Scriptures: "With trumpets and with the sound of the horn, shout joyfully before the King, the Lord" (Psalms 88:6).

2. Rosh HaShana ushers in the solemn Ten Days of Penitence. The sound of the shofar serves as a call to repentance, for such is the custom of kings: their decree is accompanied by a warning that a transgression of the law will carry punishment. Thus, a forewarned transgressor has only himself to blame for the consequences of his misdeeds.

3. The call of the shofar reminds us of the giving of the Ten Commandments at Mount Sinai, when our ancestors assumed the responsibility of carrying out the precepts of the Torah by declaring: "We shall do and we shall hearken" (Exodus 24:7). Also at the Divine revelation on Mount Sinai, the shofar was blown, as it is said: "And the sound of the horn was exceedingly strong" (Exodus 19:16).

4. The blasts of the shofar remind us of the words of the Prophets that have been likened to a trumpet call: "Then whosoever hears the sound of the trumpet but does not take warning—when the sword comes and takes him away—his blood shall be upon his own head . . . Whereas, if he had taken warning, he would have saved himself" (Ezekiel 33:4-5).

5. When we hear the call of the shofar, we are reminded of the destruction of the Holy Temple and of the war shouts of our foes, as it is written: "For I hear the sound of the trumpet, the shouting of war" (Jeremiah 4:19). And so we pray to the Almighty that He may rebuild the Temple.

6. We recall Isaac, who was ready to let himself be sacrificed for the sake of Heaven. So, too, may we ourselves be willing to offer our souls for the sanctification of the Holy Name in the hope that the Almighty may remember us and ordain a happy future for us.

7. The sound of the shofar fills us with fear and trepidation before the Creator, for such is the nature of a piercing trumpet call, as it is said: "If a trumpet is blown in a city, would the people not tremble?" (Amos 3:6).

8. The shofar heralds the approach of the awe-inspiring Day of Judgment. "Near at hand is the great day of the Lord, near and speeding fast . . . a day of the trumpet and battlecry" (Zephaniah 1:14-16).

9. The shofar symbolizes the future ingathering of the exiles and inspires us to strive for that ingathering as anticipated by the Prophet: "In that day will a blast be blown on a great trumpet; and those who were lost in the land of Assyria, and those who were outcasts in the land of Egypt, will come and worship the Lord on the holy mountain in Jerusalem" (Isaiah 27:13).

10. The shofar makes us reflect on the future revival of the dead and reaffirm our belief in it, so it is said: "All you inhabitants of the world, and you dwellers on earth, when a signal is raised on the mountains, look! When a trumpet is blown, hark!" (Isaiah 18:3).

THE SIGNIFICANCE OF THE SHOFAR IN OUR DAY
I. "the remembrance of the sound of the shofar"

THE SOUNDS OF THE SHOFAR are always the same from year to year. But their meaning and echoes change with the events of each period in Jewish history. In essence, every age has its own shofar sound. According to Saadia Gaon and Rabbi David ben Yosef Abudraham*, there are at least ten reasons for the sounding of the shofar on Rosh HaShana, but while one of these reasons may predominate for one given era, another reason may be paramount in another day. For the sound of the shofar reverberates with the echo of the times, conveying the significance of specific events, characterizing each era and accentuating its importance.

What is the significance of the shofar in our own day?

The "remembrance of the sounding of the shofar" now reminds us of the most dramatic moment in the recent Six-Day War when the exultation of the Israeli warriors reached the peak of ecstasy with the liberation of the Western Wall on June 8, 1967. This sublime shofar call was heard throughout the world, leaving a powerful never-to-be-forgotten impact on the hearts and minds of Jews the world over. It was the voice of eternity that will never be silenced.

If, in ancient times, the Prophet wondered: "If a trumpet is blown in a city, would the people not tremble?" (Amos 3:6), then most certainly the shofar sounded on that eventful day at the Western Wall stirred every Jewish heart and filled every Jewish soul with joy. All the yearning, all the fervor of centuries of faith and hope found expression in that triumphant blast of the shofar at the sacred shrine freed by the blood of the chosen sons of Israel, the gallant warriors who had sacrificed their young lives for the sanctification of the Divine Name.

* Liturgical commentator active in Spain in the fourteenth century.

78

We were reminded of the prophecy of Isaiah which Abudraham cites as one of the reasons for the sounding of the shofar: "On that day will a blast be sounded on a great trumpet; and those who were lost in the land of Assyria, and those who were outcasts in the land of Egypt, will come and worship the Lord on the holy mountain in Jerusalem " (Isaiah 27:13).

II. prayer and rejoicing

THE SOUND OF THE SHOFAR performs two functions: it is a call to prayer for redemption from misfortune, and an expression of rejoicing at deliverance. The first function is aptly explained by Rabbi Aaron HaLevi of Barcelona* in his *Sefer Ha-Hinukh:*

"Man requires great concentration in his supplication before his Creator that He may have compassion upon him and save him from peril; hence the Divine command to sound trumpets in such times of trouble. Man, by reason of his being primarily a material creature, needs a stirring summons to look to his spiritual life. Without that call, his better nature will remain dormant, and nothing can rouse it as effectively as the sound of music, particularly the sound of the trumpet which is the most powerful of all musical instruments."

The Spanish Talmudist stresses the sound of the trumpet, alluding to the Biblical injunction: "When you engage in war in your land against an adversary that is oppressing you, you shall sound an alarm with the trumpets, so that you may be remembered before the Lord your God and be saved from your enemies " (Numbers 19:9). Just as the shofar is sounded at the beginning of the month of Tishri, on Rosh HaShana, and at the conclusion of the Ten Days of Penitence at the end of Yom Kippur, so trumpets are also sounded when the army of God's people marches forth to war and when, with God's help, it returns victorious. Thus, the trumpet-call arouses the warriors to pray for victory and also expresses the joy and thanksgiving of victory, as it is written: "And on your days of celebration, on your fixed festivals, and on the first day of the month you shall blow the trumpets " (Numbers 10:10).

The sounding of the shofar at the Western Wall in our day performed the second function—to proclaim our jubilation and our gratitude to the Almighty for having given us consolation for our sufferings and having delivered us at last.

The Day of Justice. Woodcut, by Joseph Budko, inspired by Un'tane Tokef prayer recited on Rosh Ha-Shana and Yom Kippur. Woodcut shows the scales of heavenly judgment and the great shofar mentioned in the prayer.

* Spanish Talmudist (c. 1300)

79

III. calamity and salvation

CONCERNING THE OBSCURE PHRASE in Isaiah 24:16, *razi li, razi li, oy li,* Rashi comments: "Woe is me that two *mysteries* (from raz— mystery) have been revealed to me—the mystery of calamity and the mystery of salvation."

Our generation, having experienced the virtual annihilation of European Jewry on the one hand, and the glorious restoration of the State of Israel on the other, has also beheld these two mysteries— calamity and salvation. The revelation of Divine redemption was proclaimed at long last by the jubilant sound of the shofar on the day when Jerusalem became one and the cherished remnant of our sanctuary was freed from alien hands. We beheld hardened veterans of battle weeping like children at the sight of an ancient stone wall; callous fighters who had all but drifted away from the tradition of their fathers, standing motionless and gazing in silent awe, misty-eyed with wonder and rapture, at the ruined shrine. Suddenly the Wall had become a living presence, an eloquent symbol of eternal nationhood. It will assume an even deeper significance on Rosh HaShana which, according to Rabbi Nahman of Bratzlav*, "enhances the holiness of the Land of Israel, for it is written: 'A land . . . upon which are the eyes of the Lord *from the beginning of the year.*' " (Deut. 11:12).

The significance of the month of Tishri as a month of joy and mercy had its origins in the days of antiquity when the people of Israel still dwelt upon its own land. In those days it was primarily a month of national celebration, coinciding with the completion of work in the fields and the ingathering of the harvest. It was during that month that King Solomon dedicated the Temple, as recorded in the Holy Scriptures: "And all the men of Israel assembled unto King Solomon at the feast in the month *Ethanim,* which is the seventh month " (I Kings, 8:2).

It is stated in the Talmud (Tractate *Rosh HaShana* 10:2) that there seems to have been some rivalry between the months of Tishri and Nisan as to which one should mark the beginning of the year, but when the Second Jewish Commonwealth was established in the days of Ezra, the month of Tishri, with Rosh HaShana as its spiritual climax, won out.

IV. universal redemption

AT THE SAME TIME, Rosh HaShana assumed the connotation of universal redemption. On that day, the shofar proclaimed hope for the future, for the end of wars and disasters, for a day on which "all wickedness shall be wholly consumed like smoke when Thou makest

* Hasidic rabbi (1772-1811); great-grandson of the Baal Shem Tov. founder of Hasidism.

the dominion of arrogance to pass away from the earth and when Thou, O Lord, shalt reign alone . . ." This messianic hope is bound up intimately with Jerusalem, the holy city, as prophesied by Jeremiah: "At that time they shall call Jerusalem 'the throne of the Lord,' and all nations shall gather there to celebrate the name of the Lord in Jerusalem " (Jeremiah 3:17).

V. awe and joy

WHILE ANXIETY IS DEEMED appropriate for the Day of Judgment, tradition also bids the Jew hope for a favorable verdict which will bring joy to his heart.

When Ezra saw that the returning exiles were sad and wept while the Torah was read on Rosh HaShana, he bade them dry their tears and hope for God's pardon and mercy: "This day is holy to the Lord your God; do not mourn, nor weep. Go your way, eat the fat and drink the sweet, and send portions to him for whom nothing is prepared, for the joy of the Lord is your refuge " (Nehemiah 8:9-10).

Throughout the early period of Jewish statehood, the Days of Awe were days of joy. "And what great nation is there that has statutes and ordinances so just as all this code that I am placing before you today?" Scripture (Deut. 4:8) declares, and the Talmud comments: "What people is like this people? As is the custom in the world, a man who has a serious lawsuit pending against him, dresses in black clothes, wraps himself in a black cloak and lets his beard grow untrimmed, for he does not know what the verdict, and hence his fate, will be. Not so the people of Israel: they dress in white clothes, cut and trim their beards, eat and drink, knowing full well that the Holy One, Blessed be He, performs miracles for them " (Jerusalem Talmud, Rosh HaShana 1:3).

During the **Temple** period, even **Yom Kippur**, the solemn Day of Atonement, was a day of rejoicing.The maidens of Jerusalem would go to the vineyards dancing and marriage mates were chosen. (Mishna *Ta'anit*, Chapter 4, Mishna 8).

VI. homeland and exile

THE LOSS OF NATIONAL INDEPENDENCE, however, brought a change. Rosh HaShana and Yom Kippur became "Days of Awe," solemn days that struck fear in the hearts of the Jews whose fate always hung in the balance, subject to the whims of alien rulers. As the Talmud put it, "since the destruction of the Holy Temple, there is not a day without a curse" (Sota 9:12); "and each day is cursed more than the preceding day" (Sota 49:1). At the beginning of each year, the Jew would wonder what new calamities and evil decrees the new year would bring.

81

The term "Yamim Noraim" ("Days of Awe," literally "Terrible Days") was coined in the late Middle Ages. The first man to use it was the Codifier Mordecai ben Hillel Ashkenazi, known briefly as "Mordecai" who was born at the beginning of the thirteenth century and died a martyr's death in Nuremberg in 1298. The term *nora* in Hebrew also means "awesome," hence the English translation "Days of Awe." But in the context of bitter exile, the term "Yamim Noraim" conveyed not merely awe but the real terror and anxiety which dominated the ghetto life of the Jew.

VII. days of awe and days of rejoicing

THE CONTRADICTION BETWEEN the designations *Yamim Tovim* ("Festive Days") and the *Yamim Noraim* ("Days of Awe"), both of which have been applied to Rosh HaShana and Yom Kippur, and the contrast between the rejoicing urged by Ezra and the fear of a later period, are also expressed in the liturgy of Rosh HaShana. Thus, immediately following the prayer "Reign Thou over all the world" comes the assurance that we will be privileged to behold the advent of redemption, the dominion of Heaven on earth and the appearance of the Lord "in the splendor and excellence of His might upon all the inhabitants of the world." Then the joyful aspect of the holiday was stressed in the prayers usually recited on the festivals: "And Thou hast given us in love, O Lord our God, appointed times for gladness, festivals and seasons for joy . . . O Lord, our God, bestow upon us the blessing of Thy holy festivals for life and peace, for joy and gladness . . . and let us inherit, O Lord our God, with joy and gladness Thy holy festivals."

In the course of time, when the sufferings of the Jews grew unbearable, and the *Yamim Noraim* quite literally became days of terror, some religious authorities wanted to eliminate these expressions of rejoicing from the liturgy of the Days of Awe. In the eleventh century, there arose in Mayence, Germany, a controversy among the Codifiers regarding the appropriateness of these "prayers of rejoicing." Some rabbis in Germany ruled that they ought to be eliminated. The *Gaonim* of Palestine, on the other hand, sternly cautioned against tampering with the prayerbook. Finally, in the fourteenth century, the prayers of rejoicing were deleted from the liturgy of the Days of Awe almost throughout Europe. The *Mahzor Vitry* reflects this somber mood. It declares that although the Palestinian authorities opposed the elimination of these prayers, their decision should not be considered binding on the diaspora communities since "the custom of the Land of Israel may be different from that of Babylonia" (i.e., of the diaspora).

Here we see the contrast between the optimism of the Jews of Palestine, even in days of oppression, and the pessimism typical of the outlook of Diaspora Jewry.

I believe that now, the rebirth of the State of Israel affords ample justification for restoring the note of optimism to the solemnity of the Days of Awe; "O Lord our God, bestow upon us the blessing of the holy festivals for life and peace, for joy and gladness . . ."

THE HIGH HOLY DAY LITURGY

THE FOLLOWING PRAYER EXPRESSES the hope for the day when God's sovereignty will be universally acknowledged; when justice and righteousness will be firmly established and injustice and wickedness will vanish from the earth; and when Jerusalem, the Holy City, will once again become the center of the dominion of the Almighty.

"Therefore, O Lord our God, impose Thy awe upon all whom Thou hast made, and Thy fear upon all whom Thou hast created; may all Thy works revere Thee and all Thy creatures worship Thee; and may they all form one union to do Thy will with a perfect heart. For we know, O Lord our God, that Thine are dominion, strength and might; and that Thy Name is held in awe by all whom Thou hast created.

"Therefore, O Lord, grant honor to Thy people, glory to those who revere Thee, good hope to those who seek Thee, free expression to those who wait for Thy salvation, joy to Thy land and gladness to Thy city, growing strength to David Thy servant, and a shining light to the son of Jesse, Thy anointed, speedily in our days.

"May the righteous see and rejoice, the upright exult, and the pious delight in song. Iniquity shall be silenced, and all wickedness shall vanish like smoke when Thou wilt abolish the rule of tyranny on earth.

"Then Thou alone, O Lord, wilt reign over all Thy works, on Mount Zion, abode of Thy glory, and in Jerusalem, Thy Holy City, as it is written in Thy Holy Scriptures: 'The Lord shall reign forever, your God, O Zion, unto all generations. Praise the Lord.' "

The *Avinu Malkenu* ("Our Father Our King"), selections from which are given below, is read immediately after the morning *Amida* each day from Rosh HaShana through Yom Kippur. It is omitted only on the Sabbath, because its allusions to the many calamities that have befallen the Jewish people in exile were deemed inconsistent with the joy of the Sabbath, and because it contains petitions for personal favors which are considered inappropriate on the Day of Rest.

"Shivisi" plaque. Plaque placed above Reader's stand at some synagogues. Name refers to first Hebrew word of Psalm 16:8 "I have set the Lord always before me; surely He is at my right hand, I shall not be moved." This plaque is replete with various Cabbalistic quotations.

Avinu Malkenu consists of forty-four supplications for God's blessings, pardon of sins and protection from misfortunes, both national and personal. It dates to a relatively early period: already the Talmud mentions that Rabbi Akiba, the second-century Tannaite, used to recite this prayer in its original, shorter form, on fast-days. Over the centuries, additional relevant petitions were incorporated into the *Avinu Malkenu.*

"Our Father, our King, we have sinned before Thee.

Our Father, our King, we have no king except Thee.

Our Father, our King, renew a good year for us.

Our Father, our King, abolish all evil decrees against us.

Our Father, our King, frustrate the counsel of our enemies.

Our Father, our King, remove pestilence, sword, famine, captivity, destruction, iniquity and persecution from the people of Thy covenant.

Our Father, our King, forgive and pardon all our sins.

Our Father, our King, lead us back to Thee in perfect repentance.

Our Father, our King, send perfect healing to the sick among Thy people.

Our Father, our King, inscribe us in the Book of Happy Life.

Our Father, our King, inscribe us in the Book of Redemption and Salvation.

Our Father, our King, fill our hands with Thy blessings.

Our Father, our King, fill our storehouses with plenty.

Our Father, our King, open the gates of heaven to our prayer.

Our Father, our King, remember that we are but dust.

Our Father, our King, have mercy on us, on our children and infants.

Our Father, our King, act for the sake of those who were massacred for Thy holy Name.

Our Father, our King, avenge the blood of Thy servants that has been shed.

Our Father, our King, be gracious to us and answer us although we have no merits; deal with us charitably and kindly, and save us. '

The Reader's sense of responsibility as the spokesman of the entire congregation in an impassioned plea for mercy and forgiveness before the Supreme Judge is expressed in the stirring prayer, *Hineni He-Ani,* which he recites as an introduction to the *Musaf* service of Rosh HaShana and Yom Kippur. This prayer, of unknown authorship, ranks among the highlights of our liturgy. Pervaded by a spirit of awe and humility, its emotional appeal is profound and powerful.

"I, poor in worthy deeds, frightened and terrified in the presence of Him who is enthroned amid Israel's exaltations, have come to stand up and plead before Thee on behalf of Thy people Israel who have delegated me, although I am neither deserving nor qualified for such a mission. Therefore I beseech Thee, God of Abraham, Isaac and Jacob, O Lord God, merciful and gracious God of Israel, Almighty, revered and awe-inspiring, crown with success the task I have undertaken, to present myself and to seek mercy for me and for those who have sent me. Do not blame them for my sins nor hold them responsible for my transgressions for I, myself, am but a sinner and transgressor . . . May our sins of omission be pardoned by Thy love, for love atones for all iniquities. Turn all miseries and affliction, for us and for all Israel, into joy and gladness, life and peace . . . and let there be no stumbling in prayer . . . for Thou, in mercy, hearest the prayer of Your people Israel."

The heavenly judgment on the Days of Awe is described in *Un tane Tokef* ("Let Us Recount the Holiness') recited before the *Kedusha* of the *Musaf* service for Rosh HaShana and Yom Kippur. This prayer is attributed to Rabbi Kalonymus ben Meshulam of Mayence who lived in the eleventh century. According to legend, however, the author was the martyred Rabbi Amnon, who composed it as he was about to expire. It was communicated only at a later date to Rabbi Kalonymus who introduced it into our liturgy.

"Let us recount the mighty holiness of the day, for it is fearful and awesome. On it, Thy dominion is exalted, Thy throne is established on mercy, and Thou dost occupy it in truth. It is true that Thou art judge and admonitor, discerner and witness, Who inscribes and seals; Who records, enumerates and remembers all things forgotten. Thou openest the book of records, and it reads of itself; every man's signature is in it.

"The great shofar is sounded; a still, gentle voice is heard; angels rush about, seized by fear and trembling, and proclaim:'This is the Day of Judgment to bring to justice even the hosts of heaven, for also they are not blameless in Thy sight.' All human beings pass before Thee like a flock of sheep. As a shepherd inspects his flock, causing his sheep to pass beneath his rod, so Thou dost cause all living souls to pass before Thee; Thou countest and numberest them, fixing their allotted time-limit and inscribing their fate.

"On Rosh HaShana it is inscribed, and on the fast day of Yom Kippur it is sealed, how many shall pass on and how many shall come into the world; who shall live and who shall die; who shall have a timely end and who shall meet an untimely death; who shall perish by fire and who by water; who by sword and who by beast; who by

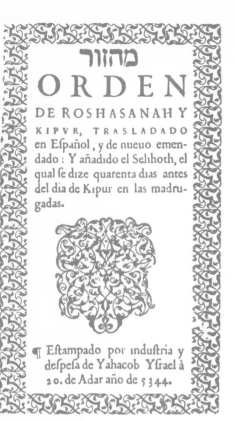

hunger and who by thirst; who by earthquake and who by plague; who by strangling and who by stoning; who shall rest and who shall wander; who shall have peace and who shall be torn by anguish; who shall enjoy tranquility and who shall be tormented; who shall become poor and who shall become rich; who shall be brought low and who shall be raised high.

"But repentance, prayer and charity can avert the evil decree.

"For as Thy Name, so, too, is Thy fame: slow to anger and prone to kindness. Thou dost not desire the sinner's death, but only that he turn from his evil way and live. Thou waitest for him until the day of his death; should he repent, Thou wilt accept him forthwith. It is true, indeed, that Thou art the Creator of men and that Thou knowest their inclinations, for they are but flesh and blood.

"Man comes from dust and ends in dust; he wins his bread at the risk of his life. He is like a fragile potsherd, like drying grass, like a withering blossom, like a passing shadow, like a fleeting cloud, like a wind blowing over, like flying dust, like a vanishing dream.

"But Thou art the King, the living and eternal God."

Heye Im Pifiyot ("Grant Aptness of Expression"), apparently first recorded by Rabbi Jacob Moellin (MaHaRil) in the fourteenth century, is another plea recited by the Reader that he may be able to present the prayers of his congregation effectively on the solemn Days of Awe. Recognizing that articulateness is a gift of Heaven, the *Hazzan* implores the Almighty to aid him in his mission, so that his representations may be worthy and acceptable before the Throne of Mercy.

"Our God and God of our Fathers, grant aptness of expression to the representatives of Thy people, the House of Israel, who stand before Thee to plead for mercy toward Thy people, the House of Israel. Teach them what they should say. Endow them with the wisdom as to what they should speak. Answer them in their pleadings. Grant them the knowledge of how to glorify Thee. May the light of Thy presence shine upon them as they bow before Thee and bless Thy people in the hope that all may be favored with Thy blessings. They pass Thy people before Thee while they themselves pass in the midst of the people. The eyes of Thy faithful are raised up to them as they place their hope in Thee. They approach the Holy Ark with reverence, to assuage Thy wrath and anger. Thy people surround them like a wall; mayest Thou look down from heaven upon them in mercy. They lift up their eyes to Thee; they pour out their hearts before Thee like streams of water. O hear them from heaven. Let them not stammer with their tongue or falter in their speech. Let them not humiliate themselves or cause their people to be humiliated. Let them not utter anything which might not be according to Thy will. For Thou, O Lord our God, art gracious and merciful to all upon Thou bestowest Thy kindness, as it is written in Thy Torah: 'I will be gracious to those to whom I am gracious, and I will be merciful to those to whom I am merciful' (Exodus 33:19). And it is also said: 'Let not those who hope in Thee be humiliated through me, O Lord God of hosts; let not those who seek Thee be disgraced through me, O God of Israel' (Psalms 69:7)."

Atah Noten Yad ("Thou Extendest a Hand") is a final moving supplication recited during the *Neila* (Concluding) Service on Yom Kippur, when, according to tradition, the gates of heaven are about to close and the fate of each individual is irrevocably sealed for the ensuing year. The authorship of this perceptive prayer, which is found in the ninth-century Siddur *Rav Amram Gaon,* is unknown.

"Thou extendest a hand to sinners, and Thy right hand is reached out to receive penitents. Thou hast taught us, O Lord our God, to confess to Thee all our iniquities, that we may discontinue our wrongdoing and that Thou mayest receive us into Thy presence through perfect repentance as Thou wouldst accept our sin-offerings, in accordance with Thy declared promise. Endless indeed are our obligatory sacrifices, countless are our guilt-offerings. Thou knowest that our end is the worm, hence Thou hast granted us abundant forgiveness. What are we, what is our life, what is our kindness, what is our righteousness, what is our salvation, what is our power and what is our strength? What can we say to Thee, O Lord our God and God of our fathers? Are not all heroes as nothing in Thy sight, men of renown as though they never existed, men of learning as though they were without knowledge, men of intellect as though they were without wisdom? For most of their deeds are futile, and the days of their life are but a fleeting breath in Thy sight; in essence, man is not superior to beast, for all is vanity.

"Thou hast singled man out from the beginning; Thou hast recognized him as deserving to stand in Thy presence. Who can say to Thee: What doest Thou? Even though man be righteous, what can it avail Thee? O Lord our God, Thou hast lovingly granted us this Day of Atonement for final pardon and forgiveness of all our iniquities, that we may discontinue our wrongdoing and return to Thee, to observe Thy laws and to do Thy will with a perfect heart; and Thou, in Thy abundant mercy, have compassion upon us since Thou dost not desire the destruction of the world, as it is said: 'Seek the Lord while He may be found, call upon Him while He is near. Let the wicked forsake his way, and the iniquitous his thoughts; let him return to the Lord, Who will have compassion on him, to our God Who will pardon abundantly'(Isaiah 55:7).

Page from High Holiday Mahzor, Germany, 14th century.

"Thou art a forgiving God, gracious and merciful, slow to anger, rich in grace and fidelity and abundantly beneficent. Thou willingly acceptest the repentance of the wicked and dost not desire their death, as it is said:'Tell them, says the Lord God, as I live, I have no desire for the death of the wicked, but that the wicked return from his way and live . . .'(Ezekiel 18:23). Thou art the pardoner of Israel, and the forgiver of the tribes of Yeshurun in every generation; beside Thee, we have no king Who pardons and forgives.

"My God, before I was created I was of no worth, and now that I have been created it is as though I had not been created. In Thy sight, I am like an object filled with shame and disgrace. May it be Thy will, Lord my God and God of my fathers, that I sin no more. In Thy abundant mercy, erase the sins I have committed against Thee, but not through grave sufferings and ailments."

THE LITURGICAL POEMS (PIYUTIM)

THE *PIYUTIM* (from the Greek *poiesis*, "poetry") are works of religious poetry introduced into the liturgy to enhance its esthetic value and emotional appeal. To this day, the *piyutim* contribute significantly to the spiritual elevation and to the devotional mood of the worshiper.

As early as in the days of the Holy Temple, psalms had been sung by the Levites on various occasions. With the establishment of synagogues during the period of the Second Temple, additional Biblical hymns and brief invocations attributed to the Sanhedrin were included in religious services. When, following the destruction of the Second Temple in the year 70 C.E. and the dispersion of the Jewish people, prayers took the place of sacrifices, the need for appropriate ritual expressions became increasingly manifest. A number of poets and scholars began to compose prayers, some of which are well-known today, (e.g. *Alenu Leshabeah, El Adon Al Kol Ha-ma'asim, Elohai Netzor Leshoni*, etc.).

The *piyutim* had their origins in Palestine, and their initial content was drawn from Talmudic and Midrashic legends dealing with law, ethics, consolation and the promise of eventual deliverance from exile. The *Gaonim** generally approved the inclusion of certain *piyutim* in the official liturgy, although some rabbinic authorities were considerably more discriminating in the selection of *piyutim* for public worship.

The two best-known early *payetanim* (liturgical poets) were Yannai and his disciple Eleazar Kallir**, who were active in the eighth and ninth centuries. The traditional High Holy Day Prayer Book is replete

---

* Religious leaders of the post-Talmudic Babylonian Jewish community (6th-11th centuries).
** Also known as Eleazar Ben Kallir.

88

with Eleazar's works. Although he was a master of rhyme, acrostics and alliteration, his style was encumbered by affectation, euphemisms, anachronisms and artificially constructed words designed to fit into that strait-jacket of formalistic pattern which became the model for other *payetanim* for the next two centuries.

The art of the *piyut* reached its peak during the Middle Ages in Spain and in Germany. The illustrious poets of the Golden Era in Spain—Solomon Ibn Gabirol, Moses Ibn Ezra, Judah Halevi and others—gave us religious poetry of sterling quality, throbbing with intense fervor and rising to sublime heights of divine inspiration. Their Hebrew was more natural, their style more fluent, their expression more spontaneous. Ibn Gabirol's *Shahar Avakeshkhah* ("At the Dawn I Seek Thee") and Judah Halevi's *Tziyon, Halo Tish'ali* ("Zion, Wilt Thou Not Ask?") are poetic gems of extraordinary brilliance.

Among the outstanding Jewish liturgical poets active in Germany were Rabbenu Gershom (965-1028), known as *Meor Ha-Golah*—"Light of the Exile"; Rashi (1040-1105), the celebrated Biblical and Talmudic commentator; Rashi's grandson Rabbenu Jacob ben Meir Tam (1100-1171); and Rabbi Simeon ben Isaac of Mayence (died c. 1015). The flowering of *Kabbala* and religious mysticism in the sixteenth century, in Safed, Palestine, inspired *piyutim* there. Rabbi Solomon ben Moses Alkabetz (1505-1584) composed the popular Sabbath eve hymn, *L'khah Dodi* ("Come, My Beloved"). Rabbi Israel Ibn Najarra ran a close second to Alkabetz. The distant Jewish community of Yemen also produced a distinguished religious poet in Rabbi Shalom ben Yosef Shabazi.

Thus, practically in every generation new prayers and hymns were added to the prayerbook. In our own day, a prayer, approved by Israel's Chief Rabbinate, for the welfare of the State of Israel was incorporated into our liturgy.

Tashlikh. A ritual performed in a small village in Eastern Europe. Painting by Chenoch Lieberman. (From the collection of Mr. and Mrs. Seymour Propp, New York City).

THE DAYS OF AWE

> "The Lord is near to all who call upon Him."
>
> (Psalms 145:18)

OF THE MANY AND VARIED attributes of God, the one particularly relevant to the Days of Awe is, most assuredly, His *nearness*. When Jews assemble in their houses of worship and, with awe and trembling, begin to recite the *Selihot*, the penitential prayers, they sense in their inmost being that "The Lord is near to all who call upon Him." This is the password that opens the heavens to their supplications. The Jew, humble and unsure of himself, stands in fear and trepidation and reflects: "How shall I reach the gates of heaven? How can my voice rise out of the depths to the loftiest of all high places?" And in the midst of his solemn meditations, he hears an inner voice calling to him: "Seek God while He may be found" (Isaiah 55:6), while your heart is attuned to His Presence. Call upon Him, for He is near. He may be found among those who seek Him.

However abject his despair, the Days of Awe raise the Jew to a level of spiritual closeness to God. They imbue him with a feeling of confidence that he is neither forsaken nor without hope in his hour of distress. There is always One to Whom he can turn for solace and succor, for "The Lord is near to all who call upon Him."

On the face of it, this seems rather strange. These are awesome days, filled with fear of the Day of Judgment. Would it not be more logical to seek to escape, to hide from the threatening wrath of the Lord, and do as the prophet would have us do—"Go into the cleft of the rock and conceal yourself?" Instead, the call goes forth to man in his despondency and terror not to seek to escape *from* God, but to escape *to* God, to flee from sin and evil and to hasten to the Lord, seeking—and finding—in Him a refuge from wrath, a shelter from peril, even as one in distress finds protection in the bosom of his family. In this connection, it is significant to note that *"karov,"* the Hebrew term used in the above-quoted Psalm to denote God's nearness, is the same as that which designates a "close" relative.

Would anyone refuse to shelter a kinsman from a violent storm on a dark night? Would your kinsman lock his door—and his heart—if, soaked and shivering with cold, you were to stand at the gate of his house and to plead: "Let me in"? The sound of your voice would be enough to have him let you into his home at once. Therefore call upon Him! He will draw you into the shelter of His abode, for "The Lord is near to all who call upon Him."

The Jew best perceives this nearness of God on the Days of Awe, a season of greatness and trembling. The Day of Judgment is great as well as awesome. The prophet Malachi speaks of the "coming of the great and awesome day." In whatever state man finds himself, whether in the smugness of conceit fostered by success, power and wealth, or in the abyss of gnawing self-doubt, of want and misery, on the Days of Awe he is prepared to place his thoughts and deeds, even his very fate, upon the crucial scales of God's judgment. For no matter how strict that judgment may be, he is comforted by a sense of nearness to its Source that bespeaks mercy since "The Lord is near to all who call upon Him."

The task of bringing man near to God was assigned to the prophets. This, too, seems strange. The prophets are the severest of all chastisers. With the searing ire of their fiery words, they rip the veil from corruption, tear the mask from sham and hypocrisy, bare crime and transgression, and expose man in all his decadence and degradation. One would think that those who would thus consign man to banishment from God's grace would consider him as being worlds apart from the Divine

Synagogue. 19th century painting of a service at a synagogue in a small Eastern European town, by I. Winter. (The Jewish Museum, New York City).

Presence. But quite the contrary. The prophets' stern words of reproof are meant to separate man not from God, but from his own base instincts and thereby draw him closer to his Creator. No matter how far he may have strayed, there is no Jew who will not feel, particularly during these Days of Judgment, the nearness of his merciful Father. For who was it that admonished man to call upon God, if not the prophets? Who lifts him up from the darkness of perdition to the light of redemption, if not the bearers of the Divine Word who inspire him with new hope and assure him that "The Lord is near to all who call upon Him"?

Consider, too, that it is precisely the existence of sin and the awareness of guilt that lead to repentance. It is these unfortunate facts of life that have given us the prophets and their timeless message. It is written in the Talmud that were it not for the circumstance that man is imperfect, we would have in our sacred literature only the Pentateuch and the Book of Joshua. Our misdeeds cost us dear, but they gave us the prophets. Our estrangement from Divine Law provided the prophets with their mission to effect a reconciliation between man and God.

The prophets, however, were reluctant to carry out this thankless, burdensome mission. They attempted to flee from their destiny. The message from God, with which they were charged, was stern and thus bound to earn them bitter resentment and even open animosity on the part of the people. Prophets were frequently spat upon, ridiculed and even stoned. Their life was in constant danger. From the first prophet, Moses, who implored, "Send, I entreat Thee, whomever Thou wishest to send" because "the Children of Israel will not listen to me," to later prophets like Ezekiel, who knew beforehand that "The House of Israel will not hearken unto me" and Jonah who vainly fled from his assignment which, most appropriately, became the subject of the *Haftara* reading for the *Minha* service of Yom Kippur. All these servants of God sought to dodge a task from which there was no escape, because they were appalled by the vast gap between the heights of Godliness and the abyss of evil, and they were not at all sure that it could ever be bridged. But God has assured us, time and again, that this gap is not unbridgable, for "The Lord is near to all who call upon Him."

Truly, at no time is this nearness so strongly felt as during the Days of Awe, the Ten Days of Penitence that begin with Rosh HaShana and culminate in Yom Kippur. At no times does the Jew hear the call, "Seek God while He may be found" as plainly as he does then. And so, on the solemn Days of Awe, every Jew, each from the depths of his own anguished soul, from the perplexities of his own troubled conscience, calls out to the Lord, confident that "The Lord is near to all who call upon Him."

Torah breastplate. In Ashkenazi communities it became customary to place a silver plaque on each Scroll of the Law to indicate the occasion or holiday for which it was to be used. Today this plaque is seen in the form of the "breastplate." This silver shield, decorated with semi-precious stones (Nuremberg, 1752) is provided with interchangeable plates to indicate the occasion on which the Scroll is to be used. The plate marking for Yom Kippur is shown here. (Hebrew Union College Museum, Cincinnati, Ohio).

And this shall be a statute for ever unto you: that in the seventh month, on the tenth day of the month, you shall afflict your souls, and do no work at all, whether it be one of your own country, or a stranger that sojourns among you. For on that day shall the priest make an atonement for you, to cleanse you, that you may be clean from all your sins before the Lord. It shall be a sabbath of rest unto you, and you shall afflict your souls, by a statute for ever.

LEVITICUS 16:29-31

YOM KIPPUR

AS IMPLIED BY ITS NAME, Yom Kippur, the Day of Atonement, is the day when Jews make amends for sins committed during the preceding year, and voice a final, impassioned appeal to God for forgiveness before the gates of Heaven close and the verdict of each individual's fate in the year to come is irrevocably sealed.

This atonement is expressed by fasting and fervent prayer. In humility and contrition, pious Jews fast from sundown to sundown and remain all day in the synagogue for penitential prayers.

The highlight of the Yom Kippur Eve service is the chanting of the time-hallowed *Kol Nidre* prayer. The solemn, haunting Kol Nidre melody, which originated among the Jews of Southern Germany in the sixteenth century, has become well known to all lovers of classical music, and a number of noted composers have created variations on its stirring theme.

The Hebrew phrase "Kol Nidre" means "All the Vows." Actually, Kol Nidre is not a prayer but a declaration absolving one from vows which one may have rashly made to God during the past year and which later proved impossible of fulfillment.

This declaration assumed a particularly poignant significance during the Inquisition, when thousands of Jews in Spain and Portugal, the so-called "Marranos," had been forced to convert to Catholicism while secretly continuing to adhere to the Jewish faith. Kol Nidre released them from the vows they had been pressed to make to the Catholic Church.

A single, prolonged blast of the Shofar, the ram's horn, marks the conclusion of Yom Kippur, thus bringing to an end the High Holy Day season. The congregation leaves the synagogue filled with hope and new resolve "to do justly, to love mercy, and to walk humbly with the Lord."

ATONEMENT

THE JEWS ARE A PEOPLE of conservationists. The very survival of the Jewish people amidst the trials of exile depended on its ability to conserve its spiritual heritage against overwhelming odds. Judaism was therefore geared to maintaining, cultivating and strengthening its sacred and timeless values against erosion from within by the tidal waves of change, and against economic, social and political pressures from without.

Religious Jews are particularly zealous to guard the principles of the Torah from any attempt at arbitrary change.

Man, by his very nature, is conservative. He clings to established traditions and to ingrained habit. He tends to walk in the furrows plowed by his predecessors and to follow accepted, conventional patterns. An ordinary person instinctively rebels against change, especially radical, revolutionary change, either in his way of life or in his patterns of thought.

Yom Kippur, however, conditions our minds in the opposite direction. The very substance of this solemn day is *change, revision*, a new look at accustomed conduct, a re-evalution of man and his deeds. In the words of Jeremiah, "Let us search and examine our ways" (Lamentations 3:40), so that we may alter them, even radically, if they conflict with the principles of the Torah.

Such is the true meaning of *Teshuva. Teshuva* is commonly translated as "penitence." Literally, it means a "return" or a "turning back." It requires a reorientation of man's thought and action, a change in one's very person. This, then, is the purpose of Yom Kippur, and this is the effect it is meant to have on human character.

Man's prayer may be intended to change the judgment decreed over him *in Heaven*, but that prayer, together with other factors of the day, should also bring about a change in man's conduct *on earth*.

"Let the wicked forsake his way" (Isaiah 55:7)—this is the Heavenly command, even though that way may have led one to "success," to personal advancement in status and to wealth. Whether that change will yield continued fruits of success is not important. What matters is that man's new way should be righteous, straight and in accordance with the fundamental morality of the Torah.

This criterion overthrows the conventional concepts of success and failure. Material possessions, status and influence mean nothing if they are not attained through the paths of righteousness. Hence the impassioned cry of the prophet: "Return, O Israel, to the Lord, your God; for you have stumbled in your guilt" (Hosea 14:1). If you have violated the ethics of the Divine Law, you must repent, change your ways and return to the Lord even if your former path led you to success in business, society or politics.

A person who boasts that he is consistent, that he will not deviate a hair's breadth from his line of thought and action, deserves nothing but pity, for he is unable to admit his errors and therefore incapable, and indeed unworthy, of feeling true penitence.

For penitence means remorse—not at the thought of personal failure or defeat but at the thought of having pursued aims that were morally wrong.

Teshuva signifies a return to a former state of righteousness. To Judaism, all things have their origin in goodness and justice. Our fore-fathers stood at Mount Sinai and witnessed Divine Revelation; there-fore, every Jew, *a priori*, is rooted in holy ground. The trouble is that he has turned aside from the straight path and has lost his way. His sal-vation lies in penitence, in his return to the rock whence he was hewn.

The heathen Balaam had agreed to curse the Children of Israel, but after having seen the people encamped before his eyes, he changed his intended curse into a blessing. He declared: "For from the top of the rocks I see them, from the hills I behold them" (Numbers 23:9). Rashi comments on this verse: "I look at their beginnings, at the tips of their roots, and I see them as strong and solid as these rocks and hills, by virtue of their fathers and mothers." Rashi also saw that "their begin-nings and the tips of their roots" were good. While Judaism is under-going constant change and periodic renewal, moving steadily onward to the "End of Days," its roots go deep into antiquity. Is there another nation on the face of the earth that asks God to "renew our days as of old" (Lamentations 5:21) when that "of old" reaches back thousands of years?

While we all possess the natural inclination to follow the inertia of established habit, there is also implanted within us an opposing tend-ency, prompted by normal curiosity, to explore new ideas, to pursue new trails. For that reason, we are urged "to search and examine our ways and to return to God" (Lamentations 3:40), and Jeremiah exclaims: "If you return, O Israel, said the Lord, you will return *to Me*" (4:1). Should you be disillusioned by alien ideologies and con-duct rooted in alien thought, you will return to Me, the Divine Source, and you will never know disillusionment again.

Turning to part of our generation, contemporary Jewry, which never had the privilege of a Jewish education, we are compelled to ask ourselves: How can they be expected to "return" to a position where they had never been to begin with? To a blind person who once had

been able to see, we can recall colors which he had seen in the past before his world grew dark. But how can one describe colors for one who was born without sight? How can we discuss a "return" with one who has no roots in Judaism? How can we talk *Teshuva* to a lost generation?

But all is not yet lost. Jewish life today shows three distinct signs of what may well be the beginnings of *Teshuva*.

In the first place, there seems to be a thirst for Jewish knowledge among the rising generation. Young Jews want to know the meaning of their Judaism. The proliferation of day schools and *yeshivot* (Talmudical academies) and the quantitive progress of Jewish education in America are not just the result of an active rededication on the part of parents and community leaders. The young student himself is becoming curious about his religious and cultural heritage and identity. In days gone by, Jewish children had to be forced to study the Torah, and even coercion did not always help. Our youth revolted against what seemed to them inconsistent with the then existing atmosphere of pragmatism, whose hallmark was the attainment of material success and social status. Torah for its own sake, or for the sake of a revitalized Judaism, had no place there. Although the present state of affairs is still far from satisfactory, we can note, thank God, an improvement in the attitude of the average Jew toward his heritage.

Secondly, we are at present witnessing a most remarkable phenomenon—the rise of a new Jewish youth, imbued with Jewish consciousness, loyal to its people, culture and homeland, out of a soil that lay fallow for long years, like wild grass growing in crevices between barren rocks, suggesting the fulfillment of the prophecy: "Your sons shall come from afar, and your daughters shall be brought along in arms" (Isaiah 60:4). Although the number of these young people is still insignificant, the fact that this is at all possible is definitely encouraging.

Thirdly, there is the impact of the State of Israel, the very fact of its rebirth and growth. Powerful though it was even after 1948, the hold of Israel on world Jewry has increased infinitely since the Six-Day War of June, 1967. It is a well-known fact that crises test the spiritual strength of men. In the hour of decision, man discovers within himself mysterious forces of a power inconceivable under ordinary circumstances. These forces arise from primeval sources, from ancient roots, from the very depths of a people's soul. They lie dormant until some dramatic hour demands speedy, decisive action. In Rashi's aforementioned words, they are "as strong and solid as these rocks and hills, by virtue of the fathers and mothers of the people."

Thus we can understand why, on the eve of Yom Kippur, prior to the solemn *Kol Nidre* service, we open the gates of prayer with the statement: "We declare it lawful to pray with the sinners." To begin with, all these "sinners" are considered capable of repentance. And even more important, incalculable forces of spiritual regeneration may well lie dormant even within the souls of "sinners," energies which may be suddenly and unexpectedly released when the hour of destiny calls.

Yom Kippur is thus a day of *Teshuva*, the kind of penitence which signifies *change*. Thus interpreted, the Day of Atonement may not only bring in a new *year*, but also bring out a new *man*.

LIGHT FOR THE RIGHTEOUS

THE HOLY CONGREGATION is assembled in awe and solemn expectation. A hush falls on the worshippers as the Ark is opened and the elders reverently remove the Sacred Scrolls of the Law. In silent awe they stand at either side of the cantor as he begins to chant the service of the holiest of days. The congregants listen intently as he movingly intones the opening verse of the liturgy. But what is it that he recites with so much fervor? Is it a prayer? Is it a hymn of praise? It is, in fact, neither. It is a formal declaration, a statement of the principles which constitute the very foundation of Jewish belief and thus appropriately serve as an introduction to the hallowed observance of Yom Kippur.

The words of the declaration ring out: *"Light is sown for the righteous and joy for the upright in heart."* (Psalm 97:11) This is the verse which opens the gates of prayer on the momentous day. Repeated over and over again, each time with more ardor, more fervor, these words act as a summons, a clarion call, and at the same time as a password to sublime, hitherto inaccessible realms.

These words proudly and confidently proclaim the fundamental device which is to guide the Jew in his Yom Kippur prayers and, if he abides by the teachings they imply, also in his life, his thoughts, and his actions throughout the coming year.

What is the meaning of this declaration? What special message does it convey?

True light, these words affirm, belies the transitory glow, the deceptive luster of wordly pursuits. It does not shine for those whose sole distinction is sophistication, superior knowledge or personal renown. True light is "sown for the righteous," however poor or humble they may be.

Joy is not found amid the money-getters, the pleasure-chasers, the power-hunters, the fame-seekers, or the achievers of success and status. Banish from your mind the illusions of contentment which possess those misguided souls. The show of gladness and delight which seems to brighten their lives is but hollow gaiety, as fleeting as a passing shadow. True joy is "for the righteous of heart alone."

On the Eve of Yom Kippur, the Jew, absorbed in prayer, purified by contemplation, trembling in the face of divine judgment, repentant over his past and anxious over his future, is assured, first and foremost, that the Light which he seeks does not come from without but is already "sown" within him. It is found in the inmost recesses of the heart of every man who leads a truly "good" life, a life of justice and righteousness. It shines forth from the soul of man by virtue of his piety and good deeds. Moreover, we are reminded that joy and righteousness march side by side, that happiness is not to be gained by immersing oneself in vain folly, in the frivolous revelry of empty pleasures.

The lesson which this day imparts emerges spontaneously, a lesson that must be unfailingly applied to everyday life throughout the year. This is the meaning of the proclamation that forms the prelude to the Yom Kippur service. Indeed, "Light is sown for the just and joy for the righteous of heart."

You shall observe the feast of tabernacles seven days, after you have gathered in your corn and your wine. And you shall rejoice in your feast, you, and your son, and your daughter, and your manservant, and your maidservant, and the Levite, the stranger, and the fatherless, and the widow, that are within your gates. Seven days shall you keep a solemn feast unto the Lord your God in the place which the Lord shall choose; because the Lord your God shall bless you in all your increase, and in all the works of your hands, therefore you shall surely rejoice.

DEUTERONOMY 16:13-15

You, Lord our God, have graciously given us holidays for gladness, and festive seasons for joy: this Feast of Tabernacles, our Festival of Rejoicing, a holy convocation in remembrance of the exodus from Egypt.

FROM THE SUKKOT LITURGY

SUKKOT

Etrog container. The etrog is kept in a special container to protect it from any injury that may render it unfit for ritual use. This etrog container, made in Germany about 1900, bears the text of the Biblical commandment with regard to the etrog: "And you shall take the fruit of a goodly tree" (Lev. 23:40). (The Jewish Museum, New York City).

THE FESTIVAL OF SUKKOT

The Festival of Sukkot, usually rendered in English as "The Festival of Booths" or "The Feast of Tabernacles," is of Biblical origin. The Book of Leviticus gives two reasons for its celebration:

"Mark, on the fifteenth day of the seventh month, when you have gathered in the yield of your land, you shall observe the festival of the Lord seven days . . . On the first day, you shall take the product of goodly trees, branches of palm trees, boughs of thick trees and willows of the brook, and you shall rejoice before the Lord your God for seven days . . . as a statute for all time, throughout the generations . . . You shall live in booths seven days; all citizens in Israel shall live in booths, in order that future generations may know that I made the Children of Israel live in booths when I brought them out of the Land of Egypt—I, the Lord your God." (Lev. 23:39–43)

Sukkot is to be observed "when you have gathered in the yield of your land." It is thus an agricultural holiday, a fall harvest celebration, much like the American Thanksgiving. Accordingly, Sukkot is known also as *Hag Ha-Asif*, the Festival of the Ingathering of the Harvest.

But the same Biblical passage which specifies that Sukkot is to be observed at harvest-time, gives yet another reason for the celebration—"in order that future generations may know that I made the Israelite people live in booths when I brought them out of the Land of Egypt." In addition to being an agricultural feast, Sukkot is a national historic holiday, commemorating the forty years which the Children of Israel spent in the wilderness before being permitted to enter the Promised Land.

Among traditional Jews outside of Israel, the festival is celebrated for nine days instead of the original seven. The first two days, Sukkot proper, are observed as full holidays on which no work may be done. The next four days, known as the Intermediate Days, or *Hol HaMoed*, are observed as half-holidays. The seventh day, Hoshana Rabba, The Day of the Great Hosanna, gradually took on some of the characteristics of the Days of Awe. On it, we invoke God's blessings for the year just begun. The eighth day, Sh'mini Atzeret, The Eighth day of Solemn Assembly, is marked by a unique liturgical feature—the Prayer for Rain. The ninth and final day is Simhat Torah, the Rejoicing in the Law, when the annual cycle of weekly Torah readings in the synagogues is completed, and a new cycle begun.

One of the most important Sukkot observances is the building of the *sukka,* the booth or temporary hut, usually erected adjacent to the home. It has a roof covering of branches or corn-stalks, and is decorated on the inside with fruit symbolizing the harvest. Observant Jews eat all their meals in the *sukka* and some even literally "dwell" there day and night during the first seven days of the festival.

Another impressive ceremony is the festive procession of the worshipers in the synagogue on the first two days of Sukkot, each man holding an *etrog,* a fragrant citrus fruit, and a *lulav,* a palm branch decorated with myrtle twigs on one side and willow branches on the other, while appropriate prayers are chanted by cantor and congregation.

On Simhat Torah, the Jew gives expression to his delight with the Law God revealed to his people. At evening services, and again in the morning of this last of the fall holidays, seven gay processions known as *hakafot,* or "circlings," are held in the synagogue. The adults who take part carry Scrolls of the Law. The children hold small, appropriately decorated flags, each topped by an apple into which a lighted candle is inserted. During the intervals between the *hakafot* processions, a general atmosphere of merriment prevails, highlighted by singing and dancing.

Etrog market. One of the Four Species of vegetation honoring the festival of Sukkot is the citron or etrog. Here a pious man in Tel Aviv examines the wares of the etrog dealer with the utmost care before making his final purchase. It is considered meritorious to acquire the most beautiful etrog available. (Israel Office of Information).

OF THE THREE Pilgrim Festivals, two—Pesah and Shavuot—are exclusively Jewish. The third festival, Sukkot, is different. It is meant to appeal to all mankind. The Prophet Zechariah had envisioned Sukkot as a festival for all the nations of the world:

"It shall come to pass that any that are left of all the nations that went up against Jerusalem, shall go up from year to year to worship the King, the Lord of Hosts . . . to celebrate the *Feast of Booths*" (Zechariah 14:17-18).

This universal aspect of Sukkot is symbolized by the offering of seventy bullocks as sacrifices to represent the seventy nations into which, according to the Talmud, the world was divided. These sacrifices had been offered by the Jews while the Holy Temple was in existence. The Talmud, however, goes further still; it predicts that "in the End of Days, in the time to come" (Tractate *Avodah Zarah* 3:1) the Festival of Sukkot will be observed not only by the Jews but by all mankind.

Why is Sukkot, of all the Festivals, given in this universal character?

The answer lies in the origin and nature of the three Pilgrim Festivals. All three are derived from a struggle for liberation, but each represents a different freedom attained.

Pesah symbolizes political and civil liberty. It commemorates the deliverance of a people from physical enslavement to the peoples and rulers of alien lands.

Shavuot symbolizes the achievement of spiritual and cultural freedom. The giving of the Ten Commandments has two basic implications: first, the circumstance that the Children of Israel assumed the obligations set forth in the Torah, and second, to observe the precepts that the Children of Israel declared themselves free to lead an independent religious and cultural life as Jews.

Sukkot symbolizes a different sort of freedom. It marks the liberation of man as such from self-imposed servitude, from slavish addiction to material excesses out of indolent habit or weakness of character. Dwelling in the flimsy *sukka* during the Festival teaches us moderation in all things. Once a man can learn to do without luxuries and to return, even if only for a short time, to the simple life, he ceases to be a slave to material wants which so often place him inextricably in the debt of others. He is no longer dependent on the favors of his fellow men. He is no longer compelled to covet the possessions of his neighbor. The mere fact that he is able to meet the basic needs of daily living gives him a sense of achievement and makes him content with his own portion in life. It is characteristic of this Jewish outlook that Jewish tradition should refer to this temporary removal from spacious, comfortable quarters to a modest, makeshift dwelling equipped with nothing but the bare necessities of primitive existence as "the season of our rejoicing."

Allusions to these three freedoms symbolized by the three Pilgrim Festivals are found in three Scriptural verses, all of which contain the key-word *P'dut*—redemption. In the Scriptural account of Pesah we read: "And I (the Lord) shall make a *distinction* between My people and your (the Egyptian) people" (Exodus 8:19). This "distinction" is the redemption of one people from enslavement by another; namely, the attainment of political freedom. In the case of Shavuot, redemption is equated with the Law that was given to the Children of Israel on Mount Sinai. "Redemption has He sent unto His people; He has commanded *His covenant* forever" (Psalms 111:9). Here, redemption has led to religious and cultural freedom. In the case of Sukkot the redemption is man's liberation from himself. "For with the Lord is kindness, and with him is *redemption* in abundance; and He will surely *redeem* Israel from all its iniquities" (Psalms 130:7-8). Iniquities, or sins, originate within man's inner self. Triggered by human instinct, they are frequently perpetuated by the force of habit.

This enslavement to habit, to inner weakness and personal convenience is not an evil peculiar to the Jews. It is common to all mankind, for it is rooted in what has been called the "human condition."

Thus, while historically Sukkot is a Jewish festival, its essential appeal is universal, symbolizing the liberation of each individual, Jew and Gentile alike, from the excesses of crude materialism. No wonder, then, that some early Jewish scholars named Sukkot the "Festival of Mankind."

DECOR OF THE SUKKA

The traditional decorations of the *sukka* are many and varied. They have changed with time and place. Some are true works of art, express-

Sukkot in Jerusalem. Seated in the gaily-decorated sukka, this youngster is reciting the blessing over the lulav. Silver containers on the table hold the etrogim. (Keren HaYesod, Jerusalem).

Folding Sukka. Built in 1825 by the Deller family of Fischach, near Augsburg, Germany, this sukka consists of numbered wooden planks which were taken down from the attic once a year and assembled into what probably was the first "collapsible" sukka. The planks, with illustrations of Jewish holidays and Biblical motifs, were found in Nazi Germany in the 1930's by the late Dr. Heinrich Feuchtwanger, of the Bezalel Museum in Jerusalem, who brought them to Israel. (top, view from outside; bottom, inside view). (The Israel Museum, Jerusalem).

ing our aspiration to that sublime beauty which Scripture has so often exalted. One motif has appeared in them over and over: the cities and towns of the Holy Land—Jerusalem, Hebron, Tiberias, Safed, Meron—and hallowed sites—the Wailing Wall, the Cave of Machpelah and Rachel's Tomb.

What did these pictures symbolize for us in our childhood and for the generations that went before us? They reminded us of a long-past era in Jewish history, and of far-off places which we hardly expected to see in our lifetime. They were images of another world which had once been ours but which had been removed from us by long centuries and vast distance.

Nor need we look back so far. Even as recently as before June 1967, Old Jerusalem, Hebron, the Wailing Wall, the Cave of Machpelah and Rachel's Tomb were forbidden territory to Jews. Now, since the Six-Day War, those of us who have visited Israel have been privileged to see these shrines of the *sukka* illustrations as familiar places recalling not only heart-warming memories of past splendor but also the miracles of recent history. Even those Jews who have not yet made the pilgrimage to the new Israel share the thrill of realizing that all these places are now ours, close to us not only in spirit but also in fact. Freed from alien, hostile domination, they are now within the boundaries of our Jewish State. Jews from all over the world may pour out their hearts before the liberated Western Wall—a Wailing Wall no more—and behold Jerusalem Reunited, the spiritual center of our people and of our exultant Homeland.

HAK'HEL—CONVOCATION

THE RITE OF *Hak'hel**, the Convocation for the Reading of the Law, is based on a Biblical commandment:

"... At the end of every seven years, in the set time of the year of release (Sabbatical Year), on the Feast of Tabernacles, when all Israel come to appear before the Lord your God in the place which He will choose, shall you read this Law in the presence of all Israel, in their hearing. Assemble the people, the men, and the women, and the children, and your stranger that is within your gates, in order that they may hear, and that they may learn how they are to revere the Lord your God, and observe to do all the words of this Law; and that their children who have not yet any knowledge, may hear, and learn to revere the Lord your God, all the days that you live in the land to which you will go across the Jordan to possess it " (Deut. 31:10-13).

Obviously, Moses proclaimed this Divine commandment as he was nearing the end of his life, for we are told directly thereafter: "And the Lord said to Moses: Behold, your days approach the time when you must die; call Joshua, and place yourselves in the tabernacle of the congregation, that I may give him a charge..." (Ibid., 31:14). It is therefore to be regarded as the last will and testament of Moses, indicating his fervent hope that the Israelites would continue to study the Law from generation to generation in order to assure their national survival.

As Rabbi Aaron HaLevi of Barcelona** most aptly commented:

"It is most appropriate and desirable that all [Jews] should assemble periodically to listen to the words of the Torah ... in order that they may study it more diligently and learn to revere the Lord " (*Sefer Ha-Hinukh*, Commandment 612, *Sidra VaYelekh*).

* Literally, "assemble."
** Spanish Talmudist (c. 1300).

This precept was, in fact, carried out faithfully throughout the days of the First and Second Temples. On the festival of Sukkot, at the close of each Sabbatical year, the Israelites were summoned by the sound of trumpets to assemble on the Temple Mount to hear the reading of the Law of Moses. Mighty throngs—men, women and children by the tens of thousands—would gather together before the Sanctuary to participate in the inspiring ceremony at which selections from the first six chapters of the Book of Deuteronomy were read.

The congregation which attended the reading was unusually large. It was to consist of *all* the people of Israel—men, women and children. The Talmud defines the respective roles of each of these: "Said Rabbi Elazar ben Azariah: Men come to study, women come to listen. But why do the children come? In order to reward those who bring them." This is a splendid educational objective. The reading of the Torah is not intended merely for passive listening but also—and primarily—for creative *study*. Rabbi Naftali Tz'vi Yehudah Berlin* interpreted the Biblical expression "in their hearing" to mean: "That the words of the Torah may enter into their ears, hence that they may comprehend and absorb the message contained therein, and learn well the ordinances and statutes of the Written Law " (*Ha-amek Davar* on the Pentateuch).

The reader was no less a person than the King himself. Unlike the monarchs of other nations of the time, who were noted mainly for their physical prowess and military skills, the rulers of Israel were expected, in addition, to possess superior qualities of spiritual leadership. When Moses pleaded with the Almighty to appoint a true leader over Israel, God selected Joshua, the son of Nun, *"a man in whom there is a spirit,"* to guide the destinies of the people (Num. 27:18) . Subsequent tradition and history have borne out the paramount role of spiritual qualifications in our leaders. The most important and best-remembered figures in our history have been men of the spirit, of intellect, of Torah.

Scripture contains the following description of the *Hak'hel* ceremonial during the reign of King Josiah, son of King David:

"And the King sent, and they gathered unto him all the elders of Judah and Jerusalem. And the King went up into the house of the Lord, and all the men of Judah and all the inhabitants of Jerusalem with him, and the priests, from the small to the great; and he read in their hearing all the words of the Book of the Covenant which had been found in the house of the Lord. And the King stood upon the stand, and he made a covenant before the Lord, to walk after the Lord, and to keep His commandments, and His testimonies and His statutes, with all

---

* Head of the famed Yeshiva of Volozhin, known as HaNatziv (1817-1893).

108

his heart and all his soul, to maintain the words of this covenant that are written in this book. And all the people entered into the covenant " (II Kings, 23:1-3).

Thus, *Hak'hel* was popular assembly and governmental function, educational program and solemn convocation all in one, emphasizing the distinctive qualities of a chosen people. It was, too, a thoroughly democratic institution, in which not only all the Israelites but also the strangers sojourning with them were eligible to participate. It was a demonstration of unity of heart and purpose, under the guidance of the chief of state who also had to be a spiritual leader of his people.

In the opinion of some Talmudic Codifiers, the *Hak'hel* commandment was to be observed only "while Israel dwelt in its land," which was taken to mean only if there was an independent Jewish State in the Holy Land. Nevertheless, even before the establishment of the State of Israel, during the period of the British Mandate, a number of authoritative rabbis advocated the revival of this valuable institution, pointing out that even if there still was no independent Jewish State, the Jews living in Palestine did dwell in their land. But other religious leaders, no less authoritative, citing other Codifiers in their support, held that the *Hak'hel* precept could be carried out only if there was a Holy Temple in Jerusalem. These leaders, including the late Chief Rabbi Isaac Herzog, maintained that as long as the Temple was not rebuilt the ceremony could be revived only symbolically as a "remembrance of the Sanctuary."

With the restoration of the State of Israel, however, the function of *vayak'hel* was partially revived in various forms and has gained recognition in ever-widening circles.

Now, with the great awakening brought about by Israel's miraculous victory in the Six-Day War of 1967, with the reunification of Jerusalem and the return of the hallowed remnant of the Temple, *Hak'hel* has assumed a new significance as the continuation of an ancient, venerated and inspiring tradition. We can visualize the magnificent spectacle of tens, perhaps even hundreds of thousands, of Jews from all four corners of the earth, solemnly assembled in the spacious square before the Western Wall for the purpose of studying and honoring the Torah, the timeless source of our people's spiritual strength.

The effect of such periodic mass assemblies as means of rekindling Jewish consciousness throughout the world, strengthening the bonds between Israel and the diaspora, and imbuing our youth with new faith and idealism can hardly be overestimated.

SUKKOT IN THE CAUCASUS

THE DAY BEFORE THE FESTIVAL, the Gentiles come to the market place with donkeys laden with moist fresh leaves to be sold to the Jews for use as a roof on the *sukka.*

Everyone builds a *sukka* by setting up four poles, to which the walls, also made of leaves, are attached. Some set up their little huts next to their own homes; others, on the roofs of their houses. But not one *sukka* there has any charm or beauty, and any little gust of wind can blow them down. A *sukka* there is just large enough for two or three to squeeze in and sit, with not an inch to spare. No one sleeps in the *sukka* hut, except for old Rabbi Isaac: he sleeps in his *sukka* every night of the Festival; in fact, he stays there all week long, except when it rains.

Before the Ashkenazic Jews from Europe proper settled there, *lulavim* (palm branches) and *etrogim* were to be found only in distant cities, brought from Persia by people who happened to come from there before Sukkot. At best there would be one *lulav* and *etrog* for an entire community. To this day, even if there should be a good supply of these objects, the Jews there will buy only one *lulav* and *etrog* for each synagogue, to be used by all the worshippers. They know nothing of our practice to have each householder purchase a set of his own.

The *lulav* and *etrog* are brought to the synagogue on a copper tray. Each person takes up the *lulav* and kisses the *etrog.* He shakes both once (to move the leaves of the *lulav*), kisses the *etrog* once again, and then puts *lulav* and *etrog* back on the tray. This the members of the congregation do, one after the other, until, by the second day, the *etrog* has become black beyond recognition from all the handling and kissing. Whoever knows the proper blessing over them recites it. Those who do not know it, merely kiss the *etrog.* The women show no interest whatever in the observance of this precept (which is obligatory only for the males), nor do they go in great numbers on Simhat Torah to see the *hakafot,* the procession through the synagogue with the Torah Scrolls.

On the eve of Sh'mini Atzeret (the eighth day of the Festival), the illiterate boors gather in several groups to make their own boisterous celebration, forcing the kosher slaughterer to keep them supplied with enough meat for half the night. Should the poor man refuse their request, they apply means of "gentle persuasion": they break his door and windows, draw their daggers, and order him to get to work. Thus they eat and drink, dance and make merry, until night gives way to the light of dawn. The women and the girls also prepare feasts of their own, at which they drink a great deal of wine and liquor, laugh, dance, and beat their drums, shouting, "Joy, oh joy!" In this condition they come to the synagogue later in the morning for the prayer service.

On Simhat Torah day, the mood is no longer as happy and gay as it was the night before. First of all, many of them, unable to read

Kiddush cup, contemporary design, by Ludwig Y. Wolpert. Hebrew inscription cut into bottom of cup is "For Thou art my praise" (Psalms).

Hebrew, did not complete the reading or study of the Torah through the year, and now must make up for lost time. Secondly, they need the entire day to reckon up how much each member of the congregation owes for the year, for the cantor receives twenty-five kopeks (a quarter of a ruble) from each and every male in the congregation as his yearly salary.

THE JOY OF SUKKOT

THE FOLLOWING ESSAY is taken from the works of Don Isaac Abrabanel (1437-1509), scholar, statesman and financier who, though held in high esteem at the Court of King Ferdinand and Queen Isabella of Spain, was unable to avert their infamous decree to expel the Jews from that country in 1492. His colorful career ended in virtual solitude and disillusionment in Venice, Italy, where he devoted the later years of his life to the completion of his Biblical commentary and to the writing of valuable philosophical treatises. Abrabanel said:

Lulav holder. (The Israel Museum, Jerusalem).

The Torah contains a triple reference to the precept of rejoicing on the Festival of Ingathering (Sukkot): "You shall rejoice in your festival" (Deut. 16:14); "You shall be only happy" (ibid. 16:15); and "You shall rejoice before the Lord your God for seven days" (Lev. 23:40). Regarding Passover, no rejoicing is mentioned at all. Why? Because at that season one is still uncertain whether the total harvest for the year will be plentiful. There is only one reference to rejoicing on the Festival of Shavuot. Why? Because although the grain had been gathered in, the later fruit harvest is still in question. But on Sukkot, when both the grain and the fruits have been fully harvested, our joy is complete, hence the triple reference to rejoicing.

Although it is commendable to rejoice on all three festivals, the Sukkot festivities at the Holy Temple were particularly joyous. A special place in the balcony was provided for the women, and all, young and old, participated in the joyous celebration from the first day of the Festival through the *Hol Ha-Moed* period. The general hilarity was resumed each day following the late afternoon offering, and continued through the night and the next morning.

Those who could sing, sang; those who could play the flute, the harp, the lyre, the timbrels, or other instrument, played. Many danced, hopped and frolicked, each according to his ability and inclination. Even great sages, heads of Talmudical academies, religious and secular leaders—all were swept into the spirit of hearty abandon and boundless mirth mingled with praise and thanksgiving to God, while the great masses—men, women and children—looked on.

The joy of fulfilling the divine commandments and of love of God is an essential element of true worship. He who does not partake of this joy is disdained by God, as it is said: "Because you would not serve the Lord your God in the joy and happiness of heart, . . . you shall serve your enemies" (Deut. 28:47). Also he who is haughty and boastful and seeks self-aggrandizement in the holy sanctuary is both a

Man holding lulav and etrog. Detail from the Rothschild Manuscript, painted on thin vellum (Italy, 1470).

sinner and a fool, as King Solomon has said: "Claim not honor in the presence of the king" (Proverbs 25:6). On the other hand, he who humbles himself in the service of the Almighty is truly great and honorable, as stated by King David: "Therefore I will disport myself even more than that and lower myself in my sight" (II Samuel 6:22). It is greatness and honor to rejoice before God, as it is said: "And King David was whirling in a dance with all his might before the Lord" (ibid.6:14).

During the celebration, nuts and sweets would be distributed among the children. Women would appear in their finest holiday attire. People feasted on meat and wine, because meat and wine are symbols of joy. And when a man eats and drinks, he is duty-bound to invite orphans, widows and the unfortunate poor to his table. But when a man locks his gates and eats and drinks with his family without feeding the poor and the bitter of heart, his joy is not the joy of performing a good deed, but merely the joy of his belly. Of such selfish people it is said: "Their sacrifices shall be unto them as the bread of mourners; all that eat thereof will defile themselves, for their food is for themselves only" (Hosea 9:4). Such joy brings disgrace upon them, as it is written: "I will strew dung upon your faces, the dung of your feasts" (Malachi 2:3).

Although partaking of food and drink on festivals is generally a positive precept, one must not overindulge in it. In the morning, one must go to the house of worship, pray and read in the Torah concerning timely topics. Then one must return home and eat. Thereupon one should go again to the synagogue, read and study until mid-day at which time the afternoon prayers are to be recited. Following the afternoon service, it is proper to return home and then to eat and drink until the evening.

When a man eats and drinks and rejoices in the festival, he should not drink wine to excess in the mistaken belief that this would tend to enhance his joy. On the contrary, inebriation and frivolity are not rejoicing, but folly and debauchery. We were not commanded to practice folly and debauchery, but to serve God with joy. One cannot serve God through light-mindedness and drunkenness.

"You shall be only happy." When you come on Passover and Shavuot for a pilgrimage to the Holy Temple, you are necessarily concerned about the grain in your field. On Sukkot, however, when your produce has been gathered in, when God has blessed the work of your hands, you shall be *only* happy, admitting no other thought that might mar your joy. For on Passover, following the first day of the festival, you are commanded: "In the morning, you are to return to your tents," namely to your work in the field. This is also the reason why Shavuot is celebrated only one day, so that one may not tarry in Jerusalem and neglect one's harvest. But on Sukkot, when you have gathered in the produce into your granary and wine-cellar, it is proper that you remain in Jerusalem for a seven days' celebration of joy and thanksgiving. No worry will distract you from your rejoicing. Hence, the commandment "you shall be only happy" should be interpreted to mean that if you rejoice wholeheartedly on the festival of Sukkot, you are assured of happiness throughout the ensuing year, and conversely, if you are sad at the beginning of the year, you will eat your bread in sorrow all the days of the year. Such is the nature of things: he who is contented with his portion in life, shall attain constant joy and gladness, and he who sighs without cause, will remain sullen for the rest of the year.

The festival of Sukkot is observed for seven days on account of the "Seven Species"[1] with which the Land of Israel is blessed.

SUKKOT IN ADEN

The city of Aden (in my day) permitted the head of each family to build one *sukka* for himself, one for his son-in-law, and one for his children. When the British legions came to take over the city, there were no houses for them to stay in. They needed huts set up at once, and the Jews were given the task of building them, for they could be trusted to have ready within two or three hours a shelter which could withstand the wind and keep out the heat of day and cold of night. A short distance from the city they found the materials they needed: bamboo, reed grass, palm leaves and trees. Tree trunks were used for the walls, hanging bamboo sticks became the "doors," the reeds provided protection from heat and cold, and the palm leaves were woven into mats to cover the walls.

Even after the new government had built houses of stone, it still maintained these huts in the hills, for the English found the hot dry climate easier to take in little houses built of grasses, and similar materials. As a result, Jewish farmers kept on hand a constant supply of such natural "building materials," ready to use at sudden notice from the government.

Hence, when Sukkot drew near, most of the Jewish city dwellers would go to Moshe Razon, the farmer, to borrow the materials they would need for the *sukka*. He would open his store of natural-grown materials, taking no payment whatever in return. He would plant himself on the threshold of his door to receive the masses of visitors who crowded and pushed, as their requests and pleas mingled in an unintelligible babble. Moshe Razon, too, shouted at the top of his voice as his workers brought out his stock of materials. He made no record of what he lent, and no borrower ever signed for what he took. Yet everyone was trustworthy; everything was returned after the festival, when a *sukka* was no longer needed.

In Aden every house was built with a flat roof accessible by a stairway. During the hot summer the rooftops were used as sleeping quarters. When Sukkot came, each rooftop sprouted a *sukka*, so that the Jewish section looked like a rooftop community.

The green leaves and boughs that formed the covering for each *sukka* gave the impression of a vegetable garden. And as the Jewish householders slept in their *sukka*, they would hear a rustling overhead that sounded like an orchard in the breeze.

---

[1] Wheat, barley, grape, fig, pomegranate, olive and honey.

Many people would decorate their *sukka* walls with tapestries embroidered with all kinds of flowers. From the beams above they would hang apples, pomegranates and citrons, until the *sukka* resembled a veritable orchard. It was well worth the trouble, for in Aden the Jews were accustomed to sit for hours at the *sukka* table, enjoying the company of relatives and friends and singing holiday songs. On the table stood one or more bottles, the contents of which were suited to gladden the heart. And in each *sukka* the people could hear all the singing from the neighboring *sukka*, since these rooftop huts were as close together as the houses atop which they stood. Thus, at any one moment, if you stopped and listened, you could hear all kinds of festival songs at once, mingling in a joyous chorus or a gay festival pot-pourri.

Every *sukka* had a few glass oil-lamps, imported cheaply from India, hung from the overhead beams The wicks burned brightly at night as they swayed in the breeze, until they flashed and twinkled through the windows like so many stars in the sky. During Sukkot it would seem to casual passers-by below that an extra story had been added to all the houses in the Jewish neighborhoods.

As for the Biblical command to take "four species"—*lulav* (palm branch), *etrog* (citron), *hadassim* (myrtle leaves) and *aravot* (willow leaves)—the Jews of Aden would obey this precept like the most religious and scrupulous of our people anywhere else. Between Rosh HaShana and Yom Kippur they made their way to Ali Awad, the dealer in Yemenite wares, to ask if the *mitzvot* had already arrived from Yemen. Eventually, Ali, too, learned to refer to the "four species" as *mitzvot*, "religious precepts."

It was this dealer's custom to receive from one city in Yemen, every year, three or four camel-loads of *etrogim* and *hadassim*, which he would proceed to sell one by one. He would open a sack and spread its contents on a mat; and the customers would sit all about, carefully picking and choosing. One *etrog* might have a fine *pitma**, but it had a diseased spot; another might be smooth and handsome, but it lacked a *pitma*; still another might be perfectly splendid, but much too large—almost as big as an infant's head! So the choosing went on for hours, as the people debated which were the most suitable according to Talmudic law. Ali Awad, though he definitely was not Jewish, had learned so much about these matters over the years that he would occasionally interrupt the arguments and give acceptable explanations, like "That is not really a diseased spot, but a bruise from pressure. The big one over there was pressed against it in the sack" . . .

(Mahalallel Ha-Adeni, *Between Aden and Yemen*)

* Crown-shaped protuberance at one end of the *etrog*.

Sukkot at the Western Wall. Thousands of Jews from the world over flocked to the Western Wall with lulav and etrog to celebrate the first Sukkot after the reunification of Jerusalem in 1967. (Israel Office of Information.)

A SUKKOT NIGHT IN VOLOZHIN

There was truth in the oft-quoted saying, "Whoever had not seen *simhat bet ha-sho'evah* in Volozhin, never saw a truly joyous celebration in his life." On the second night of Sukkot, in the famed Yeshiva of Volozhin, five hundred students would put all their youthful zeal and vigor into a celebration that truly reflected the joy of the "Feast of the Drawing of the Water" as it had been in the days of the Temple in Jerusalem.

Days before, some of the better students were chosen as *gabbaim*, or wardens, to take charge of plans. They had to prepare liquid refreshments strong enough to gladden the heart, with accompanying cakes, cookies and other delicacies. For how could they have celebrated on a sober heart and an empty stomach? Furthermore, they had to rent quarters large enough for the dancing that would go on all day and all night long.

But no matter how large the quarters they chose, it could never hold them all; and the dancing students overflowed into the streets outside. They began about noontime, gathering steam as they went along. Once the celebration was in full swing, all would go to the *roshé yeshiva*, the instructors in Talmud and ethics, to lead them in melody and song to the *yeshiva* building, where the festivities would begin in earnest.

The renowned dean, Rabbi Naftali Zvi Judah Berlin,* would join in the dancing and singing with such spirit that he inspired even the young to added fervor. At the proper time, they would recite the Evening Prayer, interrupted by spontaneous bursts of ecstatic melody. When the service was ended, the sacred songs were resumed, and the singing went on far into the night.

Rabbi Naftali Berlin would remain until the end. When finally fatigue overtook the students, he would open the Holy Ark, and they all would join in chanting the *Alenu* ("It is for us to praise the Lord of all"). This proclamation of faith was chanted exactly as it was at services on Rosh HaShana and Yom Kippur. When they reached the words, "and we bow and kneel down and give thanks before the King of Kings," all, including the dean, would kneel and fall prostrate, exactly as they had on the Days of Awe, probably to ask Heaven's forgiveness for any excesses that might have occurred in the course of the evening's merriment.

Even if the celebration went on till dawn, everyone appeared in time for Morning Services several hours later. No one was too tired or too much under the influence of liquor to come. Afterwards there would be *kiddush* in the *sukka* of the *yeshiva* over a cup of wine or liquor, along with a bite of cake or other pastry. Only the "worthies" got seats around the table, but there was room enough for all to stand crowded together. After *kiddush* and some edifying words about the festival, the delicacies were served. Hands would reach out eagerly for their share before the trays even got to those seated at the table. One wit used to say, "When they reach out and take, there is enough for all. If someone doesn't get a share—it just means he didn't reach out in the right way."

* Known as the Natziv (1817-1893).

Blessing the Lulav, watercolor by Chaim Gross.

THE SUKKA: A BOND OF FAITH

THE FESTIVAL OF Sukkot is dedicated to the physical preservation of Israel by God. It is the season when the year's harvest is almost completed and your house and granary are full. No longer do you anxiously look heavenward for your blessing, for you have already gathered it in and, relying on what you have stored, you face the winter with equanimity.

On the other hand your harvest may have been meager and, as you reflect on your want and poverty, you, as well as your wife and children, grow despondent and see nothing but destitution ahead.

Whatever your harvest has been, when Sukkot comes, you are to leave your settled abode and dwell beneath the sparse ceiling of foliage, and to consider what it is meant to commemorate; that the Lord, your God, caused your forefathers to dwell in booths in the wilderness for forty years when He led them forth from Egypt, and that He sustained them in these booths, thus revealing Himself as the Divine Providence which sustains us all.

117

If you are wealthy, be aware that neither riches nor possessions, and certainly not the talents of which man is so proud, can be the gods which make life secure. It is God alone who can sustain—even in booths—those who commit themselves to Him in complete faith. Remember that it is to God that you owe your wealth, distinction and your treasures, and that they will be yours only as long as God wills it. Remember that fortunes change, and that the forefathers from which you, the man of wealth, are descended, once lived in booths in a wilderness for forty years. Cling to these ideas. They will make it easier for you to free yourself from indolence and the treacly ties of wealth to follow Him, even though the path may lead you through wastelands and deserts. In the end, if you establish your prosperous home not upon the foundations of riches and comfort, but upon the Lord, who watches over your household even through roofs of stone, and through whose loving-kindness alone you have not only acquired your possessions but are enabled to keep them, then you will learn, even in the midst of wealth and opulence, to put your trust in God alone, Who is the sole Sustainer of all things living.

And if you are poor, my fellow Jew, and in despair, still move, I pray you, into the foliage-topped booth. Leave the shelter of your roof; and of your own accord choose a life of even greater poverty and remember: God sustained your forefathers in booths in the wilderness. That same God still lives; He is also your God, and even as the twinkling stars shine through the roof of foliage, so does He tenderly look down upon you with His watchful eye; He beholds your sufferings, sees your tears, hears your sighs and knows your cares. And even as He did not forsake your forefathers, so He will never forsake you. Are you in despair because you do not possess those things upon which men build their lives? Then I say to you: did not your forefathers, who were nourished on *manna*, learn in their booths that man lives not by man-made means but only by each and every utterance of the Lord: Will you not learn this lesson, as your forefathers did, for your own wanderings on life's stony paths? Enter the *sukka*; learn to be strong and cheerful even in suffering, and to trust in God Who can sustain life even in booths and in wilderness . . .

What is it that alienates us from God in our lives, makes us conceited, robs us of hope or causes us to become so deeply concerned about our well-being that we have no time to think of our true happiness? It is the delusion with which we cling to worldly possessions and place them upon a pedestal to worship as the gods of our life; it is the delusion with which each and every one of us rears his own tower of Babel, believing ourselves secure only beneath sham shelters of our own making. It is from this delusion, from this worship of wealth and of human skills, that Sukkot is to set us free. May our fulfillment of the precept to dwell in booths lead us to accept God as the sole foundation of our life; may it teach us to put our trust in God alone.

Samson Raphael Hirsch

118

SIMHAT TORAH IN JERUSALEM (1742)

ON SIMHAT TORAH the last *sidra* (portion) is read from the Scroll of the Law in the synagogue. It is a great honor to be called to read the final passages of this portion. The man so honored is called the *Hatan Torah,* the "Bridegroom of the Law"; and as a rule this mark of esteem is sold at auction to the congregant who makes the highest bid for it.

In Jerusalem in 1742, however, the custom was entirely different, as we learn from the following letter written by the cabbalist Rabbi Hayyim ibn Attar, who went there earlier that year to establish a Talmudical college:

Simhat Torah Scene in Jerusalem, by Chaim Gross. These Israelis are of the "Old Yishuv," Jewish communities that have been part of the Jerusalem scene for many generations.

"On Simhat Torah I was called to be the 'Bridegroom of the Law.' The heads of the community sent word to ask me to accept this honor. They wanted no donations or contributions from me in return, they said, but sought only to give glory to the Torah. May the Almighty give them the reward they deserve. But in return I pledged to provide oil for the synagogue lamps in honor of the *Bet Midrash K'nesset Israel** (may the Almighty protect it), that it might be a good omen . . .

"The night after the conclusion of the Sabbath we had held a joyous celebration in the synagogue. All the rabbis and pious men danced before the Scroll of the Law with all their might and fervor. It was all sanctity and light—never before had there been anything like it.

"On the second night of Sukkot, we had *Simhat bet ha-sho'eva* (the 'celebration of the drawing of water,' to recall the celebration held in the days of the Temple), and there was great rejoicing."

(Abraham Yaari, *Igg'rot Eretz Yisrael,* p. 269)

* The congregation to which Rabbi Hayyim ibn Attar addressed this letter.

Rejoicing with the Law. Members of a settlement of Habad (Lubavitcher) Hasidim with the Torah Scrolls at the end of Simhat Torah.

Torah Scrolls from many lands. This exhibit of Torah Scrolls on display at The Israel Museum in Jerusalem features (left to right) a Torah Scroll with mantle, breastplate, pointer and finials (Augsburg, Germany, 18th century); a silver, partly gilt Torah Scroll case (India, 19th century); and a velvet covered case with silver and partly gilt decorations (Iran, 1799). (The Israel Museum, Jerusalem).

SIMHAT TORAH DECORATIONS

IN THE DAYS OF THE GAONIM (6th to 11th Centuries) it was customary to adorn the Scroll of the Law with special ornaments on Simhat Torah. In communities where this custom was followed the Scrolls would be wrapped in beautifully embroidered bridal gowns.

Finely wrought chairs were set out for the *Hatan Torah* (the "Bridegroom of the Law") who was called up for the reading of the final verses of the Book of Deuteronomy and for the *Hatan B'reshith* (the "Bridegroom of Genesis") who was called up immediately after the *Hatan Torah* to read the opening verses of the Book of Genesis from a second Scroll.

Rabbi Hayyim Joseph David Azulai (1724-1806) describes the "celebration of the *Hatan Torah*" in which the man so honored would march in an impressive torchlight procession. One such procession, which took place in Amsterdam at the beginning of the 18th Century, is pictured in a copper engraving by the French artist Picard.

The Simhat Torah flags which the children carried in the *hakafot* were made by the children themselves. Designs would be cut with a knife in paper or wood, drawn with pens or painted in bright colors. Even the sticks of the flags were gaily decorated.

Thus even the lowly Simhat Torah flag became an object of folk art in the finest sense of the word.

The following hymn for Simhat Torah, of unknown origin and authorship, is chanted between *Hakafot* on Simhat Torah eve and morning.

"Rejoice and be glad on Simhat Torah
And render honor to the Torah,
For it is more profitable than worldly goods,
More precious than gold and jewels.

Let us be glad and rejoice in this Torah
For it is our strength and our light.
I will extol my God, find joy in Him,
In Him will I place my hope.

Amidst His people I will glorify Him,
My God, my Rock in Whom I trust.
With all my heart I will sing of His justice,
His praises will I declare.

All my life I will tell of His wonders,
Of His kindness, of His truth.
Let us be glad and rejoice in this Torah
For it is our strength and our light."

Ark of the Law, by Chaim Gross. This Ark is in the Ari Synagogue, the oldest synagogue in Safed, Israel.

Torah crown, Amsterdam, 19th century, gold with precious stones. (Hechal Shlomo Museum, Jerusalem).

THE LAST DANCE

THIS HAPPENED ON THE last Simhat Torah, in 1942. Only a handful of Jews had remained alive out of the five hundred thousand, formerly in the Polish capital.

Twenty Jews were gathered in the home of Rabbi Menahem Zemba, the last remaining rabbi in Warsaw, to observe Simhat Torah. Among them was Judah Leib Orlean, former director of the Beth Jacob Teachers' Seminary, who had devoted his life to religious education. At the proper time they brought forth the Scrolls of the Torah; and, sorrowfully reciting the verses, which in former years had been joyously chanted, they wearily plodded the *hakafot* about the table.

Suddenly a boy of twelve appeared in the room. This was astonishing, for the Germans had already slain or deported for extermination all the Jewish children in the ghetto. Who could he be, and where had he come from? No one knew.

Orlean ran to the boy and, embracing him together with this Torah, cried out, "Young Jew with the holy Torah!" He swept him along in an exultant *hassidic* dance. The other joined the dance one by one, until all had formed a circle about the unknown boy, Orlean, and the Torah.

Bereaved fathers who had lost their entire families danced, with tears rolling down their faces, while the great educator reiterated, "Young Jew with the holy Torah! Young Jew with the holy Torah!"

This was the last dance of the Jews on their last Simhat Torah in Warsaw.

(from HILLEL SEIDMAN'S DIARY OF THE WARSAW GHETTO)

In the days of Mattathias. Illuminated by Sol Nodel.

In the days of the Hasmonean, Mattathias, son of Yohanan, the High Priest, and his sons, when the evil government of Greece rose up against Thy people Israel, to cause them to forget Thy Torah and to transgress the laws of Thy will—Thou, in Thy great mercy, didst stand by them at the time of their distress. Thou didst champion their cause, defend their rights, avenge their wrong; Thou didst deliver the strong into the hands of the weak, the many into the hands of the few, the unclean into the hands of the pure, the wicked into the hands of the righteous, and the arrogant into the hands of those engaged in the study of Torah. Thou didst make for Thyself a great and holy Name in Thy world, and for Thy people Israel Thou hast performed great acts of redemption and deliverance unto this day. Thereupon Thy children came to the sanctuary of Thy house, cleansed Thy Temple, purified Thy Holy Place, kindled lights in Thy sacred courts, and designated these eight days of Hanukka to give thanks and praises to Thy great Name.''

HANUKKA

Modern menora, silver, for oil lamps by Ludwig Y. Wolpert. The Hebrew inscription reads: "To Thee all praise is due" (from Hanukka Hymn Maoz Tzur).

Hanukka Lights. Hanukka is also known as Hag HaUrim—the Festival of Lights. The lights—which may be either candles or oil lamps—are kindled on each of the eight nights of the festival. They commemorate the miracle of Hanukka—the victory of the Maccabees and the one day's supply of pure oil which miraculously burned for eight days after the reconstruction of the Holy Temple. Originally Hanukka menorot were adaptations of the simple Roman terra cotta oil lamp. Later, lamps and eight-branch candelabra (with a ninth branch holding the light used to kindle the other lights) were made of pewter, tin, copper or silver.

HANUKKA, THE FESTIVAL OF LIGHTS, is celebrated for eight days to commemorate the victory of the Jews over the Hellenist Syrians in the year 165 B.C.E.

"Hanukka" is the Hebrew term for "dedication." Following their victory, the Maccabees, the sons of the priestly Hasmonean family which led the Jews in their revolt against their Syrian overlords, entered the Holy Temple which had been defiled by the Syrian invaders, cleansed it and dedicated it anew to the service of God. Then, to signalize their victory, the Maccabees celebrated the first Hanukka.

The successful outcome of the Maccabean revolt against the Syrians signified much more than a mere military victory. It was above all else the triumph of the spirit over brute force, of the belief in One God over paganism. It brought the Jewish people not only political independence but also religious and cultural liberation from Hellenism which, following the conquests of Alexander the Great in the 4th Century B.C.E., had gradually spread to all the corners of the ancient Greek Empire.

The most important observance associated with Hanukka is the kindling of the Hanukka lights in the *menorah*, or *hanukkiya*, a nine-branch-candelabrum, accompanied by the chanting of appropriate benedictions and hymns. On each night one more light is kindled, beginning with one candle on the first night of Hanukka and ending with eight on the final evening. The ninth branch is reserved for the *Shamash*, the "servant" light which is lit first and which is used to kindle the other lights of the *menorah*.

The Talmud relates that when the Judean heroes, led by Judah Maccabee, made ready to rededicate the Temple, they were unable to find enough undefiled oil to light the lamps. Finally, in one of the Temple chambers, they came upon one small cruse of oil, which under normal circumstances would have lasted for only one evening. By miracle this small amount of oil kept the Temple lights burning not for one night, but for all of eight nights, until new oil fit for use in the Temple could be readied. This is the miracle commemorated by the kindling of the Hanukka lights.

In the broader sense, however, the Hanukka lights symbolize the light of religious, national and cultural freedom won by the Maccabees for their people.

126

Silver menora for candles or oil (Italy, 18th-19th centuries). (The Jewish Museum, New York City).

Hanukka is also a gay home festival. Gifts are exchanged, parties are given, and "latkes" (potato pancakes), a delicacy long associated with Hanukka, are served. The children play *dreidel*. The *dreidel* has four sides, each bearing a Hebrew letter—*nun, gimmel, hay* and *shin*—the initials of *ness gadol haya sham*—"A great miracle happened there."

127

WERE IT NOT FOR THE Hanukka lights that observant Jews have kindled for generations, it would not have been possible for the magnificent Menorah, proud symbol of Israel reborn, to rise anew in our own day, spreading its glorious light to the ends of the earth. Hanukka is the miracle of victory and the victory of miracle.

The miracle of the cruse of oil which seemed barely enough to last one day but burned for eight whole days, and the triumph of a handful of partisans over the might of a brutal foe are not two opposing concepts but, together, form one glorious whole.

There were centuries when the commemoration of the miracle of the cruse of oil eclipsed the remembrance of the heroic Maccabean wars. But in our own day when the lights of Hanukka shine upon an Israel restored and thrice preserved from annihilation, the emphasis shifts again to the glorious victory of the few over the many.

There is a striking parallel between the perils that beset our people in the days of the Maccabees and the mortal danger with which they were faced in our own time. In the days of the Maccabees, too, the Jews were surrounded by enemies who plotted to destroy them. There were the Samaritans to the north, the Edomites and the Nabateans to the south, and the Ammonites to the east. Greece, the strong naval power of those days, even closed the sea to them. Jerusalem, our capital, was held in an iron vise. Jaffa, Gaza and Acre were all in Greek hands, as were the Galilee and all the coastal cities. And above it all, there was the hostile alliance of two powers—Hellenist Syria and Egypt.

The tiny land of Israel, hemmed in by foes on all sides, was only a small part of the *Eretz Yisrael* as defined in the Bible. The other nations considered the Israelites an insignificant sect. Aristotle called the Jews "the philosophers among the Syrians," dismissing them as a group of philosophers huddled around the Holy Temple.

The political and strategic situation in which the small, weak Jewish State found itself was almost hopeless. Its foes ringed it from all directions and threatened it with invasion and enslavement.

The wars won by Judah Maccabee and his brothers, and the subsequent victories of Simon, his son Yohanan Hyrcanus, Judah Aristobulus and Alexander Jannaeus wrought a decisive change in the situation of the Jewish State. During the reign of Alexander Jannaeus, Israel's borders were extended far beyond those of the kingdom ruled by David and Solomon. But these conquests were not made for the sake of territorial expansion; their purpose was to provide effective protection from an aggressor who had menaced the very existence of the nation.

Menora, contemporary design, by Ludwig Y. Wolpert.

Edom, Samaria, the Galilee and all the coastal cities—Acre, Haifa, Jaffa and others which had been held by the Greeks, reverted to their legitimate owners, the people of Israel. These conquests strengthened the political, cultural, religious and social independence of the Jewish State. The opening of a gate to the west through the liberation of the Eastern Mediterranean ports gave new impetus to the country's economy. Maritime commerce rapidly forged ahead. Immigration from foreign lands swelled the population of Palestine, and the trend of Hellenization was not only stopped but reversed by the mass conversion of heathens to Judaism.

This phenomenal progress in many spheres of Jewish national life parallels a similar development which we ourselves witnessed during the two decades that have passed since the establishment of the modern State of Israel. But unlike the birth of the present Jewish State, the Hasmonean era was marked also by a religious revival. The "miracles and redemption" commemorated by Hanukka gave new force to the faith that had waned under the influence of Hellenism. Jewish culture began to flourish. The Hebrew language, which had been largely supplanted by Greek, came into its own once more. That period saw the composition of several Hebrew classics, among them the *First Book of Maccabees, Tobias, Judith,* the *Book of Hanoch,* the *Book of the Jubilees,* and the *Testament of the Twelve Tribes.* This too, was the period of the famed *Zugot*[1] and *Eshkolot*[2], of giants of learning, from Jose ben Joezer and Jose ben Yohanan to Shemaya and Abtalyon and Hillel and Shammai. The rabbinic courts wielded great authority; their decisions were recognized and enforced by the government. It is noteworthy that the marriage and divorce laws as formulated and interpreted by the rabbinic courts of that period are accepted even in the modern State of Israel today.

It may be said without exaggeration that the Hasmonean wars were a potent factor in the molding of the very soul of the Jewish people. While its effect on the nation's political destinies was of only temporary duration, its impact on Israel's religious and spiritual life persisted through long centuries of exile and persecution.

Before the Hasmonean period, Judaism as a religion had been confined to a limited circle. This, in itself, was no calamity. On the contrary, limitation can lead to greater concentration and intensification. But in the then existing circumstances, limitation posed the threat of deterioration and alienation. For Jews and Judaism had come under the pressure of Hellenic cultural influences backed by formidable political and military power. The far-flung dissemination of Greek culture during the second century B.C.E., which resulted in the Helleni-

Menora, contemporary design, by Ludwig Y. Wolpert.

---

[1] *Zug* (pl. *Zugot*), Lit. "pair," the two Heads of the Supreme Rabbinical Court in the early Talmudic period.
[2] Lit. "grape clusters." The illustrious scholars of the early Maccabean period.

Stone menora made in Yemen, 18th or 19th century.

zation of large numbers of Jews, including acknowledged leaders and intellectuals, wrought havoc particularly among the youth, thus increasing the threat of total assimilation.

The Maccabean victory wrought a radical change in the situation. Judaism regained its cultural strength to an extent rarely experienced in the annals of the Jewish past. The foundations of *Mishna* and *Gemara* were laid, shaping the cultural and spiritual destiny of the people of Israel for many centuries ahead. It was this body of Jewish law that was to be a shield and protection to the Jewish people, enabling it to survive even the destruction of the Temple and the loss of political independence.

It can be said without hesitation that the seeds of the extraordinary heroism shown by Israel's defenders of our own time were planted then, "in the days of Mattathias, son of Yohanan, the Hasmonean High Priest, and his sons." The similarities between the two critical contests, two millennia apart, are clearly discernible. The miracle of the Hasmoneans lay not only in the victory of the inspired Maccabean partisans, but also *in the fact that they fought at all.* According to all the calculations of military experts, based on the strategic and political situation of the time, and according to all the rules of logic, the Maccabees did not have the slightest chance of defeating the Hellenic Empire. Then, as they did now, the strategists stood gaping: Where did a band

130

of hopelessly outnumbered, poorly trained and inadequately equipped fighters get the courage to wage war against a mighty empire? What madness was this?

And when Israel emerged victorious then, and again in the War of Independence, in the Sinai Campaign, and finally in the Six-Day War, the learned theoreticians conceded that the miracle of Israel's triumph consisted in the fact that the defenders dared to wage the fight. This evaluation has found its expression in the prayer of thanksgiving we offer on Hanukka. We give thanks to God not only for "the miracles and for the redemption," but also "for the mighty deeds and for the battles." We give thanks for the spirit that enabled the fighters for the cause of the Lord to plunge courageously into an unequal contest, into a "David-against-Goliath" battle rather than submit without putting up a fight. The "mighty deeds" refer not merely to heroism on the field of battle but, first and foremost, to the decision to fight against countless odds despite sober opinions of experts and objective rules of logic. Heroism is active resistance to force; it is spiritual strength pitched against physical might. He who possesses that spiritual strength is the true hero.

Such is the heroism that inspired the Maccabees of the past as well as Israel's defenders of the present. Hanukka therefore symbolizes not only the miracle of victory, but also the victory of the miracle—of faith

Menorot, Morocco, 19th century. Top, marble; bottom, stone.

Menora, cast bronze, Western Europe, 14th century, for oil lamps. This is one of the oldest European menorot extant. Inscription: "For the commandment is a lamp and the Law is a light" (Prov. 6:23). (Courtesy Temple Emanu-El, New York City).

Flower–shaped menora (Persia, 18th century).

in the supreme power of Providence that passes human understanding.

Some still tend to stress only one aspect of Hanukka, the spiritual aspect, symbolized by the miracle of the cruse of oil, and virtually ignore the political phase of the Hasmonean revolt; namely, the miracle of the wars and triumphs. Others go to the opposite extreme glorifying Israel's triumph on the field of battle without giving thought to its spiritual victory. Either of these views is narrow, and subject to misinterpretation. Actually, there have been very few historical occurrences in which the spiritual and political aspects were as closely intertwined and interrelated as in the chain of events that is commemorated by Hanukka. Both aspects, the political and the spiritual, are vital parts of the Festival of Lights. Even as the miracle of the lights symbolizes the triumph of the Jewish spirit, so do the lights themselves recall the heroism and self-sacrifice so gloriously manifest in the wars and victories of the Jewish people—from the Maccabees of old to the State of Israel today.

Menora with glass cups for oil (Bagdad, 18th century).

WINTER IS STILL WITH US. Nature is asleep. The fields are covered with snow and slush. The trees, bereft of their leaves, stand with naked branches against the winter sky. But in the Land of Israel, spring is almost here. Nature, awakening from its winter sleep, is about to come back to life.

In the northern lands of his dispersion, the Jew, looking through his frosty window panes at the snow piled high outside, gazed with his inner eye upon a brighter scene in the Land of Israel. He could almost feel the warmth of spring, smell the fragrance of the verdant vineyards, and see the young leaves heralding the rebirth of nature. It might be winter all around him, but spring had come to his homeland and it was time to celebrate Tu Bi'Sh'vat, the New Year of the Trees. And as he welcomed the advent of spring in the land of his fathers, the Jew also renewed the timeless bonds that linked him with the land throughout the centuries of his exile.

Hamisha Asar BiSh'vat. (Hebrew Arbor Day). The fifteenth day of Sh'vat, which falls about the month of February, is known as the New Year of the Trees. Israeli children by the thousands observe the holiday by planting trees.

In Israel, Tu Bi'Sh'vat is marked by the planting of trees. Most fittingly, this ritual is performed by the children of the land, who, themselves in the springtime of life, symbolize the eternal hope of mankind. It is an act of creation, in which, according to Judaism, man works in close partnership with God Himself.

Basing their view, no doubt, on the Biblical dictum that man was formed in the image of God, and on the fact that God planted a garden in which man was to dwell, the Sages of the Talmud declared that it was mandatory for the Jewish people to plant trees in their land. "When you first come into the Land of Israel," they said, "you are to engage in no other work than planting" (*Midrash Rabba*, Leviticus 25) .

In the same vein, the Midrash indicates that trees must be planted in the Land of Israel not merely for the sake of the fruits they will yield, but for their own worth. "Said the Holy One, blessed by He, to Israel: Even though you may find the land filled with abundance, you must not say: 'We shall not concern ourselves with planting,' rather even as others planted [trees] for you, so shall you plant [them] for your children." (to Leviticus 28) .

The stress which Judaism has always placed on creative work stands in striking contrast to the ways of the other nations of the once "Fertile Crescent" who were content to submit to the whims of nature to the point where they thought it sinful to harness the forces of creation for the welfare of their own peoples. This fatalistic view of the world moved them to destroy the wells dug by Abraham and Isaac three thousand years ago and, more recently, to thwart the endeavor of Abraham's descendants to use the waters of the Jordan for the benefit of the entire Middle East.

Now that the Jewish people has returned to its land, Tu Bi'Sh'vat has taken on a new significance. Not only has the New Year of the Trees come to signify the rebirth of the Land of Israel, but the State of Israel itself has become the symbol of rebirth and revival to men of good will everywhere.

Rabbi Yochanan ben Zakkai was wont to say: if a seedling were in your hand and you were told the Messiah is at hand, come and plant the seedling and then go and greet him.

AVOT D'RABBI NATHAN

CUSTOMS OF TU BI'SH'VAT

HAMISHA ASAR BI-SH'VAT, the "Arbor Day" which celebrates the annual rebirth of nature, provides a welcome break in the monotony of the dreary winter months that separate Hanukka from Purim. The Sephardic Jews call it *Frutas*, the Feast of the Fruits, or, in accordance with the Mishnaic characterization of the day, the New Year ("Rosh HaShana") of the Trees, Rosasana dos Arbores. Children are given little bags embroidered with their names and filled with fruits, particularly hazelnuts and almonds, to wear as festival pendants around their necks. *

In Bagdad and elsewhere in the Orient, wealthy Jews would hold feasts at which over fifty different kinds of fruit would be served, in addition to wine and bread. Each guest would read a chapter from the book *P'ri Etz Hadar* ("The Fruit of a Goodly Tree") before reciting the proper blessing and partaking of one of the fruits.

In what is now Iran, Jews would gather on the eve of the holiday at the home of some affluent member of their community. The host would have prepared for them a lavish spread of fruits, vegetables and cereals, including roasted wheat kernels, peas and pumpkin seeds, and delicacies such as roast fish.

The Sephardim mark Hamisha Asar Bi-Sh'vat with an all-night vigil, during which appropriate portions from the Bible, Talmud and Zohar are read. They attach particular importance to fruits grown in Israel, especially the carob fruit.

Ashkenazim partake of fifteen different kinds of fruit.

Sephardim in the Balkan countries would go in festive procession with their families to some large outdoor place where they would slaughter a sheep and hold a picnic.

Schools in Israel and Talmud Torahs in the Diaspora countries observe Hamisha Asar Bi-Sh'vat with outings and tree plantings.

And Mordecai wrote these things, and sent letters unto all the Jews that were in all the provinces of the King Ahasuerus, both near and far, to establish this among them, that they should keep the fourteenth day of the month Adar, and the fifteenth day of the same, yearly, as the days wherein the Jews rested from their enemies, and the month which was turned unto them from sorrow to joy, and from mourning into a good day; that they should make them days of feasting and joy, and of sending portions one to another, and gifts to the poor.

ESTHER 9:20-22

With the beginning of Adar rejoicing is increased.

TAANIT 29A

Rabbi Joseph taught: Joy and feasting and a good day (Esther 9:19): joy, to signify that mourning be forbidden; feasting, to signify that fasting be forbidden; good day, to signify that servile work be forbidden.

MEGILLA 5:72

PURIM

Purim plate. Pewter plate (Germany, 1753) used for carrying Purim gifts to neighbors. Decorations show the signs of the Zodiac and main events in the story of Purim. In the center: King David with his harp, and a quotation from the Book of Esther (9:22) "[and they should make them days] of sending portions to one another, and gifts to the poor."

THE FEAST OF PURIM celebrates the deliverance, some 2500 years ago, of the Jews of the Persian Empire from total annihilation plotted by Haman, Prime Minister at the court of King Ahasuerus. This last-minute rescue was brought about by the intercession of beautiful Queen Esther and by the steadfast faith of her foster-uncle Mordecai, a devout Jew well-known and esteemed in court circles. In the end, Haman's evil plot was exposed, Haman was hanged, and Mordecai succeeded to his high post. This event is recorded in the Book of Esther, which has been incorporated into the Bible.

Purim is the Hebrew word for "lots." According to the account in the Book of Esther, Haman cast lots to decide the date on which he would exterminate the Jews. The date he chose was the thirteenth day of the Jewish month of *Adar*.

The dramatic impact of this miraculous rescue on the Jewish people was so great that its commemoration through the Feast of Purim has become an integral part of Jewish tradition. Over the centuries many interesting customs have evolved in connection with Purim observance.

Whenever the name of Haman is mentioned in the reading of the *Megillah* (Scroll of Esther) in the synagogue on Purim eve and morning, children twirl *graggers* (noise-makers), and adults stamp their feet or strike their fists on the lecterns, literally "drowning out" the name of the archfiend.

At home Purim day is celebrated by a lavish banquet—the Purim *seudah*. A special Purim delicacy are *hamantashen* ("Haman's Pockets"), triangular pastries filled with a mixture of ground poppy-seed and honey, or with fruit preserves.

Another popular Purim custom is *Mishloach Manot* (in corrupted Ashkenazic usage—*Sh'lach Mones*) literally "the sending of portions," in which relatives, friends and neighbors exchange gifts of fruit and sweets.

Some forty years ago, a new Purim observance was introduced in Tel Aviv. On Purim day, a festive parade, miles long, with colorful floats, bands, choruses and costumes, winds through the main thoroughfares of the city, as tens of thousands watch from street-curbs, windows and balconies. This procession has become known as the *Adloyada*, literally "Until-One-Knows-Not," an expression derived from a facetious Talmudic remark that one should partake of strong drink *until one knows not* the difference between "blessed be Mordecai" and "cursed be Haman." This annual parade has become so popular that tourists from all over the world come to view it each year.

In schools, children participate in carnivals and masquerades, including "Queen Esther beauty pageants," starring, of course, the girls.

The real significance of Purim consists in the moral and religious lessons it imparts, namely that tyrants who seek to destroy others are ultimately destroyed themselves, and that faith is a source of great spiritual strength which can help us overcome the many adversities that are part of the life of men and nations.

THE DUAL SIGNIFICANCE

THE SPIRITUAL PREPARATION for Purim is accomplished through two things: a spirit of rejoicing in accordance with the rabbinic adage, "When the month of Adar enters, joy is increased," and, on the Sabbath before, a reading of the part of Chapter 25 of the Book of Deuteronomy which bids us to "Remember what Amalek hath done to thee."

The joy of Purim is entirely different from the exultation of other holidays which is expressed by the precept, "thou shalt rejoice in thy Holy Days" (Deut. 16:14). It contains an element of rebellion against reality and at the same time a call to faith in the ultimate triumph and the downfall of evil. The joy of Purim actually borders on a forgetting of self. The Talmud enjoins us to make merry on Purim *"ad d'lo yada"* —"until one knows not the difference between 'cursed be Haman' and 'blessed be Mordecai.'" Such merriment obviously implies a deliberate effort to forget reality, the unhappy facts of exile.

139

Megilla case. Some Megillot are kept in cases of carved wood, embossed silver or filigree work. This decorated silver case (early 19th century, Eastern Europe) depicts the story of Purim. The design in the center shows Mordecai, cousin of Queen Esther, in royal garb riding through the city of Shushan. The design at the bottom, left, shows Haman and his ten sons on the gallows. (Hebrew Union College Museum, Cincinnati, Ohio).

On the other hand, we are bidden to "remember" Amalek. "Remembering Amalek" serves as a warning not to forget persecution, not to let ourselves be lulled into a false sense of security, not to escape into a fool's paradise when danger threatens. Nor should we be so spineless as to forgive and forget an implacable foe. This is not vindictiveness, it is merely self-defense against a recurrence of persecution. To remember Amalek simply means to remember reality, to guard against the wrong kind of forgetfulness and to steel oneself against the storms that may lie ahead in the precarious existence of our people in exile.

It is in the light of this dual significance that we should view Purim and its observance.

THE SCROLL OF ESTHER

THE BIBLICAL CANON includes five *Megillot* ("Scrolls"), of which each is read in the synagogue on a specific occasion during the Jewish year. Three are read on major festivals. The Song of Songs is read on Pesah, the Book of Ruth on Shavuot, and *Kohelet* (Ecclesiastes) on Sukkot. The connection of each of these three with the festivals on which they are read is a rather tenuous one; it is apparent neither from the content of the *Megillah* itself nor from the simple, direct meaning of the festival. Primarily, the links between these Scrolls and "their" festivals are rooted in tradition and in rabbinic interpretation.

Not so the other two *megillot*—Lamentations and the Scroll of Esther. Both of these are closely interwoven with the events their reading commemorates. Particularly the Scroll of Esther, both in its content and in the act of its reading, constitutes the very substance, the core of the holiday of Purim. The practice to read the Scroll of Esther on Purim has been established by precept and devolves upon the Jew by divine commandment as indicated by the benediction that is recited before the Scroll is read. All the other precepts pertaining to the observance of Purim, such as the exchange of gifts and the distribution of charity to the poor, are derived directly from the Scroll of Esther.

The Scroll of Esther is the only one of the Five Scrolls to which a special tractate has been devoted in the Talmud. *Tractate Megillah* includes not merely the laws pertaining to the way in which the Scroll itself is to be written and read, but beyond this, a wealth of explanations, laws and legal interpretations pertinent to the observance of Purim, all based on the material contained in the *Megillah*.

Various ingredients are blended in the Scroll of Esther to produce the fascinating, dramatic story of a vicious—and unsuccessful—plot to annihilate an entire Jewish community. Out of the various elements of the plot—political, religious, personal, diplomatic—there emerge three dominant motifs: hatred for the Jews to the point of a war of annihilation, as it were, deterrent action by Jews of great wisdom and courage and self-defense on the part of the Jewish masses. All these elements are well-known to us Jews from various periods of our history of blood and tears, to our very own times.

The historical event narrated in the *Megillah* was not an isolated happening. In essence, it has recurred in different epochs and, in so recurring, has taught us some lessons of eternal significance.

Legend has embellished the holiday of Purim with both fanciful tales and instructive ideas—ideas that have proven eminently relevant also to subsequent days of wrath and salvation, distress and deliverance, exile and redemption.

Indeed, Jewish communities in many lands and at many different periods have instituted local "Purim" festivals of their own to commemorate miraculous deliverances from evil plots similar to the one related in the story of the original Purim.

The incessant persecution of the Jews in the lands of their dispersion, the persistent need for miraculous intervention from a higher power, the continuous struggle for individual and group survival—all these have found their concrete expression in the observance of Purim. Purim has served as a demonstration of the ultimate triumph of good over evil, and the Scroll of Esther has become the symbol of the Jew's eternal hope for redemption.

THE OBSERVANCE OF PURIM

PURIM BECAME ROOTED in the Jew's national consciousness both in its actual meaning and in its historic significance. On Pesah we are reminded that "every man is duty-bound to regard himself as if he personally had gone forth from Egypt." On Purim we need no such instruction, for numerous communities have lived through trials and tribulations quite similar to those of the Jews of Persia in the days of Mordecai and Esther and then found themselves delivered by sheer miracle at the eleventh hour.

There appears to be a contrast between this serious aspect of the Purim story on the one hand, and the commentaries, interpretations and customs relating to the merry celebration of Purim, on the other. The *Megillah* is pervaded with sadness, for it deals with hard fact and tragic reality. It has no lighter moments. Even the so-called "happy ending" is presented in a sober mood, as an object lesson for future generations. Miraculous deliverance from attempted genocide is no laughing matter.

Megilla case. This silver Megilla case is the work of Ludwig Y. Wolpert (Congregation Beth Shalom, Oak Park, Michigan).

141

Purim plate, by Ilya Schor. (Courtesy Mr. and Mrs. Isadore M. Marder, Philadelphia, Pa.).

But in the realm of classical commentary, particularly literature dating from the Middle Ages and more recent times, as well as in the various customs evolved for Purim celebrations, fun and hilarity predominate. The atmosphere is one of jest, play, masquerades and light-hearted entertainment. Purim became an occasion of escape from burdensome reality but also one of active protest and rebellion against that reality. It came to symbolize profound dissatisfaction with the *status quo*, among our people and in the world at large, and our effort to change it through practical action.

A striking illustration of this spirit is the manner in which Purim was celebrated in the *yeshivot* (talmudic academies) of old, particularly in Eastern Europe. These *yeshiva* celebrations often served as catalysts for intellectual ferment. One of the students would be accorded the honor of impersonating a scholar of the Law whose authority was universally unchallenged. This "hero of the day" was dubbed "Purim Rabbi" and, as such, he was allowed complete freedom to heap open and severe criticism on everything and everybody not only in the *yeshiva* but also in the Jewish community outside. With extraordinary wit, humor and satire, this "rabbi-for-a-day" would lash out against the faults and weaknesses of the existing order of things, all to the boundless merriment of his audience which included the butts of his merciless ridicule. Here, then, was a once-a-year opportunity to overstep the

Purim rattle. Whenever the name of wicked Haman is mentioned in the synagogue reading of the Scroll of Esther, the congregation literally "drowns out" his name with noisemakers ("graggers"). This silver and wood gragger, executed by Ilya Schor, bears the inscription, "Blessed be Mordecai the Jew."

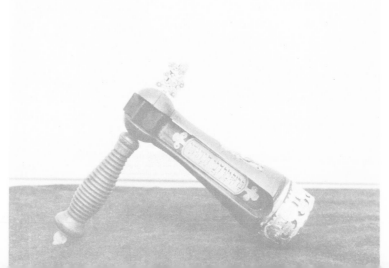

limits of fixed routine and rigid convention and to express, albeit face-tiously, revolutionary ideas obviously prompted by a spirit of rebellion against authority and reality. The only weapon employed was laughter, but that often proved remarkably potent.

It is fair to assume that the *Rashei-Yeshiva*, the heads of the academies, many of whom were excellent practical psychologists, adopted a permissive attitude toward these uninhibited obloquies by the "rabbi-for-a-day." This was a way of providing an outlet for their students' pent-up emotions, pet peeves and frustrations, of opening the safety-valve for a while to let off excess steam. This was good psychology, and more often than not these Purim "entertainments" resulted in constructive action in response to justified complaints.

Many brilliant students, endowed with a keen sense of humor, a rare aptitude for satire and a discerning eye for faults and weaknesses in others as well as in themselves, excelled in their Purim discourses and diatribes. A number of non-conformists and rebellious spirits, too, utilized this opportunity to protest vigorously against the discipline and authority to which they had to submit all year long—except, of course, on Purim, when "anything went."

In the general community, too, Purim was the time to wield the weapon of humor and satire, of indignation tempered with jest, against evil, tyranny and persecution. Laughter was the only means of revenge which the Jews could employ not only against the Haman of the *Megillah*, but also against the Hamans of their own time—those who had already met their doom as well as those who, though still in power, were sure to share the fate of all the others of their ilk.

The Scroll of Esther, popularly known simply as the "Megilla," has provided inspiration for many an artist. This Scroll depicting the characters in the story of Purim is the work of a Polish scribe and dates back to 1748. Illuminated Scrolls such as these were mostly used at home; the undecorated ones were considered more appropriate for reading at the synagogue service. (Hebrew Union College Museum, Cincinnati, Ohio).

Purim ball. Purim masquerades gave rise to Purim balls in many communities. This fancy-dress affair was held in New York in 1865.

The Jew fought against his oppressors with the weapon of laughter, but his laughter was mingled with tears. In the *Megillah* story, Esther, in danger of her own life, implores the king: "Let my life be sacrificed at my petition, and my people saved at my request." But commentators and celebrants of subsequent generations have turned even these elements of tragedy into comedy. Ignoring the intensely dramatic character of the Scroll of Esther, including its "happy ending," they converted its serious mood into a riot of clowning and buffoonery.

144

PURIM DECORATIONS

THE YEARNING FOR BEAUTY which throbbed in the hearts of the Jews in their narrow, crowded ghettoes sought expression especially in their observance of Purim.

It manifested itself in various forms of art: illuminations for the Megillah and illustrations of scenes from the Purim story; woodcuts and copper engravings portraying characters and events from the Scroll of Esther; exquisite silver Megillah cases finely wrought by master craftsmen; theatrical and musical Purim presentations; elaborate costumes for Purim masquerades and table decorations for the Purim *Seudah,* the festive Purim banquet; and, more recently, in fascinating, colorful floats for the *Adloyada* parade that is held each Purim in Tel Aviv.

Not only Jews, but non-Jewish artists, too, have created masterpieces on Purim themes. Some of these may be seen in leading museums of European capitals, such as the Louvre in Paris and the Renaissance Museum in Florence.

Since Purim symbolizes the confrontation between fact and fancy, it is only natural that artistic creativity, which similarly reflects the contrast between things as they are and things as one might wish them to be, should have found ample inspiration from the story of Purim.

Indeed, today we are hard put to conceive of Purim without the beautiful decorations that represent centuries of skilled and imaginative craftsmanship.

Purim carnival. Tens of thousands in Tel Aviv turn out each year to watch the Adloyada, Israel's Purim parade complete with marchers, elaborate floats and costumes. (Israel Office of Information).

TAKING REVENGE ON HAMAN

Title page of a popular book on Purim in the Ladino language.

THERE WAS AN interesting custom in Frankfort-on-the-Main. On Purim eve, as the *Megillah* (Book of Esther) was to be read aloud in the synagogue, they would have a most unusual, unique object standing on the great table or lectern at the front of the synagogue. Made of wax and painted with gold color, it was an artistic representation of an open hollow castle, in which the figures of Haman and his wife Zeresh stood beside a hangman. When the *Megillah* reading began, the two figures were set aflame. At the two sides appeared two other figures, made of wax, about nine inches tall; they had black hats, yellow beards, and manes of white hair. The one at the right was dressed in red, with a pipe in his mouth and a large sword at his side. The one at the left had green clothing, with a royal scepter of gold in his right hand and a tobacco pipe in his left. The first figure was Mordecai; the other was obviously King Ahasuerus.

PURIM IN DAMASCUS

ON THE NIGHT OF Purim (here called the Festival of Haman) Evening Services in the Damascus synagogue lasted until midnight. In addition to hearing the *Megillah* (Book of Esther) chanted aloud with its chant, they would pray to the Almighty that He take Haman and punish him, so that the scoundrel and villain might never rise again.

In the morning they would set up next to the synagogue an effigy of Haman—a large figure made of rags and other flammable materials. After the holiday meal the Jews would gather to shoot this "Haman" with rifles and stab it with drawn swords.

REVENGE IN YEMEN

HERE THE YOUNGSTERS would make a figure of Haman out of plaited wood, which they plastered over with mud, until it was the actual size of a man; and they would lacquer it in various colors. Similarly they made a figure of Mordecai riding his horse, with Haman running before him as a herald. The figures of Haman they hung from a tall tree in the synagogue courtyard and then shot arrows and threw stones at it, until it fell apart. So the children played all that happy day, striking Haman (in effigy) and hurling invective at him, while they sang the praises of the righteous Mordecai and Esther . . .

146

מה יעשה לאיש אשר המלך חפץ ביקרו

The Triumph of Mordecai. Contemporary, pen-and-ink wash by Leonard Baskin.
Hebrew inscription: "Thus shall it be done to the man whom the king delights
to honor" (Esther 6:11). (The Jewish Museum, New York City).

THE GRAGGER

IN THE EARLIER communities of France and Germany, Italy and Egypt, Algiers and Amsterdam, it was the custom for our people to "beat Haman" by stamping their feet, rapping with a stick, banging with a hammer and stones, erasing his likeness or his name, and so on. In recent generations, however, the *gragger* (noisemaker) has gained importance. They took to "beating Haman" with this instrument in communities all over Germany, and from there the practice spread to many Sephardic and Eastern communities.

The *gragger*, it would seem, had its origin in ancient Greece. In the Middle Ages the Catholic Church used to call its people to worship in the four final days of Holy Week, when church bells could not be rung. Then the sextons would sound large *graggers* from the steeples instead.

So it was that in time Jewish children learned a new, "improved" way of "beating Haman," adapting the instrument to their own needs, and giving it a Jewish appearance, according to their time and place.

Haman begging Queen Esther for mercy (Esther 7:7) after his plot had been exposed, England, 19th century.

HAPPINESS IS THE REALM OF FREEDOM

TRUE TRANQUILITY AND peace of mind are achieved essentially through joy. For in happiness a person can direct his intelligence as he wishes, and can compose his mind to meditate on his ultimate purposes beyond the boundaries of time. For happiness is the realm of freedom; and therefore, when a person fixes his thoughts on joy, his mind is liberated, and is not confined by the bonds of exile. In melancholy and sorrow, the intelligence and the mind are in exile.

Hence a person must rally his strength to dwell in happiness as much as he can; he must strive to find some good in himself so that he can achieve joy . . .

It is even often necessary to find happiness through wit, humor and jokes. Amidst the over-abundant suffering and troubles that come to everyone concerning health, money, and spirit, as a rule, one cannot gladden his own heart without sharp, humorous sayings and witticisms to achieve a happy state.

(Rabbi Nahman of Bratzlav)

PURIM IN PERSIA

THE FIRST SIGNS OF this merry holiday already appeared weeks before. All kinds of sweet Purim pastries were put on sale in the shops. In the schoolrooms the children took to studying the *Megillah* (Book of Esther) and other texts connected with Purim. Purim melodies could be heard from every house. And the children, big and small, busied themselves in their leisure hours making a proper effigy of wicked Haman. One sewed two hands; another, two feet; a third worked on the head; and a fourth on the torso. They stuffed the body with straw, stubble, and all kinds of rags; then they stitched all the parts together—and Haman rose to his full height, with every part in place ready to accept his sentence to death by hanging.

The triumph of Mordecai. "Then Haman took the apparel and the horse, and arrayed Mordecai and caused him to ride through the streets of the city and proclaimed before him: 'Thus shall it be done to the man whom the King delights to honor.'" (Esther 6:11) This etching by Rembrandt (ca. 1640) shows Mordecai, holding the King's scepter, riding in triumph through the city of Shushan. Leading the horse is Haman who had plotted the destruction of Mordecai and the entire Jewish people because they had refused to bow to him as a divine being. (The Jewish Museum, New York City).

The hanging of Haman. Copper engraving. Holland, 1725. Gallows with Haman can be seen in the background.

Other children, ten years of age and younger, would prepare scrolls from which to follow the reading of the *Megillah* in the synagogue. For several weeks they would sit each day, hours at a time, copying the Book of Esther in the square Hebrew characters used by Torah scribes, toiling away until the scrolls were completed. Then, happy as only children can be, they eagerly awaited the time when the Book of Esther would be read in the synagogue.

On the Sabbath before Purim, special prayers were recited to a chant that set the holiday mood. At the mention of Haman's name, fists already beat the tables and walls. And the Torah reading that Sabbath ended with the command of the Almighty to "blot out" the memory of the people of Amalek, from which Haman had sprung. (Deut. 25:19).

That Sabbath afternoon, young and old crowded into the synagogue to hear a reading of *Targum Sheni*, the Aramaic translation of the Book of Esther that embellishes the story of Purim with Midrashic additions. The women stood in the courtyard outside, listening as the reader explained it all. This reading would continue until late in the day.

The Fast of Esther the day before Purim was observed as strictly as Yom Kippur. Even the sick refused to take food, and children frequently had to be forced to eat.

At evening time, old and young would gather in the synagogue. In the Jewish quarter not a soul was to be seen in the streets. The children were armed with little "explosives": paper caps for guns, firecrackers, and so on. Before the Evening Service began, the sexton passed through the synagogue with a brass tray, on which everyone put some coins to recall the half-shekel that each Israelite contributed toward the upkeep of the Holy Temple in Jerusalem. The money went for the maintenance of the synagogue or to the charity named after Rabbi Meir Baal Ha-ness (the Miracle Worker).

Each synagogue had one *Megillah* of parchment, from which the cantor would read the *Book of Esther* aloud, while the congregation listened without any texts from which to follow. As the reading began the children prepared for "action." All ears would strain to catch the first mention of Haman's name, and even before the cantor could utter it, the "fireworks" began, as adult fists pounded the tables and walls, until the very air shook.

The ten sons of Haman standing in front of the tree that was to serve as their gallows. This drawing is from an edition of the Book of Esther published in Poland several years before the outbreak of World War II.

King Ahasuerus extends his golden scepter to Queen Esther (Holland, 15th century).

In Hamadan (160 miles west of Teheran) most of the Jews would gather that night at the tomb of Mordecai and Esther, crowding into the tiny space for the *Megillah* reading. Many would remain there throughout the night studying the holy books.

One who had recently lost a relative, particularly a parent, would invite a *minyan* (quorum) of ten people to his home for the *Megillah* reading. The guests would be served a kind of *halvah*, after which they would recite a special prayer for the soul of the departed. In many cases the mourner would distribute the *halvah* in his synagogue after the services on Purim eve and again on Purim morning.

After evening prayers the merriment began. Bands of children would dress up in all kinds of gaily colored costumes, paint their faces in various colors, particularly black, and go from house to house, beating drums and dancing. The adults, having fasted all day, waited before beginning their festivities. In some cities, such as Shiraz and Bulgurd, they would arise at midnight for feasting and celebration till morning—to recall that midnight hour when sleep eluded King Ahasuerus, that sleepless night which started the chain of events leading to the miraculous deliverance of the Jews from Haman's evil plot.

On Purim morning, after prayers and the *Megillah* reading, all would be quiet in the city until noon. What little exchange there was of *mishlo-ah manoth*, Purim gifts of food—took place mainly between betrothed couples. The bridegroom would send to the bride's family

Purim rattle. This elegant silver version of the "gragger" was made by a British artist in the early part of the present century.

a large wooden tray laden with all kinds of baked goods and sweets, fruits wrapped in gold-colored foil and, most important, jewelry. If he was a man of prestige in the community, he might send not just one tray but as many as four or six to the bride's house, each borne aloft on the shoulders of four men.

(Jews there had no skill in baking, and all year long only Gentiles' wares were available. But at Purim time whoever had an oven would hire a Gentile to bake sweet wafers, long cookies, rice cakes and nut cakes for him—which he then offered for sale.)

On Purim night, the people would gather at the home of someone who happened to be celebrating a joyful occasion in his own family. The tables were set with bottles of wine and beer, seeds, fruit, preserves, and roasted tidbits. As a rule the drinking was not wild, but the guests insisted on being served in large goblets. If a guest thought his cup was too small, he would ask his host with a smile, "Would you water a camel with a spoon?" Satiric ditties from *Esther-Naamah*, a well-known Persian play mocking Haman, were sung. Everyone would join in Vashti's reply to the king's invitation to appear before his guests to show her beauty:

> Too drunk are you a camel to see;
> How can you send me this decree?
> In a stable you worked ere I was your wife,
> Till my royal father saved your life.

Then there was King Ahasuerus' response to his officers:

> Vile has she been to husband and lord;
> I'll burn her, behead her with naked sword.

Thus, the company would spend the night in singing, dancing and all kinds of entertainment, while the liquor flowed freely until the guests could no longer tell the difference between "Cursed be Haman" and "Blessed be Mordecai."

The children also knew how to have fun on Purim. Their stuffed effigy of Haman was now ready for hanging from a wood or iron beam. Then they would douse the effigy with oil and set it afire. As it burned, a mass of children gathered around it, beating drums, clapping hands, and shouting, "O Haman, wicked Haman." Nor was this their only amusement that day. In the morning, after the *Megillah* reading, each child received "Purim money" from his father and all his relatives; and all day there was no end to the bustle and excitement.

Hand towel to be used at Purim dinner, embroidered linen, Southern Germany, 1812. (The Israel Museum, Jerusalem).

153

And Moses said unto the people: Remember this day, in which you came out from Egypt, out of the house of bondage; for by strength of hand the Lord brought you out from this place; no leavened bread shall be eaten.

EXODUS 13:3

And you shall relate to your son in that day, saying, This is done because of that which the Lord did unto me when I came forth out of Egypt. And it shall be for a sign unto you upon your hand, and for a memorial between your eyes, that the Lord's law may be in your mouth; for with a strong hand has the Lord brought you out of Egypt. You shall therefore keep this ordinance in its season from year to year.

EXODUS 13:8-10

In every generation everyone ought to look upon himself as if he personally had gone out of Egypt.

PASSOVER HAGGADAH

PESAH

Cup of Elijah. A prominent place at the Seder table is occupied by the Cup of Elijah. This cup honors the prophet who, according to tradition, is to herald the coming of the Messiah. Unlike most of the vessels used for this purpose, the cup in this picture (Germany, 17th century) is not made of silver but of ivory. The carving shows Messiah, the scion of the Davidian dynasty, accepting the homage of the people. (Hechal Shlomo Museum, Jerusalem).

THE SEDER

THE FESTIVAL OF PASSOVER commemorates the deliverance of the Israelites from Egyptian bondage, followed by their exodus from Egypt under the leadership of Moses, about the 13th Century before the Common Era.

The Biblical account in the Book of Exodus relates that after Moses had unsuccessfully pleaded with Pharaoh to release the Israelites from slavery, God smote the Egyptians with ten plagues in rapid succession. Only then, in desperation, did Pharaoh relent and let the Children of Israel go.

Before the tenth and most devastating of all the plagues—the slaying of Egypt's firstborn—each Israelite family was commanded by God to offer up a lamb. The blood of this animal was sprinkled on the doorpost of each Israelite home so that the Angel of Death would "pass over" the dwellings of the Children of Israel as he stalked the land. Hence the name Pesah which, quite literally, means "Passover."

Aside from the special prayers recited at services in the synagogue, Passover is primarily a home festival. The first two nights of Passover (in Israel and among Reform Jews, the first night only) are marked by a home ceremony known by its Hebrew designation, *seder*, meaning "order" (of rituals).

The exact "order" of the home celebration of Passover is set down in detail in the *Haggadah* which, as the Hebrew term implies, is literally a "recital" of the miracle of the Exodus. It contains readings, prayers and hymns compiled over a period of centuries, which are read and chanted by the entire family seated around the festive board.

Covered with a shining white cloth and set with the family's best silver, crystal and Passover china, the *seder* table has as its "centerpiece" the *seder* plate which bears the visual symbols of the festival. Most important, there are the three things without which the celebration is considered incomplete—the *matzot* or unleavened bread recalling the thin unleavened cakes the Children of Israel baked in the sun when they went forth from Egypt in too great a haste to permit the dough to rise; *maror*, "bitter herbs," usually horseradish, to denote the bitterness of slavery; and *z'roa*, the roasted shankbone which recalls the Paschal lamb. In addition, the *seder* plate holds a dish of *haroset*, a mixture of chopped or ground nuts and apples, cinnamon and

156

Passover Haggada. Title page, Amsterdam, 1695. Copper engraving shows Aaron (in priestly vestments) and Moses (bearing Ten Commandments). Medallions above show scenes from the Bible: Adam and Eve driven from Paradise (top); the Flood (upper left); Jacob's dream (center); the Tower of Babel (upper right); Sodom (lower left) and Abraham and Melchizedek (lower right).

Page from Passover Haggada. This richly illuminated medieval Haggada is part of the Rothschild Manuscript Collection now in The Israel Museum in Jerusalem. Picture on top, right, shows the head of the household with candle and feather sweeping away remnants of leaven; picture at right, center, shows the kashering of kitchen utensils for Passover. Picture at bottom shows the preparation of matzot for the festival.

wine, meant to commemorate the mortar from which the Israelite slaves made their bricks for construction work; and a green vegetable, usually parsley, which is dipped into salt water and eaten to symbolize the coming of springtime. The salt water has been variously interpreted as recalling the tears of servitude, or signifying the salty water of the Red Sea which the Israelites crossed when they went forth from Egypt.

Another prominent object on the *seder* table is the special cup of wine—usually of silver—reserved for the Prophet Elijah, who is invited to enter every Jewish home on this night. At one point in the *seder* the main entrance of the home is opened wide to usher in this guest who is considered the herald of freedom and deliverance.

The *Haggadah* opens with an invitation to all those who are hungry—no matter what their race or creed—to "come and eat" and celebrate the Passover festival with the family. It has been a time-honored custom to invite not only relatives and friends but also strangers who might lack the means to have their own Passover celebration.

The youngest child recites the Four Questions—known as the *Ma Nishtana* after the opening words "Why Is This Night Different . . ."—inquiring into the reasons for specific *seder* observances. In reply, the rest of the family joins in reading from the *Haggadah* the account of the triumph of freedom over slavery. "In each generation," we read, "every person must regard himself as if he personally had gone forth from Egypt." Every person has before him a goblet of wine from which he sips on four different occasions during the *seder*, to recall the four Biblical expressions of God's promise to free the Children

Passover Haggada. Prague, 1849. This picture shows the Children of Israel doing slave labor in Egypt. Israelite in foreground is being beaten by an Egyptian taskmaster.

Seder Plate. Glass and silver, contemporary design. Hebrew lettering: "Pessach, Matzot and bitter herbs," by Moshe Zabari. (Gift of Mr. and Mrs. A. Kanof to The Jewish Museum, New York City).

of Israel from slavery. At various intervals, all join in singing joyous hymns—some dating back hundreds of years—to time-hallowed melodies.

The story of the Exodus, which Passover celebrates, has taken an honored place in world history as the first recorded instance of rebellion against tyranny. The leaders of the American Revolution made frequent references to it. In fact, the original design for the Seal of the United States submitted by a committee of the Continental Congress—John Adams, Benjamin Franklin and Thomas Jefferson—depicted the Children of Israel crossing the Red Sea.

160

Seder plate for matzot and ceremonial symbols, silver, Austria, 1815. (Hebrew Union College Museum, Cincinnati, Ohio).

THE HOLIDAY OF FREEDOM

UNTIL THEIR ENCOUNTER with Egypt, the Children of Israel had dwelt among tribes to whom they were related ethnically and culturally, and whose way of life bore some semblance to their own, though, of course, they had always been set apart from their pagan kinsmen by their belief in One God. With their arrival in Egypt, however, the Israelites met, for the first time, a people with a culture, form of government and social structure in direct conflict with the outlook, the beliefs and the customs of the peaceful Hebrew shepherd tribes. Consequently, as soon as they arrived in Egypt, the Israelites declined the generous offer Pharaoh had made to Joseph: "The Land of Egypt is before you; in the best part of the land make your father and brothers to dwell" (Genesis 46:6).

Instead, they elected to live in their own compound in Goshen, the first ghetto in history, a ghetto they chose of their own free will. This was one of the first of many times that Jews were to take up residence in self-imposed ghettos, fortresses built to keep out alien influences, not prisons imposed by an unfriendly world from without.

After the failure of the Goshen experiment, which ended in their enslavement, the Israelites, as at many subsequent junctions in their history, had the choice between two alternatives—either to give up their newly-emerged individuality or to assert their identity and consolidate their spiritual forces for meaningful survival. They chose the latter.

For the first time in history, the Children of Israel linked the belief in God with opposition to bondage and the pursuit of liberty—a revolutionary idea which inspired them to rebel against every form of tyranny.

But the enslaved Hebrew masses did not grasp the full significance of this revolutionary concept all at once. They hesitated before submitting to the daring, dedicated leadership of Moses. Out of the dark depths of bondage, the Children of Israel were elevated to the heights of freedom *of* faith and *in* faith.

Matza cover. Gold and silver silk embroidery on velvet, Germany, 19th century. Hebrew legend reads: "And thou shalt keep the Feast of Unleavened Bread." (The Israel Museum, Jerusalem).

Seder Plate. Modern, glass and silver, by Ludwig Y. Wolpert. Plate holds matzot; cups on edge of plate hold Passover symbols. Silver lettering on plate reads: "This is the bread of affliction."

An unbridgeable chasm opened between the people of might and the people of the spirit, between a system based on slavery and a society founded on human freedom.

Out of trials and tribulations, struggles and sufferings, there emerged a distinctive Jewish national identity which has remained alive and strong to this very day. What Genesis was to the creation of the universe, Exodus became to the birth of the Jewish people. Each time the clash between the two opposing philosophies—slavery against the dignity of man—which first occurred in Egypt, recurred elsewhere in later epochs of Jewish history, the statement of the Haggadah that "every man should regard himself as if he personally had gone out of Egypt" assumed added significance and reflected the permanent actuality of the redemption from Egyptian bondage.

Therefore, changing times and conditions left the significance of Passover unaltered. Indeed, Passover frequently became a shining symbol of fearless contemporary struggle for freedom. Today, for instance, it is on Passover that we remember and most vividly experience the plight of our brethren in Soviet Russia. The eloquent plea "Let my people go" is as timely, as urgent and as compelling in our day as it was in the days of Pharaoh four thousand years ago.

Passover Cup. Silver repoussé, Germany, 17th century. Figures are those of t[he] Four Sons mentioned in the Passover Haggada; the Wise Son (top, left), t[he] Wicked Son (top, right), the Simple Son (bottom, left) and the Son Who Does N[ot] Know Enough to Ask (bottom, right). (The Israel Museum, Jerusalem).

THE HAGGADAH

THE *Haggadah* (literally "narrative," "recital") is intended not only as a prayer book in the conventional sense of the word but also as a guidebook for the observance of the Passover ritual.

Mindful of the fact that the Passover *seder* is essentially a cheerful home celebration with special appeal for children, and of the rabbinic adage that "the more one tells of the Exodus from Egypt, the more praiseworthy he is," our sages have left ample room for informality and flexibility in the Haggadah text. Throughout the ages, the Haggadah has been open to additions of legends, homilies, parables, hymns, learned commentaries and jolly songs in which the entire family can join.

Innumerable artists of every generation have created illustrations—some impressive, some humorous—to embellish the Haggadah, and composers in every land have written musical scores to beautify the recitation of the seder service.

Among the most notable recent additions to the Haggadah are the Ritual of Remembrance for the six million Jews who perished in the Nazi holocaust, the Prayer for the State of Israel and expressions of solidarity with the Jews of Soviet Russia who have been denied religious freedom. In Israel a number of non-Orthodox kibbutzim have composed Haggadot of their own, containing traditional elements and items of timely interest in proportions depending on the philosophy by which the kibbutz is guided.

No book of Jewish liturgy has been published in so many editions, and in such an endless variety of formats, styles and pictorial decorations as the Haggadah. Before the invention of the printing press, wealthy patrons had private copies laboriously written out by hand and illuminated by gifted artists, often at considerable cost. Since the advent of modern printing,

164

the output of Haggadot has increased to incredible proportions. Abraham Yaari, in his monumental *Bibliography of the Passover Haggadah**, enumerating the editions of the Haggadah from the earliest printed text (ca. 1475) to 1960, lists as many as 2,713 different editions.

Each Haggadah represents a faithful reflection of Jewish history through the past five centuries, a chronicle of the sufferings, the faith and the courage of our people over ages of exile and dispersion.

The Haggadah opens on a note of hospitality. "Let him who is hungry come and eat. Let him who is needy come and celebrate the Passover." In fact, it is a time-honored tradition to invite needy strangers to the family *seder*. For what Jew could truly celebrate the Festival of Freedom if he remains indifferent to those of his brethren who are enslaved by poverty and privation?

But the central theme of the Haggadah is redemption. The *seder* service is replete with specific references to deliverance—from the past and of the hoped-for future. The faith in the ultimate coming of redemption gave comfort and spiritual sustenance to generations of Jews crowded into ghettoes and beset with enemies on every side. Generations of artists have captured Israel's longing for the Messiah in naively conceived pictures of the coming of the Redeemer from the House of David, accompanied by the Prophet Elijah, and of Jerusalem restored, with the Third Temple resplendent in the center ** captioned *LeShana HaBa'a BiY'rushalayim - Next Year in Jerusalem.*

* Jerusalem, 1960, Bamberger & Wohrman

** *Studies in Bibliography and Booklore, Vol. VII*, pp. 52-55. Library of the Hebrew Union College—Jewish Institute of Religion, Cincinnati, Ohio

The parting of the Red Sea. Moses (staff in hand) and Aaron (wearing priestly mitre) watch as Pharaoh (wearing crown) and his hosts, drown in the Red Sea. (Illustration from Haggada, 1849).

אִלּוּ נָתַן לָנוּ אֶת הַתּוֹרָה
וְלֹא קֵרְבָנוּ לִפְנֵי הַר סִינַי
אִלּוּ קֵרְבָנוּ לִפְנֵי הַר סִינַי
וְלֹא נָתַן לָנוּ אֶת הַתּוֹרָה דַּיֵּנוּ
אִלּוּ נָתַן לָנוּ אֶת הַתּוֹרָה
וְלֹא הִכְנִיסָנוּ לְאֶרֶץ יִשְׂרָאֵל דַּיֵּנוּ
אִלּוּ הִכְנִיסָנוּ לְאֶרֶץ יִשְׂרָאֵל
וְלֹא בָנָה לָנוּ בֵּית הַמִּקְדָּשׁ דַּיֵּנוּ
עַל אַחַת כַּמָּה וְכַמָּה טוֹבָה כְפוּלָה
וּמְכֻפֶּלֶת לַמָּקוֹם עָלֵינוּ הוֹצִיאָנוּ

Woodcut from old Haggada. Picture shows the Egyptians afflicted with lice —the third of the Ten Plagues.

THE FAMILY FESTIVAL

THE MIGRATION OF THE Children of Israel from Canaan to Egypt was essentially a family event. So, too, the celebration of their deliverance from Egyptian bondage was ordained and observed as a *family feast*. We read in the Torah that the Children of Israel first came to Egypt "each *with his household*" (Exodus 1:1), and that, as part of their observance of the first Passover, the Israelites were commanded to "provide for themselves one lamb *for each of their families*, a lamb *for every household*" (Exodus 12:3). In Judaism, the individual was always considered within the framework of his family.

But one might expect that the redemption of the entire people and its collective triumph over its enemies would be celebrated by some sort of mass observance—a "community *seder*" in present-day parlance. But this was not the case: we were commanded to observe the Passover holiday primarily within each family circle. This mode of observance best served to strengthen and help stabilize the family unit as the basis of our national existence.

This singular approach brings into sharper focus the *educational* purpose of Passover. The responsibility for its proper and effective celebration falls not upon the leader or the teacher of the community but upon the father, the head of the household. It is he that is entrusted with the conduct of the *seder* ceremony. He must therefore be conversant with its laws and customs—he must *study* in order to *teach*.

This obligation which the father must fulfill in order to teach his children is implicit in numerous precepts ("and thou shalt tell thy son" [Exodus 13:8], "and ye shall teach them unto your children" [Deut. 11:19], et al). The Talmud, too, stresses this paternal duty: "His father must instruct him in the Torah."

Owing to various social and economic circumstances, this responsibility was later relegated to the professional schoolteacher. But this does not mean that the father is exempt from the obligation of working at the informal education of his children through the medium of home observances.

The Passover *seder* affords a splendid opportunity for the child's informal training in Judaism. On the *seder* night the family, which is usually dispersed during the remainder of the year, reunites under one roof to join in the commemoration of a decisive event in the history of the Jewish people.

Several factors combine to enhance the educational importance and effectiveness of the *seder*.

First, although *seder* literally means "order" and thus implies a fixed procedure, there is nothing rigid about it. On the contrary, its most endearing qualities are informality, warmth and intimacy—an atmosphere of family togetherness.

Second, the *seder* is not an abstract lesson in history. Replete with concrete, meaningful symbols, it becomes a valuable educational experience, impressing the story of the Exodus from Egypt upon the minds and hearts of the children. The *Haggadah* itself points up the importance of the visual aids provided for the festive *seder* table by stating that one may retell the Passover epic only "when *matzot* (unleavened bread) and *maror* (bitter herbs) are placed before thee."

Third, the *seder* utilizes the cardinal pedagogic principle of *learning by doing,* of the child's active participation in the perpetuation of Jewish tradition. As a result, the child becomes deeply imbued with the sense of continuity of his people's history and with the obligation of personal commitment to living Judaism. No amount of abstract learning can achieve this aim.

Hence, the *seder* is primarily an *educational* process in which the father assumes the role of *teacher.* Like any good teacher, he is aware that he would miss his mark if he were to deliver a mere lecture, a lengthy monologue before a bored audience. The *Haggadah* prescribes the format of the *seder;* it is to be a dialogue between father and child.

The most effective method of initiating such a dialogue is to arouse curiosity, to stimulate an urge for knowledge, to generate questions. Accordingly, the *Haggadah* begins with a key question to be asked by the youngest child in the family: *Mah nishtanah halailah hazeh?* "Why is this night different from all

Page from Haggada, 1629.

The coming of the Messiah. Page from Haggada printed in 1561. "Pour out Thy wrath upon the nations that do not know Thee and upon the kingdoms that do not call upon Thy name . . ." Picture shows the entry of the Messiah into Jerusalem as tradition describes it—on a white donkey followed by attendant sounding the ram's horn.

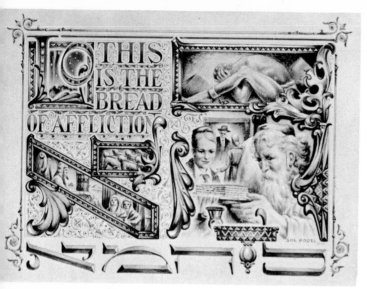

other nights of the year?"

Once the dialogue has been opened, and the father has answered the first basic question, it is the child's turn to ask the next question. Here the anonymous author of the *Haggadah* gives us the parable of the Four Sons, representing four categories of children, classed by attitude and intellectual capacity and disposition. The Wise Son asks a provocative question; the Wicked Son acts the cynic; the Simple Son wants to know "what this is all about"; and the son whose intellectual capacity is so limited that he "does not even know how to ask" is passive and must be instructed although he lacks the initiative to pose questions of his own.

The wise teacher treats each of his students as an individual, according to his personal abilities, temperament and inclinations. Similarly, the father at the *seder* table and in other "educational" situations, too, must find the right answer for every type of child. It is his duty to clarify uncertainties, to dispel doubts and to reconcile conflicts. Thus, even the "Wicked Son" must not be rejected. Through patience and understanding, even the antagonism of the cynic can be overcome. By proper education, he can be won over and transformed into a useful, constructive member of his group and of society in general.

But what about the son "who does not know how to ask?" This poses a real problem, particularly in view of the fact that a good part of our youth today belongs to that category. The *Haggadah* imposes upon the father, in his role as teacher at the *seder*, the task of prompting the non-questioning son to ask, to inquire, to be curious about his Judaism: "It is up to you to begin for him, as it is written: 'And thou shalt tell thy son: This is because of what the Lord did for me when I came out of Egypt'" (Exodus 13:8).

In like manner, one of the main objectives of Jewish education, *as a lifelong process*, is to open the minds of those of our young generation who were estranged from our people and from its faith.

Seen in this light, the festival of deliverance from physical slavery also becomes the symbol of liberation from the spiritual bondage of ignorance that gradually leads to the abandonment of Judaism.

A fascinating aspect of the *seder* service is the symbolic appearance of the Prophet Elijah for whom the door is opened at the climax of the celebration. Why Elijah of all our prophets?

The *seder* dialogue is no mere intellectual interplay of intellects. It is a renewal of the mutual trust between successive generations, a reaffirmation of the harmonious relationship between parents and children and of the respect and reverence due the head of the household as manifested in his title in Jewish tradition: "My father and teacher."

And it is none other than the Prophet Elijah who, according to popular belief, will come to herald the advent of the era of Messianic redemption and of *perfect* understanding between parents and children, as is foretold in the last verse of the Book of Malachi: "Behold, I will send you Elijah the Prophet before the coming of the great and awesome day of the Lord; and he shall turn the hearts of the fathers toward their sons, and the hearts of the sons toward their fathers " (Malachi 3:24).

Pilgrimage to Mount Zion. To the sound of massed ram's horns (foreground) pilgrims from all over Israel make the journey to Mount Zion during Passover week.

The first five plagues (top to bottom): transformation of water into blood, frogs, lice, wild beasts, cattle plague.

PASSOVER NIGHT
By Isaac Breuer

EVERY YEAR there recurs in the life of the Jews a night which is set aside for Jewish fathers to explain to their children what it means to be a Jew. This night is pervaded by the spirit of a nation of indestructible vitality; it echoes the mournful lament of a nation tried by sorrows and surrounded by enemies at every turn; through it, too, resounds the proud triumphal anthem of an unconquered nation which has outlasted mighty empires, the hymn of thanksgiving arising from a nation that is close to its God, serene even in misfortune and certain of its eventual deliverance. He who has grasped the meaning of this night has come to understand the essence of Judaism.

On this night the father gathers his children around the seder table. On this table there is the unleavened bread which our forefathers ate when they went forth from Egypt because the Egyptians had not given them time to let their dough rise in the ovens. There are also the bitter herbs, as bitter as the servitude in which Pharaoh held our ancestors. And there, too, is all the family silver, which the Children of Israel have never been entirely without since the day when they took the silver of the Egyptians with them into the wilderness. The questioning eye of the children travels over the candle-lit board and comes to rest upon the father's face. "What does all this mean?"

And then the father begins to tell the story as it is set down in the Haggadah, the ancient document of the freedom of the Jewish nation:

"Slaves we were unto Pharaoh in Egypt, and the Lord, our God, took us out from there with a strong hand and an outstretched arm. Now if the Holy One, blessed be He, had not taken our fathers out from there, then we, and our children, and our children's children, would still be enslaved to Pharaoh in Egypt. Therefore it is incumbent not only on our fathers but also on ourselves, no matter how wise, understanding, mature and knowing we may be, to tell the story of the Exodus from Egypt, and whoever enlarges on the story is worthy of praise . . ."

To the Jewish nation, the miraculous exodus from Egypt is not some fairy tale out of a long-dead past, but a historic fact which it has personally experienced. It is as a witness to this truth that the father stands before his children on this night. He himself heard the story from the mouth of his own father, and he constitutes but another link in the long chain which, spanning the millennia, joins the slaves of the ancient Egyptians with their youngest descendants of our own day.

"In every generation the Jew is duty-bound to regard himself as though he had personally come out of Egypt, for it is said: 'And thou shalt tell it to thy son in times to come that it was on this account that the Lord did for me when I went forth from Egypt.' For not only our forefathers did the Holy One, blessed be He, redeem, but also ourselves did He redeem with them, for it is said: 'And us did He take out from there, to lead us home to the land which He had sworn unto our fathers ' . . ."

What the father then proceeds to tell his children stems from his own personal experience. He does not speak to them now as an individual, weak and mortal, confined to one narrow segment of time, but as the spokesman for the nation, as the bearer of the nation's history, and as he does so, he demands of his children that loyalty which not he but the nation has a right to expect of all its members. Woe to the child who, on that night, when his nation addresses itself to him, turns away with a shrug of the shoulders and dismisses the unleavened bread and the bitter herbs with a superior air, saying: "I admit that this service may have had some meaning for your ancestors, but what good it is to you? "To you," he says, and not to himself. By thus excluding himself from the nation he has denied the essence of Judaism. Exclude thou him then also, for it is written: 'It is because of (my) faithfulness that the Lord did it for me when I went forth from Egypt!' *For me and not for him.* For had he, faithless as he is, been in Egypt, he would not have been redeemed."

You must remember that we are not a nation like the other nations. Who knows how those other nations arise? They are rooted in the natural prerequisites for their survival. They worship the soil which nourishes them, the sun which shines on them and the physical strength that protects them. But what of us? Behold Terah, the father of Abraham and Nahor. He dwelt on the other side of the river, remaining with Nahor and sharing the fate of the other nations. Not so Abraham, your father. The Lord took him away from the other side of the river, and led him through the whole land of Canaan. Then, from the multitude of Abraham's progeny, the Lord chose Isaac, to whom in turn He gave Jacob and Esau, giving to Esau the land of Seir while He brought Jacob and his sons down to Egypt. There hatred and envy caused us to be enslaved, and while the descendants of Esau were already enthroned as kings in Seir, we, in Egypt, were nothing but a horde of slaves, bereft of all human rights. "And the Egyptians did evil to us, and tormented us, and laid hard labor upon us." But we were helpless, for theirs was all the power and strength. According to the laws of history, we were lost. We had nothing left but the God of our fathers. "And we cried out unto the Lord, the God of our fathers, and the Lord heard our voice, and He saw our distress, and our travail, and our oppression, and He took us out of Egypt with a strong hand, and with an outstretched arm, with great terror, and with signs and with wonders . . ."

Hallelujah! Join in the Jewish anthem which was first sung by David, King of Israel. Join in the hymn which proclaims the providence of God in history. Ours is history and ours, too, is the future! In Egypt we have vanquished the death that comes to nations. From Mount Sinai we brought down that light which, wherever we may be, turns our slavery into freedom, our sorrow into joy, our mourning into festivity, our subjection into redemption, and our darkness into great light. Hallelujah!

The last five plagues (top to bottom): boils, hail, locusts, darkness, death of the first born.

Anyone who has ever lived through this night which has been sacred to Israel from the very beginning will be permanently disabused of any doubt as to whether or not the Jews are indeed a nation. Let him who does not know this night refrain from passing judgment here. It is dedicated to the children so that wherever they may have been born physically—they may complete their spiritual birth on the sacred soil of Israel. On that night when, year after year, the national unity of Judaism is built up anew from rock bottom for each succeeding generation, there is no mention of dogmas or of a mysterious personality who founded a religion and rose to the level of ideal communion with God. This night is all history, the history of a nation. Abraham, Isaac and Jacob, whom an arid theology would turn into mythological figures, this night presents them, supported by the testimony of his own father, to the Jewish child so clearly and vividly as if it had been only yesterday that they had blessed their sons in farewell and lain down to rest in the Cave of Mahpelah. While scholars are deep in debate as to whether the Jews were ever really enslaved by Pharaoh, the Jewish child shares with his ancestors the bread of Egyptian servitude, tastes the bitterness of slavery, and, thus inspired, joins in the song of thanksgiving which Moses sang long ago on the banks of the Red Sea. And finally, what is the meaning of that line of distinction which scholarship has so painstakingly drawn between the ancient people of Israel and the Jews of today? It is meaningless in the face of that unity of national consciousness which on this night links the very youngest Jew of our own day with Moses and the Prophets, with David and with the Temple of Solomon. The Jewish religion is only a history of the Jewish people. And to be a Jew conscious of his heritage means to have experienced the history of the Jewish nation and to devote one's self to the task of being its bearer and of taking part in the shaping of its future.

Seder plate. Pewter, Germany, early 19th century. Objects on table are the symbols placed on the Seder dish. (The Israel Museum, Jerusalem).

LAG B'OMER

THE ORIGINS OF THE celebration of Lag B'Omer are shrouded in mystery—political and spiritual. The political aspect is linked to Bar Kokhba, who led Israel's first revolt against Rome; the spiritual aspect is bound up with the person of Rabbi Simeon Bar Yohai, to whom the authorship of the Zohar, the classic work of Jewish mysticism, has been attributed.

The political origin of the holiday, which apparently should have been obvious to all, was destined to remain a secret, for the Bar Kokhba rebellion began as an underground movement and emerged as as open insurrection only toward the end. This rebellion was not crowned with victory, and the Roman conqueror extended his dominion over the entire country. On the other hand, the very fact that the rebellion took place at all certainly justified a celebration, but that celebration of necessity had to be clandestine. It was, in essence, a continuation of the underground revolt, expressing, as it did, the determination of the freedom fighters not to yield to Roman domination. In the course of time, the memory of the leaders of the revolt grew dim, and only feeble

Tomb of Rabbi Simeon ben Yohai, Meron, near Safed.

echoes of these erstwhile heroes remained alive in the Talmud. Also, the fact that there was a difference of opinion between the sages of the Talmud concerning the positive aspects of the personality of Bar Kokhba and of the rebellion he had led contributed to the paucity of specific documentary material pertaining to the event.

As a result, the rabbis recorded only the one quasi-legendary detail that "Rabbi Akiba had twelve thousand pairs of disciples from Gevet to Antipatrus, and all of them died during one period of time, namely between Passover and the Day of Convocation"* (*Yevamot* 62:67). Other early post-Talmudic sources indicated that "the calamity" (of these deaths)—which they attributed to the war against the Romans—had occurred sometime between Passover and Lag B'Omer. On the basis of this latter calculation, Lag B'Omer was instituted as a minor festival.

The anniversary of the second event associated with Lag B'Omer, the death of Rabbi Simeon Bar Yohai, the late illustrious disciple of the martyred Rabbi Akiba, was also traditionally fixed for that day, the eighteenth of Iyar, and commemorative observances take place at the tomb of Rabbi Simeon in Meron, near Safed. We may assume that these observances at Meron had originated not too long after Rabbi Simeon's demise but later fell into desuetude until the saintly Ari (Rabbi Yitzhak Luria) came to Safed in the sixteenth century and revived the ancient tradition, infusing Lag B'Omer with new content and spirit. As a result, its observance was embellished by new rituals; it came to attract masses of celebrants who soared to high peaks of enthusiasm and ecstasy as they took part in the celebrations. From Safed these observances spread to Jewish communities throughout the world. In time, they assumed overtones of mysticism; thus, the custom of lighting candles in synagogues on the occasion of the *Hillula* (celebration in memory of Rabbi Simeon Bar Yohai) arose in many congregations.

Another Lag B'Omer custom—to have children armed with bows and arrows, march like so many soldiers into field and forest—is obviously associated with the Bar Kokhba rebellion.

This uprising was the last revolt by the Jews against a foreign enemy until the rebellions of *Haganah, Irgun Tzvai Leumi* ("Etzel") and *Lohamei Herut Yisrael* ("Lehi") against the British mandatory power in Palestine in our own day.

As mentioned above, the Rabbis were divided in their views regarding the significance of the Bar Kokhba rebellion, the personality of its leader and his strategy. Both the protagonists and the antagonists were extreme in their opinions. Bar Kokhba's supporters saw in him a re-

* Shavuot—The Festival of Weeks.

deemer and a liberator, while his opponents denounced him as a daredevil, who had brought misfortune upon his people.

One of the staunchest supporters of Bar Kokhba was the eminent Talmudic sage, Rabbi Akiba who, in describing the rise of the revolutionary leader, quoted the scriptural verse: "A star has come forth from Jacob" (Num. 24:17). Rabbi Akiba was not only a giant of the spirit but also a zealous patriot and champion of freedom for his land and people. He hated the Roman aggressor and prayed for the coming of the day of retribution when the conquerors would be routed, and the people of Israel would regain their freedom and rebuild the Holy Temple.

The advent of Bar Kokhba inspired Rabbi Akiba with new hope. He immediately pledged his moral support and lent his enormous per-

Lag B'Omer in Meron. Pious pilgrims celebrating Lag B'Omer at Meron, near the tomb of Rabbi Simeon ben Yohai, a disciple of the martyred Rabbi Akiba. It was on Lag B'Omer that the plague which had killed thousands of Rabbi Akiba's students suddenly ceased. The hasidim in this picture observe the custom of giving a three-year-old boy his first haircut at Rabbi Simeon's tomb on Lag B'Omer.

sonal prestige to the cause of the rebellion. Thousands of his disciples joined the ranks of the fighters, and their great teacher imbued them with courage, lifting their morale to new heights of self-confidence and self-sacrifice.

But when the revolt failed, and the heroic freedom fighters fell in battle, the conquering despot Hadrian, enraged and bitterly revengeful, was determined to crush the very spirit of the vanquished. He outlawed the study of the Torah, the chief source of our people's inner strength, throughout Judea, on pain of death. Rabbi Akiba, who openly defied this cruel edict even as he had earlier resisted the Roman rule of force, paid with his life for his disobedience. He was one of the hallowed "Ten Martyrs" who were tortured to death for their refusal to give up their God.

For fear of Roman reprisals, the story of the Bar Kokhba rebellion and the account of Rabbi Akiba's anti-Roman activities were toned down, so that students of traditional sources today have little more than vague, fragmentary Talmudic references to go by.

The Bar Kokhba revolt was not a conventional war in the open field of battle. It was a desperate fight of dauntless partisans against the formidable might of the Roman legions. Hadrian's commander-in-chief, Julius Severus, sought to conquer the rebels by starvation. The Judean partisan fighters, who had been plagued by privation, lack of supplies and inadequate communications even before, were further weakened by this strategy, but they were not subdued.

The bloody, decisive battle of Betar marked the tragic end of a revolt that lasted three and a half years (132-135 C.E.). Half a million Jews were slain. Many more were led into captivity.

But like a flickering candle that flares up briefly before it finally goes out, so, too, this historic rebellion, in its last flash of heroism at Betar, lit up the darkness of exile and oppression with a hope and faith that blazed forth in the years between 1940 and 1948 into a revolt against another oppressor and culminated in the glorious rebirth of the State of Israel.

THE FESTIVAL OF RABBI SIMEON BEN YOHAI

AS MYSTICISM AND THE *Zohar* grew in popularity, so did the meaning of its reputed author, the Talmudic sage Rabbi Simeon ben Yohai. Study and faith in *kabbalah* (mysticism) led men of piety to return to the Land of Israel, and from the 15th century on, they made it a custom to stream to Rabbi Simeon's tomb in Meron, to recite fervent prayers on certain occasions such as the beginning of a Jewish month and the three Pilgrim Festivals (Passover, Shavuot, Sukkot). Rabbi Isaac Luria (the *Ari*), one of the great masters of mysticism, would go there regularly with his disciples.

Lag b'Omer became the most popular day for visiting the tomb of Rabbi Simeon ben Yohai. This day was especially consecrated to his memory for tradition had it that three important events in his life had all taken place on Lag b'Omer—his rabbinic ordination, his marriage and his death. (It is related in the Midrash that in the days of Rabbi Simeon the Romans sought to ban the study of Torah in Israel. The authorities decreed that whoever gave or received rabbinic ordination would be slain, and that any town harboring such people would be wiped out. Many defied the edict, particularly Rabbi Judah ben Bava. Somewhere between two towns—so that neither town should be destroyed if he were to be found out—Judah conferred ordination on five disciples of Rabbi Akiba, among them Rabbi Simeon ben Yohai. The Romans discovered them. The five newly-ordained rabbis escaped but Rabbi Judah ben Bava was too old to flee, and he died, his body riddled by 300 enemy spears. According to an old manuscript in Spain, his martyrdom took place on Lag b'Omer.)

In the olden days the devout mystics would go to Meron several days before, visit all the holy graves there, and then spend Lag b'Omer at the tombs of Rabbi Simeon and his son. Such a pilgrimage was described by a visitor from Candia (Crete) in 1473. In 1522 another traveler found over a thousand people making the trip together, remaining in Meron for two days and two nights.

In time only the Lag b'Omer celebration at the tomb of Rabbi Simeon remained as an annual event. The yearly pilgrimage to Meron obscured former observances connected with this holiday which had been sanctioned for generations by the scholars of Spain and of the Provence.

It had always been customary to hold a happy feast at the tomb this day. In the course of time Lag b'Omer became known as the day of the *hillula*, the festival honoring Rabbi Simeon ben Yohai. In the Talmud, *hillula* denotes a wedding celebration. In the case of Lag b'Omer the word came to signify "rejoicing" not only in honor of the anniversary of Rabbi Simeon's wedding, but also in honor of his ordination, when profound mysteries of the Torah were revealed to him; and in honor of the anniversary of his passage from earth into the world of eternal life.

Omer calendar, Mediterranean, 19th century. Gilded metal brass, set with colored stones. On both sides of the case is the Star of David. Photo: Frank J. Darmstaedter. (From the collection of Mr. and Mrs. Max Stern, New York).

Before he departed this world, the *Zohar* (*Book of Splendor*) relates, Rabbi Simeon disclosed profound and sacred mysteries to his friends and colleagues. As he spoke, he was surrounded by a ring of fire, whose brilliant light never left the chamber. As his spirit departed, the *Zohar* further states, his disciples saw a huge fire burning in heaven in his honor.

To recall this legend, the thousands who revered Rabbi Simeon ben Yohai and the mystic teachings handed down in his name, light a huge bonfire at his tomb every Lag b'Omer, until this very day, to commemorate the great blaze that was seen on the Lag b'Omer when Rabbi Simeon departed from this world. In time, the annual bonfire became an accepted, honored custom for all who streamed to Meron to celebrate this anniversary.

It is interesting to read early accounts of these annual pilgrimages. Hayim Vital, a disciple of Rabbi Isaac Luria (the *Ari*, 16th century), writes, "It is an accepted practice in Israel on Lag b'Omer to go to the tombs of Rabbi Simeon ben Yohai and his son Rabbi Elazar, who lie buried in Meron . . . and they would eat and drink happily there . . . I have seen my own master (the *Ari*, Rabbi Isaac Luria) going there for the past eight years with his wife and family . . ." Apparently the great teacher of mysticism thought the custom important and lent it new prestige by his personal adherence to it.

A traveler of a later period recorded in 1762: "About two hours' journey from Safed there is a place called Meron. It has a cave where Rabbi Simeon ben Yohai and his son Rabbi Elazar lie buried . . . three times a year people come there from every part of the Land of Israel: once in the month of Elul, once in the month of Nissan, and once on Lag b'Omer, the day which they call the festival of Rabbi Simeon ben Yohai. They have an old tradition from long ago that on this day one must be happy and arrange large feasts, with music and ceremonial dancing, to rejoice as much as possible."

In 1774 another traveler wrote, "Near Rabbi Simeon's tomb stands a column of a wall, with a large bowl upon it. Into this vessel they pour oil into which they put a wick. They then light the wick and the great flame casts its light over a considerable distance . . . This is done on Lag b'Omer, the anniversary of Rabbi Simeon's passing, which is called his festival day."

LAG B'OMER IN OTHER LANDS

ADEN

ON THE EVE OF Lag b'Omer it was our custom to kindle lights in the synagogue as on a full festival, and all would gather there to study the entire *Book of Proverbs.* Then we would chant the hymn of *Bar Yohai*, after which we studied portions of the *Zohar* (*Book of Splendor*). The next day, after Morning Services, we would read excerpts of the *Zohar* that extolled Rabbi Simeon ben Yohai.

HADRAMAUT

LAG B'OMER as a holiday is unknown to the Jews of Haban, Hadramaut (between Yemen and Aden). They celebrate the following day, the 34th day of the *Omer*, with song and feasting and the reading of the *Zohar*. On that day, too, the men cut their hair since they do not do so during the rest of the *Omer* period.

YEMEN

THE GROUP OR sect which reveres the *Zohar* rises early on Lag b'Omer. All have their hair cut and then proceed to the synagogue to study the *Zohar*. A great many candles are lit in honor of Rabbi Simeon ben Yohai and other holy, pious men of the past. The day is marked by celebrations with ample food and drink, during which weddings and family gatherings take place.

Those who reject the *Zohar*, on the other hand, hold no celebration at all on Lag b'Omer. The men go to work as usual, the children study at the religious school all day and there are neither banquets nor weddings.

RHODES

ON LAG B'OMER it was customary for the Jews in Rhodes to bury their *genizah*, fragments of sacred books and scrolls that could no longer be used but were too holy to destroy or discard. They would gather from their homes all their old, tattered volumes, torn leaves of religious works and prayer-books, and bring them to the *genizah*, the official "hiding place" for such things in the synagogue. The entire collection would then be given a "burial" in the ground during which the congregation sang mournful hymns and Psalms and recited a special prayer. Together with the old sacred volumes, old record books and ledgers of the congregation, and outdated resolutions and by-laws would be buried. Due to this practice, much important documentary material pertinent to the early history of the Jewish community of Rhodes has been lost to us.

TUNISIA

FROM ALL PARTS of this country, Jews travel for Lag b'Omer to the old synagogue on the island of Jerba, near Tunis. There they spend the entire day in prayer. Toward evening they give a large repast for the poor.

Those who cannot travel to Jerba gather in the synagogues in their own localities. Each person prepares a little nook or corner in his House of Prayer for himself and his family. In this corner, which is called "the corner of Rabbi Simeon ben Yohai," each person lights a special lamp, called "the *menorah* of Rabbi Simeon ben Yohai," so that the merits of the pious sage might protect the family the entire year. Similarly, a huge candelabrum holding dozens of candles or oil lamps, and decorated with tulips, is lit in the home. In the afternoon each person takes his candelabrum from his home to the synagogue, to study by its light in honor of the great sage. After the study period, a feast is held, mainly for the youngsters.

MOROCCO

IN MOROCCO Lag b'Omer is considered a holiday. The evening before, the people gather in groups to study Torah all through the night, and they eat, drink, and make merry.
IN TETUAN, a walled seaport in northeast Morocco, Lag b'Omer eve is known as "the night of the Festival." Until midnight the people read the *Zohar* and other sacred books. Thereafter they go to the home of their chief rabbi for a festival meal, at which the rabbi recites a memorial prayer for all members of the community who died during the past year.

IZMIR (SMYRNA)

HERE IT WAS the custom for Jewish communal officials to make the rounds of the city after Lag b'Omer to prevent people from continuing the dancing and singing of the day before.

LAG B'OMER WITH THE MARRANOS IN SPAIN

THE CONVERTS AND descendants of converts whom the Spanish Inquisition had forced to abandon their Jewish faith secretly remained loyal to the ways of their forefathers. They would celebrate Lag b'Omer in secrecy with dancing, feasting and the lighting of candles. Perhaps they did it to make up for the joy of Passover, which they had ceased to observe out of fear of the spies of the Inquisition.

One Lag b'Omer a group of Marranos celebrating the day was apprehended and brought to trial before the court of the Inquisition. Among those arrested was Don Frederico Morgano, one of the leaders of the Jewish community and son of a judge in Barcelona. He undertook to speak in defense of the group. "According to Jewish custom," he told the court, "the days between Passover and Shavuot are a time of sorrow, when it is forbidden for Jews to rejoice, to marry, to put on new clothes, and so forth. We, however, wishing to demonstrate our loyalty to the Catholic faith, made it a point to arrange a day of celebration and rejoicing precisely in the middle of this period when the Jews are in mourning."

The prisoners were acquitted.

THE FEARLESS TRADITION OF STRENGTH

RABBI SIMEON BAR YOHAI, the disciple of the martyred Rabbi Akiva, continued the tradition of Israel's earlier era of strength and national awakening. His many homilies are noteworthy for their spirit of deep piety coupled with fervent nationalism. The anti-Jewish excesses of the Roman conquerors drew from him some harsh remarks about the pagan world which he considered the embodiment of all evil. In his opinion, the Jewish people alone were capable of establishing absolute righteousness in the world, and that only by the strength of its Judaism.

The true personality of Rabbi Simeon bar Yohai has been somewhat eclipsed in the minds of later generations by the image of the man created by more recent tradition. One account of Rabbinic literature tells that Rabbi Simeon bar Yohai once sat together with Rabbi Judah bar Ilai and Rabbi Yose ben Halafta and pondered the worth of Roman culture. Rabbi Judah began, "How splendid are that nation's deeds: They have built highways and market-places, constructed bridges, erected bath-houses . . ." Rabbi Simeon cut him off saying: "Whatever they have built has been only for their own need . . ." When the Roman governor heard of this, he decreed that Simeon was to be put to death for his impertinence. (Talmud, Shabbat 33b). Rabbi Simeon bar Yohai fled and hid in a cave for thirteen years. Only when a new government came to power and the decree against him had been forgotten did he return to the Galilee to serve on the *Sanhedrin*, Israel's supreme court of law,

Rabbi Simeon frequented the baths of Tiberias to obtain relief from the ailments he had contracted during his years of hiding. He later lived in Tiberias and Meron, near Safed, and participated in the deliberations of the *Sanhedrin* at Usha. At one time he went to Rome on behalf of the *Sanhedrin* to intercede with the authorities for the repeal of new and harsh decrees against his people.

Intrigued by the Talmudic account of Simeon's long sojourn in the dark cave, medieval folk tradition credited him with mystical teachings and miraculous powers. In 14th century Spain he was regarded as the author of the wondrous *Zohar* or "Book of Splendor," which was accepted as the "Bible" of Jewish mysticism. From the 16th century onward, when the mystics in the Land of Israel began to spread the teachings of the *Zohar*, Rabbi Simeon's fame in this regard grew even greater. Since that time his tomb in Meron has been the object of particular reverence.

The first of the first-fruits of your land shall you bring into the house of the Lord your God.

EXODUS 23:19

And you shall observe the feast of weeks, of the first-fruits of the wheat harvest.

EXODUS 34:22

Seven weeks shall you number unto you; begin to number the seven weeks from such time as you begin to put the sickle to the corn. And you shall keep the feast of weeks unto the Lord your God with a tribute of a freewill offering of your hand, which you shall give unto the Lord your God, according as the Lord your God has blessed you; and you shall rejoice before the Lord your God.

DEUTERONOMY 16:9-12

SHAVUOT

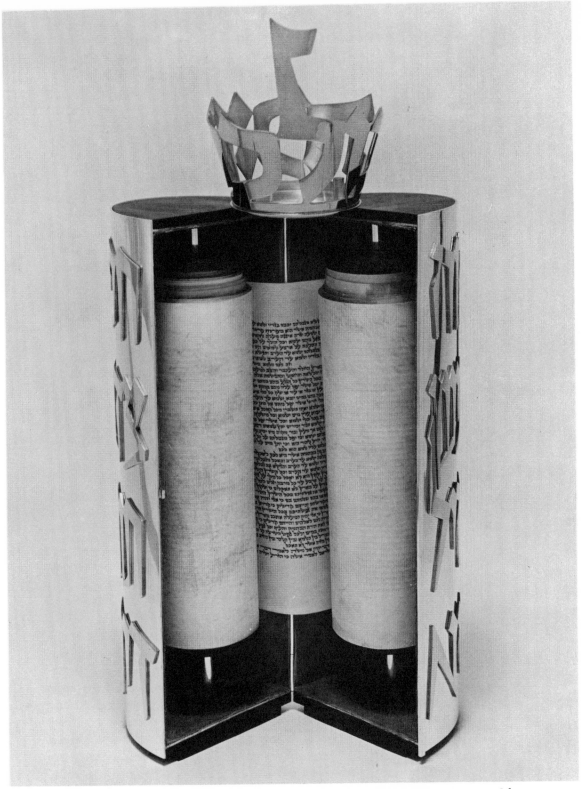

Torah case and crown. This modern sterling silver Torah Scroll case, executed by Ludwig Y. Wolpert, is patterned on the Torah container used in Sephardic communities to house Scrolls of the Law. Hebrew inscriptions on body of the case reads: "The Lord was pleased, for His righteousness' sake to make the Torah great and glorious" (Isaiah 42:21). The crown is formed of the words "And ye shall write down for yourselves . . ." (Deut. 31:19) from which is derived the Rabbinic commandment that every Jew should write a Scroll of the Law, or at least have a share in the writing of one. (From the collection of Rabbi and Mrs. Amos Edelheit, Willimantic, Conn.).

SHAVUOT

OF THE *Shalosh Regalim*, the three Pilgrim Festivals, Shavuot is the one prescribed by the Bible for the late spring when the Israelites brought their offerings of wheat and first fruits to the Holy Temple of Jerusalem. For this reason, the festival was also known as *Hag HaBikkurim*, the "Festival of the First Fruits."

It is celebrated exactly seven weeks after the second day of Pesah, the day of the first *Omer* (early barley harvest) offering, hence the name Shavuot—"Festival of Weeks," or, in the Greek version, *Pentecost* ("Fiftieth Day").

However, the chief significance of the festival is of a religious nature: Shavuot marks the anniversary of the Revelation at Mount Sinai—it is *Z'man Matan Toratenu*, "The Season of the Giving of our Torah." The Ten Commandments, proclaimed in that Revelation, are considered the 120 most important words in the Bible as they constitute not only the foundation of Jewish ethics, but the basic moral code for all mankind.

Unlike the other two Pilgrim Festivals, Pesah and Sukkot, the observance of Shavuot had not been marked by as imaginative a symbolism as the *seder* or the *sukka*, until the institution, in modern Israel, of the splendid *Bikkurim* ceremonial, recalling the rite in the ancient Temple. In this celebration, farmers come in colorful procession to bring gifts of their produce to a designated central area where, amidst song and dance, these offerings are redeemed for monetary contributions to the Jewish National Fund. The participation of gaily costumed, garlanded children enhances the joy of the occasion.

Another post-exilic Shavuot custom, faintly reminiscent of the Biblical *Bikkurim* festival, has been the decoration of homes and synagogues with green plants and flowers.

The religious aspect of Shavuot as the anniversary of the giving of the Torah is also recalled. The Ten Commandments are recited in the synagogue. Pious Jews spend part of the first night of Shavuot in the reading of selections from the Bible, as well as from Rabbinic and Cabbalistic literature. This service is known as *Tikkun Lel Shavuot* ("Shavuot Night Preparation".)

On the first day of Shevout, the mystical poem *Akdamut* ("Introduction"), composed by Rabbi Meir Ben Isaac of France, who lived in the eleventh century, is read in the synagogue. The poem appropriately extols the majesty of God and the excellence of His Torah.

In Conservative and Reform congregations in the United States today, confirmation exercises are held on Shavuot since the central theme of confirmation is self-dedication to the study and ideals of the Torah. Formerly, throughout the diaspóra, a child's Jewish education would be begun on Shavuot, so that

Torah Ornaments. Torah mantle, brocade (Italy, 17th century); Torah crown, silver repoussé, partly gilt (Italy, 1742); Torah finials, silver repoussé (Padua, Italy, 18th century). (The Israel Museum, Jerusalem).

the anniversary of the Revelation of the Law to His people might mark his own personal initiation into the study of Torah.

Finally, the reading of the Book of Ruth in the synagogue on the second day of Shavuot is related to both the agricultural and the religious aspects of the festival. The main action of the story centers around farm life during the period of the Judges. The heroine is Ruth, the Moabite, who forsook idolatry, embraced the Covenant of Sinai, and became the ancestress of David, King of Israel.

THE BOOK OF NAOMI

WHO IS THE HEROINE of the Book of Ruth? Ruth, you'll certainly say. I beg leave to disagree. The heroine of the Book of Ruth is not Ruth, but Naomi. If you are in doubt, please read with me carefully what happened in the Book of Ruth, and how and why.

Ruth's role in the book is a passive one. She takes no action of her own initiative. Her one independent act is to say to her mother-in-law: "Whither thou goest, I will go" (1:16).

True, these heart-warming words were the most fateful in Ruth's life and the most consequential in the Book which bears her name. But from that point on, everything that Ruth does, she does on the prodding of Naomi. It is Naomi, and not Ruth, who manipulates the events.

Naomi plans everything with wisdom, tact and infinite care. She figures out in detail all the possibilities, risks and dangers. In her wisdom, experience and knowledge of human nature, she anticipates Ruth's every step and every doing.

There is no doubt about it. Naomi and no one else is the driving force behind all the events, doings and happenings in the book that is called—not too accurately—the Book of Ruth.

But what force drives *her*? What impels Naomi, aged and broken by the tragic loss of her husband and her sons, to embark on the plans and acts which we witness in the Book of Ruth?

It was three qualities of heart and mind—goodness, kindness and genuine love.

The Sages of the Talmud said that the Book of Ruth was written to honor the virtue of kindness it describes. But they failed to explain *whose* kindness.

We read about the kindness of Ruth. Boaz said to her (3:10): "Thou hast shown more kindness in the end than at the beginning." We are also told about the kindness of Boaz (2:20): "Blessed be he of the Lord, who has not left off His kindness . . ." Even the kindness of Orpah is mentioned (1:8): "And Naomi said to her two daughters-in-law: '. . . May the Lord deal kindly with you, as ye have dealt with the dead and with me.'" But not one word is mentioned of the kindness of Naomi.

Such has ever been the fate of the Jewish mother-in-law. She works and worries, suffers and sacrifices herself, but she remains in the background. Self-denying and self-sacrificing, she stays on the sidelines. As she is, so is her devotion—unobtrusive and anonymous.

Mothers-in-law are usually the target for uncomplimentary gibes. Even some of our own people have picked up this non-Jewish custom, along with many others foreign to the spirit of Judaism.

How wrong! Look at Naomi. Not the meddlesome crone, but the selfless matriarch, is the typical Jewish mother-in-law. How much goodness and love is there in her personality! How much warmth and devotion in her every word and deed! We know how indebted we are to the many Jewish mothers-in-law who, down through the generations, worked day and night and endured great hardship and deprivation that their learned sons-in-law should be able to devote all their time and ability to the study of the Torah. Do you know, for example, that one of the greatest commentators on the Talmud, and on the Tosafot— the Maharsha (1555-1631), proudly and gratefully bears the name of his mother-in-law—Edel's!

And all the familiar mother-in-law jokes to the contrary, Jewish mothers-in-law who live by the spirit of Judaism have been no less kind to the *daughters* they acquired through the marriage of their sons.

Still, Naomi insists on remaining at the sidelines. She desires nothing for herself. At first, she refuses to accept the sacrifice of Ruth when she vowed not to part from her. She pleads with her to return to her mother's house. Naomi wants to bear the burden of her fate alone: "For it grieves me much for your sakes, for the hand of the Lord is gone forth against me" (1:13).

Scribes at work in Jerusalem. These scribes are correcting imperfections on old Torah Scrolls brought to Israel from Jewish communities in Europe and Asia that no longer exist.

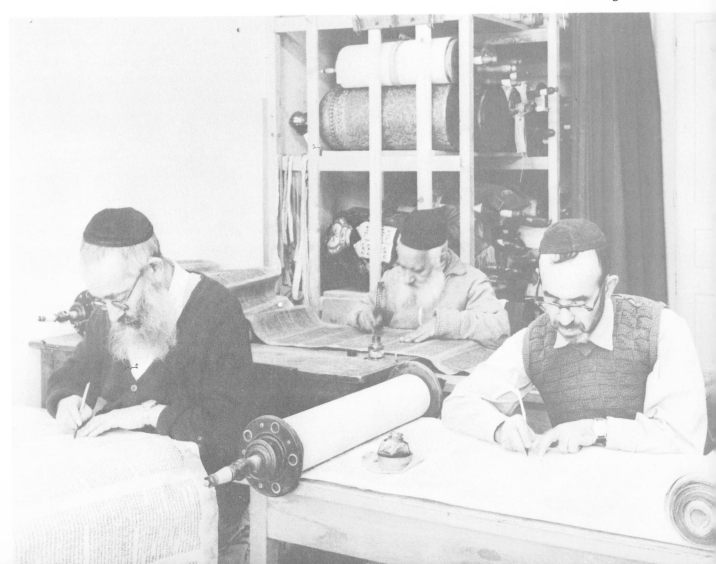

Thus they stand at the parting of the ways—we know now, at the crossroads of history—these three, lonely, grieving widows. Had Ruth taken just one step—the logical one—*not* in the direction of Naomi—here the story would have come to an unhappy end—and there would be no story and no Book of Ruth.

But Ruth took the illogical step—the right one, as we know now. She said "Whither thou goest, I will go . . . thy people shall be my people, and thy God my God . . ." (1:16) and what might have been the end, became the beginning. What could have been the tragic severance of a relationship became the start of a chain of events which culminated in the Kingdom of David.

Now let us ask: What prompted Ruth to forsake her family and country for Naomi? What impelled this young woman to give up her loved ones and her homeland for this lonely widow, so cruelly stricken by fate?

The answer is this: the tragedy that befell Naomi was the most cruel that could come to any woman—her loved ones, her husband and sons all died within a short time of each other. Yet, though she felt that "the Almighty has dealt very bitterly with me," she was not bitter. She lost everything, but she had not lost herself. Catastrophe could not rob her of her goodness nor of her love of people and her will to help and to serve those she loved.

Even though she asked her countrymen not to call her Naomi any more because it meant "pleasant," but Mara, which means "bitterness," there was no bitterness in her. Even in her darkest hour, she was Naomi.

What is more, she had grown in her sufferings. So did her goodness. And this was what attracted Ruth. This made her decide to join her fate with that of Naomi.

As soon as Ruth has announced her irrevocable decision, Naomi sets a new goal in her empty life: to find new happiness for her faithful daughter-in-law.

This goal becomes the moving force in her life, the aim of her very existence. She acquires new energy and a new sense of purpose. From then on she takes matters into her own hands. She plans everything beforehand with foresight and shrewdness. She directs Ruth's every step. She rehearses every word Ruth is to say, tells her how to say it, and when. She is careful not to rush things, not to precipitate the flow of events before their time. Correct timing is very important in such matters, as we all know, or should know. (By the way, here you have a perfect guidebook for matchmakers—amateurs and professionals alike.)

But aside from the clever management of things, deeds and people, one factor, though unseen, is always present here—love. This is the force that guides every step of Naomi, who guides and directs Ruth.

188

Ruth was sent, by Naomi, of course, to gather stalks of wheat in the field. But she finds more than wheat. She finds goodness, friendship, kindness. Through the capable guidance of Naomi, she is led by Divine Providence to her destiny and happiness.

Ruth does nothing more than to implement Naomi's planning. She meticulously carries out Naomi's detailed instructions. She acts automatically, like a robot. She does only what Naomi tells her to do—and that is enough. "And she [Ruth] said to her [Naomi]: 'All that you say to me I will do' " (3:5).

As you see, then, the moving spirit is Naomi—not Ruth.

Now, you will ask: Why is this story called "The Book of Ruth" and not "The Book of Naomi"? We know that our Sages, of blessed memory, were very careful to give credit where credit was due. Where did they err here?

Apparently, this question also seems to have troubled the author of *Megillat Ruth*. He sought, therefore, to correct matters. As the story approaches its climax, it is not Ruth and not Boaz who occupies the center of the stage. When the child is born to the happy couple, the parents step aside. And whom do we see in the spotlight at the happy ending? Naomi!

When the well-wishers come to offer their congratulations, they turn to Naomi: "And the women said to Naomi: 'Blessed be the Lord, Who has not left you this day without a near kinsman . . . And he shall be to you a restorer of life and a nourisher of your old age; for your daughter-in-law, who loves you, who is better to you than seven sons, has borne him' " (4:14,15).

And the Book of Ruth concludes: "And Naomi took the child, and laid it in her bosom, and became nurse to it" (4:16). A rather too idyllic climax for a dramatic story. But how moving is this picture of good, old Naomi, once so stricken by fate and so happy now, cuddling this infant, which is not even related to her by blood, yet owes its very life to her goodness. How fitting for her, and for the destiny of the child, that it was blessed to be the ancestor of the Kingdom of David.

And who knows? Perhaps the Psalms of David, singing the praises of goodness, carry a faint echo of the lullabies that Naomi sang to "Obed, the father of Jesse, the father of David" (4:17).

SHAVUOT

THE OFFERING OF THE FIRST FRUITS

THESE WERE THE VERSES from the Scriptures which the Israelites would chant as they went up to Jerusalem in the days of the Temple to offer up the first fruits of their fields.

On the way they would sing: "I was glad when they said to me: Let us go to the House of the Lord" (Psalms 122:1).

As they entered the city of Jerusalem they would chant: "Our feet are standing within thy gates, O Jerusalem!" (Psalms 122:2).

When they had reached the Temple Mount, they would sing: "*Halleluya*—praise God in His sanctuary, praise Him in the firmament of His power" (Psalms 150:1).

And when they finally arrived at the Temple, they would exult: "Let everything that has breath praise the Lord, *Halleluya!*" (Psalms 150:6).

Jerusalem Talmud, Tractate Bikkurim 3:2

SHAVUOT DECORATIONS

THE FOLLOWING CUSTOM is widely observed in Jewish communities throughout the lands of our dispersion.

On the day before Shavuot synagogues and homes are decorated with boughs, branches and leaves of trees. This custom is based on the Mishnaic teaching that on Shavuot Heaven decides the fate of the fruit trees and the crops of the orchards for the coming season. Thus the practice had its origins in Israel's ancient agricultural life, the greenery in synagogue and home serving as a reminder of the need for prayer in order to receive the help of Heaven for a good harvest.

Rabbi Elijah ben Solomon Zalman, the Gaon of Vilna (1720-1797) sought to root out this practice because the Christians did much the same thing on their festival (which made him suspect a strong Christian influence behind the Jewish custom). But he did not succeed in his efforts for by all accounts the custom is very old, and is intertwined with the agricultural significance of this festival of early harvest.

THE AKDAMUT MELODY

THE BIBLICAL PORTION read in the synagogue on the first day of Shavuot is the account of the Revelation at Mount Sinai in which the Ten Commandments were given. The reading is preceded by a prelude: the *Akdamut,* a long mystical poem* chanted to a special tradi-

---

* This Aramaic poem, an acrostic of 90 lines containing a double alphabet and the poet's name, was written by Meir ben Isaac of Worms in the 11th Century.

tional melody—one of the most beloved and revered old synagogue chants with which we honor our festivals. Just as the chant of *Kol Nidre* sets the mood for Yom Kippur, so does this musical setting cast its spell over the festival of Shavuot.

While we know it only as the melody to which *Akdamut* has been chanted for generations, there is reason to believe that the melody was not originally composed for this liturgical poem but was derived from older traditional sources. However, it happened to suit this poem so well that it became the universally accepted setting for *Akdamut,* and melody and words fused into one. This ancient plaintive chant, which culminates on a note of exultant triumph, remains forever alive and new, even as it conveys echoes of legends and traditions from days of yore. Blended with the exalted words, the melody—which has a range of just six notes—has become firmly established as a vital element of our festival tradition.

Although it is used only on Shavuot the *Akdamut* melody bears a certain resemblance to other chants, such as the Festival *kiddush,* the Torah reading on Rosh HaShana, and the chant used in some regions for the reading of the Passover Haggadah.

Torah crowns. The custom to surmount the Scroll of the Law with a silver crown (keter or atara) to symbolize the supremacy of God and His Law dates back to the post-Talmudic period (6th - 11th centuries C.E.). This silver crown was made in Venice or Padua, Italy, in the 18th century and is embossed with various symbols and patterns, particularly the menora. (Hebrew Union College Museum, Cincinnati, Ohio).

Memorial Lamp for the Six Million Jewish Dead. Cast bronze, 1960, by Moshe Zabari. Inscription: "I will give them an everlasting memorial that shall not be cut off"(Isaiah 56:5). Photo: Frank J. Darmstaedter.

SHAVUOT IN JERUSALEM

TRADITION (ETHICS OF THE FATHERS 5:8) has it that ten miracles occurred again and again without fail in and around the Holy Temple in Jerusalem. According to Rabbi Simeon ben Zemah Duran (1361-1444), a scholar who was active in Spain, at least one of these ten miracles persisted even after the fall of the Temple. Just as in days of the Temple, he writes, so in his own day, too, no one in Jerusalem ever complained to a neighbor that he found the city too crowded during the festival seasons.

All year long, he explains, the tiny synagogues of Jerusalem in his day could barely hold the worshipers; they were always filled from wall to wall. When Shavuot came, room had to be found for an influx of over 300 visitors from Egypt and elsewhere, who had kept up the ancient practice of making the pilgrimage to the Holy City for this festival. And the age-old miracle recurred, year after year. Everyone who came to the synagogue found that he had plenty of room in which to sit. No one ever found it necessary to complain that he felt crowded.

"For," the Spanish-Jewish scholar concludes, "Jerusalem retains its ancient holiness. And this is a sign that the people of Israel will be redeemed a third time."

SHAVUOT IN THE DESERT

IN THE DESERT OASES OF ALGERIA the most interesting Jewish settlement is at Mzab. A whole Jewish tribe dwells there, in a region hidden amidst rocky ravines in the heart of the Sahara. Some 800 Jews live in a ghetto in Gardaia, the region's capital. Several hundred more are found in other places, notably Laghuat.

It is the tradition of these Jews that their forebears were brought into the desert when the holy Temple in Jerusalem was destroyed (70 C.E.). In their synagogue they will show you a sacred Scroll of the Law which, they believe, was taken along with all the plunder and booty of Titus, the evil Roman conqueror. Along with the Torah and the code of religious law which their scholars know, they retain several traditions and memories from earlier generations.

At Shavuot time the Jews of Mzab have a singular ceremony, called (with tongue in cheek) *The Jewish Capture of Gardaia.* The morning after the festival, all the Jewish inhabitants come riding on mules and donkeys—their own, or animals borrowed from their Berber neighbors. They pass through the city streets with a great clamor and tumult, sprinkling each other, and passers-by, too, with water.

Thus they proceed to the gardens and fields, where they recite a special blessing so that the date palms may yield good fruit. Then they chant songs and hymns; and as the day wanes, they return to their homes, accompanied by many Berber neighbors, as they continue sprinkling and spilling water all about and singing their songs and chants.

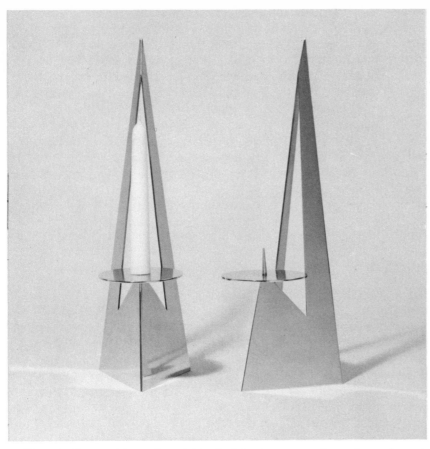

Modern candlesticks, contemporary, nickel silver, by Moshe Zabari. (Gift of Dr. and Mrs. A. Kanof to The Jewish Museum, New York City).

They believe with perfect faith that their prayers have been heard, and that the fruit of the date palm will grow well in the summer ahead.

* * *

In most Jewish communities of North Africa, the day after Shavuot is a holiday dedicated to trees and gardens. A prominent feature of the day's ritual is a ceremonial sprinkling and pouring of water. In Tripoli, for instance, all the Jews go out to their fields and orchards to pray over their trees, and to douse one another with pitcherfuls of water. They believe this will improve the growth of crops, and the more water spilled, the better. The Gentiles share their belief, and join in the pouring with merriment and shouts of joy.

A similar custom exists in Tel Massan and many northern cities, but the ancient tradition is best preserved among the scattered, isolated communities in the oases of the great Sahara desert. The Jewish settlements in southern Algeria are very old; many probably date back to the time of the destruction of the Temple in Jerusalem. They claim that their people came then to Africa directly from the Holy Land.

* * *

In one oasis of the Sahara, the Scriptural portion about the Ten Commandments read on the first day of Shavuot is prefaced by a special liturgical poem which begins, *Yom ma'amad Sinai* ("The Day We Stood at Sinai"). The cantor chants, "Who would believe what we heard? And to whom has the arm of the Lord been revealed? (Isaiah 53:1). He declared His word to Jacob, His statutes and laws to Israel; He did not deal thus with any [heathen] nation; they do not know His laws. Praise the Lord!" (Psalms 147:19-20). Then the cantor proclaims in Arabic, "O Israelite brethren, listen to the sound of these Ten Commandments that were given to Moses at Sinai amid the crash of thunder and lightning." He recites the verse, "The chariots of God are myriads, thousands upon thousands: the Lord was among them at Sinai, in holiness" (Psalms 68:18). And he adds: "Honor the Lord, and honor the Torah!"

The congregation remains standing throughout the Torah reading.

R. Simeon b. Zemah Duran (1361-1444)

SHAVUOT IN YEMEN

WE WOULD ARISE BEFORE DAWN to go to the synagogue, so that we could read through Maimonides' list of the 613 Precepts of the Torah before the service started. Later in the morning, after readings from the Pentateuch and the Prophets, we would chant *Az-harot* by Saadya Gaon*. The first day we read the stanzas enumerating the positive precepts; the second day, we read the prohibitions. We had a special melody for this that went straight to the heart; and when the cantor would sing, "On Galilee's hill we'll go with the trill of the shepherd's pipe," all would hum the tune along with him. The eyes of the very pious were filled with tears of grief, joy and yearning for Zion and Israel.

The first afternoon of the festival, we read the *Book of Ruth* in the synagogue, along with its Aramaic translation. In keeping with a custom of more recent origin we added Saadya Gaon's Arabic version so that all might understand the beautiful, moving story.

The second night of Shavuot was called "the Night of the Reading." After the evening service in the synagogues there was a festive dinner at home. Thereafter the people would return to the synagogues, each bringing some food or delicacy according to his means. One might carry a flask of spiced sweet coffee for all to share; another would bring candy; a third came with rose-water to sprinkle over the people in the later hours amid their reading and study so as to refresh them with its pleasant fragrance and awaken those who might have dozed off.

At first the custom was to read Maimonides' *Book of Precepts* in the original Arabic in which it was written, and the people would finish it the following afternoon. Then the custom lapsed, until it was eventually revived. In general, the night was to be spent at sacred study, sleep being forbidden. Young lads would make the rounds of the synagogues all night long to see which congregation was the most alert and wide-awake and the next morning arguments could be heard as to which group should be given first honors for wakefulness.

* Hebrew: "Exhortation," Liturgical poem enumerating the 613 Biblical Precepts.

This night was holy to the people, especially to the women. They believed that whoever slept this night would lose his livelihood. For this night, at an hour chosen by the Holy One, blessed be He, the heavens were supposed to open, releasing the angel in charge of income and livelihoods, to soar through the world and assign each person his lot and portion. Should he find someone sleeping, the angel would give him nothing, but would leave some small portion with his assistant, to be doled out on the morrow among those who now slumbered . . .

Now, when the heavens opened for the angel (so the belief went) the stars would scatter to make way for him. Hence the people, especially the women, would watch the heavens all night long for a falling star—a "sure sign" of the time when the heavens were supposedly opening. Once they caught sight of a falling star, each and every one would address the wishes of his heart to his Maker, believing with perfect faith that all his desires would be granted him. There is even an anecdote that one woman put her head out the window, and seeing a falling star, cried out, "O Lord, give me a large head!"— whereupon her head grew so much that the wall had to be broken up to allow her to get her head back inside.

This hand-colored woodcut from a Sephira book (Germany, 1801) shows a procession of pilgrims entering Jerusalem to bring their offerings of first fruit. Hebrew caption is "The Day of the Offering of First Fruits."

The Priestly Blessing. In the Temple of Jerusalem, the Birkat Kohanim or Priestly Blessing was pronounced each day by the Priests from a special platform (dukhan). In synagogues outside Israel today, the blessing is recited by the Kohanim on festivals only; in most places in Israel it is still pronounced every day. The Kohanim (facing the congregation) cover their faces with the Tallit as they stand on the platform in front of the Ark, reciting the benediction: "May the Lord bless you and keep you. May the Lord let His countenance shine upon you and be gracious to you. May the Lord lift up His countenance to you and give you peace" (Num. 6:24-26). This picture shows the benediction recited at a synagogue in Israel during weekday morning services (note phylacteries worn by the worshippers).

THE PRIESTLY BLESSING

THE PRIESTLY BLESSING (*Birkat Kohanim*) is one of the most meaningful prayers in the holiday liturgy. It comes as the climax to the *Musaf Amida* on Pesah, Shavuot, Sukkot, Rosh HaShana and Yom Kippur. Derived from the Bible (Num. 6:24–26), it dates back to a period of great significance in the history of the Jewish people—the days when the Children of Israel prepared to enter the Promised Land after forty years of wandering in the wilderness. Obviously, at this crucial point in its history, the new-born nation was particularly in need of Divine favor.

The Blessing consists of a threefold invocation: "May the Lord bless thee and keep thee. May the Lord cause His face to shine upon thee and be gracious unto thee. May the Lord lift up His face toward thee, and grant thee peace." In the Hebrew original, these three terse sentences contain three, five, and seven words respectively. Interestingly, this increase in the number of words corresponds to the significance of the Divine favors for which we pray. The first and shortest verse asks that God may "keep thee," the next asks "that He may be gracious unto thee" and the final verse, that He may "grant thee peace," the most precious, though unfortunately most elusive attainment within the reach of man.

Another noteworthy aspect of the Priestly Blessing is that it is phrased in the singular form, as a personal blessing, addressed to the needs and desires of each individual separately, as it is said: "... according to the blessing of the Lord thy God which He hath given thee" (Deut. 12:15). Thus, the Almighty blesses the merchant with

Laver for Kohanim. Before ascending the platform in front of the Ark to recite the Priestly Blessing, the Kohanim wash their hands. This laver is the work of Ludwig Y. Wolpert.

prosperity, the student of Torah with scholarly achievement, and the scientist with success in his search for new discoveries. This is meant by the benediction "May the Lord bless thee." "May He keep thee" refers to the hope that all these blessings will come true and remain with the recipient. The rich man hopes that he may be permitted to "keep" his wealth; the scholar, that he may preserve and utilize his knowledge and abilities for the good of mankind; and the scientist, that his investigations and discoveries may be immortalized by finding constructive application. Furthermore, this blessing implies the wish that every individual who has been granted success will be kept free from arrogance.

The second benediction, "May the Lord cause His face to shine upon thee," refers to spiritual attributes. A comment in *Sifre* interprets this phrase both here and in Psalms 67:2, "May He cause His face to shine toward us" to mean: "May you and all the members of your family, be illumined by the shining light of the Divine Presence."

"May He be gracious unto thee" means: "May He graciously accept your supplications," as it is written: "O Lord, be gracious, we have hoped for Thee." (Isaiah 33:2). Another interpretation is: "May you find grace in the sight of God and man."

"May the Lord lift up His face toward thee": "May the Almighty be amiable to thee." "And grant thee peace," as pointed out previously, is the highest blessing of all. It implies not merely the avoidance of strife, but the active pursuit of peace and harmony, both physical and spiritual. "Peace," according to our sages, "is a vessel that contains all blessings."

The brief but eloquent words of the Priestly Blessing convey volumes of faith and trust in God. Their poetry and majestic solemnity are designed to inspire and uplift the congregation.

The Priestly Blessing was one of the most important and impressive rituals of the Divine Service in the Holy Temple. It is noteworthy that this ritual should have been preserved in the synagogue to this day. In fact, with the elimination of sacrifices, the Priestly Blessing is the only remaining functional link between the present-day synagogue and the Temple in Jerusalem—a symbol of the unity and continuity of the Jewish people throughout the generations.

RARELY IN THE HISTORY of human relations has there been such an extreme contrast between two national philosophies and ways of life as that which existed between Rome and Judea; brute force, power and uninhibited greed as opposed to the laws of fundamental morality for national and individual conduct, and a belief that mere existence, even on a high level of affluence, cannot be an end in itself as opposed to lofty spirituality permeated by deep religious faith and based on the reality of the Messianic ideal.

The Romans did not recognize, indeed they could not even grasp, the concepts of good and evil. It is for this reason that the Jews saw Rome as the embodiment of evil on earth, the incarnation of the opposite of goodness and morality.

Jerusalem. "Hierosolima" with Holy Temple in the center, woodcut by Hartmann Schedel, 1492.

Destruction of the Temple. Dutch engraving.

In the encounter between these two antagonistic forces, worlds apart, a clash was inevitable, particularly since it occurred in the arena of international power play, dominated by Rome's imperialistic designs. When the collision finally came, it took place in more than one area and on several planes—religious, political, social and military.

The superhuman heroism, the fierce fighting, the dogged determination of the Judean defenders not to surrender even in the face of overwhelming odds, were undoubtedly inspired and sustained by religious ardor.

Nonetheless, partly by osmosis and partly by way of reaction, the stark materialism characteristic of Rome fostered a correspondingly materialistic attitude also among the Judeans, an attitude which, as pointed out above, had never been typical of Jews. The worship of power, typical of Rome, came to influence the Jewish fighters who had formerly believed in the invincibility of the spirit.

The urgency of self-defense, the struggle for survival as a national and religious entity, transformed these other-worldly mystics, immersed in religious contemplation and ecstasy, into fierce fighters. The conflict was shifted from the sphere of beliefs and ideas to the field of military combat. Thus, by force of necessity, the spiritual and ideological conflict was transformed into a political and military confrontation. The zealous patriots could no longer remain aloof from the harsh reality of the situation.

200

Gone was their estrangement from this world and their passionate longing to master the temporal by means of the eternal. The concept that evil could be overcome by good, immorality by morality, and force by ideas, was thrown overboard, and replaced by the bloody fight against a brutal aggressor. Physical force had to be met by physical force.

Although the defenders of Judea ultimately lost the war, their heroism had not been in vain. Their refusal to surrender to a vastly superior power resulted in their destruction, but the ideals for which they had fought could never die. The debacle on the battlefields was not followed by the disintegration of the Jewish people or of Judaism. Their struggle ended in failure but not in humiliation. Indeed, they emerged from defeat as true heroes.

In this fateful struggle, the individual faded into insignificance, and the people as a whole, though divided into opposing factions, was molded in the crucible of suffering into a strong national entity.

The Wailing Wall. "Rabbi Aha said: 'The Divine Presence never leaves the Western Wall of the Holy Temple.'" (Shemoth Rabba). The yearning for the lost Temple has been the theme of artists for countless generations. This etching of the Wailing Wall by Jeremiah Halpern (ca. 1900) is in The Jewish Museum, New York City.

This was even more remarkable in view of the political and military chaos which had afflicted the divided defense, as contrasted against the unified command in the camp of the aggressor. A violent conflict arose between the idealistic Essenes and the cloak-and-dagger Sicarii even as both fought the common enemy with extraordinary self-sacrifice.

The heroic fighters for Judea's independence thus left a heritage cherished and cultivated throughout generations. The vivid memory of the destruction of the Temple and of the loss of statehood became a constructive force in maintaining the cohesion of the dispersed people, and an indestructible link with its ancient homeland, *Eretz Yisrael.*

And so it came to pass that Tisha B'Av, the day on which the Jewish people mourns the destruction of its Temple and the loss of its statehood, became a significant factor in the rebuilding of the Holy Land and in the rebirth of the State of Israel.

REFLECTIONS AT THE WAILING WALL

MY FEET ARE STANDING within thy gates, O Jerusalem, at the Western Wall, for the first time in my life, on the Ninth of Av in the historic year 1967, only a few hours after my arrival at Lod airport. I am now in reunited Jerusalem, amongst my people who have assembled here by the tens of thousands for the first time since the rebirth of the State of Israel nearly two decades ago, for the first time under Jewish rule since the destruction of the Holy Temple nearly twenty centuries ago. We have gathered here on the day of fasting and lamentation, painstakingly following all the rules prescribed by our Rabbis for the observance of Tisha B'Av. But despite the traditional signs of mourning, the thick, three weeks' growth of beard upon our faces, our shabby garments and stockinged feet, our doleful chant of the Book of Lamentations, the sobs of the many Jews around us who cling to the hallowed stones as if snuggling close to their mother's breast—despite all this, we do not genuinely feel the sadness appropriate to Tisha B'Av.

Instead, beneath our outward obedience to the tradition which has designated Tisha B'Av as a day of mourning, there is an air of ... rejoicing! True, it is muted, restrained, subdued, but it is definitely there. From earliest childhood, we have associated the eve of Tisha B'Av with the melancholy flickering of tiny candles in the synagogue. On this Tisha B'Av, in reunited Jerusalem, a powerful floodlight plays upon the cherished stones of the Western Wall. "A new light shines upon Zion..." Our hearts throb with overwhelming joy.

Though our souls are deeply moved and our eyes filled with tears, we are under the spell of that strange emotion so aptly described by the Psalmist's words: "And rejoice with trembling" (Psalms 2:11).

This time, it seems, *Shabbat Nahamu*—the Sabbath of Consolation—has arrived early, after we had waited for it two thousand years in vain. After many centuries during which our joys were always tinged with sorrow, we have suddenly discovered that, at last, our sorrow can be mingled with joy.

As I recite the Lamentations, I am overcome by a sense of guilt. Either I am being dishonest with myself, or else my ears have grown impervious to the utterances of my mouth. I chant: "The roads to Zion are in mourning, without pilgrims coming to the feasts; all her gates are desolate." (Lament. 1:4). But is it really so? I see the roads to Zion before me today, crowded with visitors who have gathered from all the four corners of the earth. Am I not witnessing the fulfillment of the

Jerusalem reunified. Premier Levi Eshkol (in dark suit) visiting the Western Wall hours after the liberation of the Old City of Jerusalem in June 1967.

Kiddush cup with engraving of the Western Wall, Jerusalem, 1900.

prophecy of hope: "Your children shall come from afar, and your daughters shall be brought along in arms" (Isaiah 60:4)? Are not all the gates of the Eternal City filled with my brethren, faces shining and hearts overflowing with joy?

In my mixed emotions over the contrast between the words I am reading and the reality around me, a sudden remembrance tears through my brain and clamps itself like a vise around my heart. Exactly on this date, at the same hour of evening, twenty-five years ago—Tisha B'Av in the year 1942—there had begun the most horrible catastrophe in the annals of our people—the brutal destruction of the most illustrious center of Jewish life in the diaspora—the Jewish community of Warsaw.

"I am the man who has seen affliction" (Lamentations 3:1). In my *Diary of the Warsaw Ghetto*, I have thus recorded the dismal mood of that Tisha B'Av—the twenty-second of July 1942:

"Evening has descended. I walk home, and my mind is filled with terrifying thoughts.

"I cross the courtyard of our house and pass by our small synagogue (since it is dangerous now to walk through the streets, every house has set up its own small synagogue). Sitting on overturned benches are some two *minyanim* of Jews. Tonight is the eve of Tisha B'Av... Two dim candle-flames flicker on the lectern. The Jews sit with heads bowed, eyes staring into the bleak distance. And suddenly there arises the ancient, heart-rending dirge of the Lamentations, the melody that may first have been intoned by the exiles who were carried off into Babylonian captivity, the melody which like a sponge has absorbed the tears of every generation.

"*Eicha* ...*

"Every generation has had an *Eicha* of its own. But the *Eicha* of our generation has a mood no other generation has ever known before. Perhaps this will be our last *Eicha* ...

"Alas, how does the city sit desolate that was once so crowded with people ... How lonely, how forlorn are we today ... All her pursuers have overtaken her in the midst of her troubles ... I called on my friends, but they have deceived me ... How timely are these ancient words ... How aptly do they express our misfortune ...

"It all began on Tisha B'Av, 1872 years ago, with the loss of our statehood and homeland. What we behold now is merely the last link in the chain.

"We sit on the ground—we, the Jews of Warsaw, descendants of the exiles of Jerusalem, and mourn for our own destruction, the destruction of the Jewish community of Warsaw, a mother of cities in Israel—a

---

* Lit: "Alas, how." The Book of Lamentations attributed to the Prophet Jeremiah who, according to tradition, had witnessed the destruction of the First Temple, begins with the words: "Alas, how does the city sit desolate..."

confirmation of the destruction of Jerusalem. We lament our fate, the
fate of a homeless people in the clutches of the most cruel foe we have
ever faced; the fate of a people doomed to death. We sit and weep over
the ruins of the Holy Temple and the loss of our own lives—lives of
intense suffering but also of hopes, now lost forever. We mourn for our
lives—lives fraught with hardships but which, in spite of everything, we
managed to make spiritually rich and rewarding...lives which the
ruthless foe is determined to crush."

The bitter jeremiad befits the unprecedented holocaust of our
times. But it does not, it cannot fully reflect the enormity of the Nazi
crime against the Jewish people. Yitzhak Katznelson, the great poet of
the ghetto who perished in the holocaust, poignantly voices this thought
in his *Pinkas Vitel** which he wrote on the eve of Tisha B'Av in 1943, a
year after the start of the mass extermination of the Jews of Warsaw.
These are his words:

"Today I read through the Book of Lamentations. It struck me as a

* Tel Aviv, 1957, p.195.

*Tisha B'Av in the synagogue of Amsterdam. Copper engraving by Bernard Picart,
18th century. Congregation is reading the Book of Lamentations, and is sitting
on the floor as a sign of mourning for the destruction of the Temple. Cross-section
of women's gallery can be seen at upper right.*

felicitous work of poetry. The enemy fought us. We were defeated. The conqueror destroyed our Temple, the House of our Glory atop the mountain. He struck down our elders—though not all of them by far, for he exiled most of our people to Babylonia. But the brutal German did not defeat us in war. He spills our blood without war by working us to death for his sinister purposes. He transports us in trains of tens of boxcars to Treblinka and other such hells, to kill us, along with our wives and children . . . to gas us to death in Bergen-Belsen and Auschwitz . . . Cursed be this nation of murderers that has made even the Lamentations seem a festive anthem!"

Indeed, even the most moving lamentations composed through the centuries to mourn calamities and massacres that had been visited upon our people in various epochs, are totally inadequate to convey the insults and the savagery unleashed upon our people by the German *Herrenvolk*. For there is a limit to suffering and also to man's capacity for pain. There are researchers to study every phase of man's activity and historians to record human events. A future historian making a study of sadism will be hard put to discover anything in ancient archives or archeological excavations to parallel the shocking perversities perpetrated upon us by the "cultured" Germans, in the twentieth century, the so-called age of enlightenment. Even a writer endowed with boundless imagination would not be able to conjure up tales of horror to match the barbarism of the Nazis. What makes these crimes even more cold-blooded is the fact that they were not the result of a fit of rage, or blind hysteria, but the culmination of detailed diabolical planning and scientific organization. The Germans applied themselves to the work with cheerfulness and merriment, with "laughter that Satan knew not." Such terror defies expression; such violence beggars description.

At certain moments even now, this inconceivable horror returns to haunt us. Thus, as I stood before the Western Wall, reciting the Lamentations, I recalled the recent annihilation of European Jewry rather than the long-past destruction of the Temple. There came to my mind two scenes of Warsaw, the once-great center of vigorous, vibrant Jewish life—scenes that neither I nor, I am sure, any other human being can describe in all their drama and tragedy, for such incidents have never occurred before in the annals of mankind, not even in the history of any other living creature, including the wild beasts of the jungle!

I see again the tens of thousands of men, women and children herded through the main thoroughfares of Warsaw for "deportation"—a euphemism used by the German "nation of philosophers" for fiendish mass-murder.

Jews praying at the Wailing Wall. Drawing, 1854.

"I am the man who has seen affliction" such as to reduce to sheer insignificance the sufferings the prophet Jeremiah witnessed in his day. I recall Warsaw on that day a quarter of a century ago. I remember that the sun was shining, but to us who watched and trembled, the day seemed dark and dismal. We asked the sun: Are you not ashamed to shine upon this rotten world? Why do you not hide your face behind the darkest of black clouds? Here thousands of innocent human beings are about to be done to death by the scum of mankind, and you dare look down and smile on our calamity!

I saw my brothers and sisters in this enormous, satanic caravan moving through the streets of Warsaw. The streets that once teemed with vigorous, flourishing Jewish life, were now clogged with helpless, tormented Jews led to their death. He who has seen this sight will not forget it to his dying hour.

As I stood at the Western Wall a quarter-century later, all these sainted martyrs rose before me out of the abyss of death and oblivion and fixed me with a cold, mute, wide-eyed gaze, reflecting the utter senselessness of their sacrifice to an insane world. Again I heard their last agonized gasps.

They had not been wrapped in shrouds: they did not receive a Jewish burial. The *Kaddish* was not recited over them and no monument was erected in their memory. No word of eulogy was uttered over them. Their groans that had remained suspended in mid-air re-echoed in my ears as I stood, absorbed in meditation, at the sacred Wall . . .

The tidings of the rebirth of the Jewish State, of the redemption and unification of Jerusalem the Eternal, and of the liberation of the Temple Mount did not reach their ears. Alas, the good news came too late for those who were most deserving of consolation. Alas, the cultural and spiritual backbone of the nation, its brain and its heart, are gone. One of our Sages said: "The Messiah will come, but I do not wish to live to see him" (Sanhedrin 98:1) on account of the tribulations that will precede his coming. These martyrs had suffered the pre-Messianic agonies as no other generation before them—yet they were not given to live to behold the dawn of their people's salvation. If even Rachel, our mother, "refused to be comforted for her children because they are gone" (Jeremiah 31:14) how can we find consolation for our own stupendous loss?

Surely there is a striking contrast between the mourning of the Lamentations and the new, inspiring reality of Israel. While complete redemption is yet to come, we have beheld the beginnings of our deliverance. But what came to pass here in Jerusalem on that day of Tisha B'Av in the year 70 is very much relevant to what happened on Tisha

Silver coin issued in Palestine during the final revolt of Bar Kokhba against Rome (134 C.E.) Obverse (left) shows a building with four columns and an arched structure within—possibly the Temple and the Ark of the Covenant. Legend: "Jerusalem." Reverse (right) shows lulav and etrog. Legend: "Year 3 of the Redemption of Israel."

207

B'Av 1942 in Warsaw. There is a direct link between the destruction of the Temple and the annihilation of European Jewry, between the loss of our political freedom and the loss of the most creative and enterprising Jewish community in the diaspora.

The origin of the tragedy of our people can be traced directly to that early period in its history when the Temple, the symbol of our national independence, was destroyed. That day was the beginning of the disastrous succession of discrimination and persecution, oppression and expulsion—a trail of tears and blood—that finally culminated in the most appalling mass-murder of all time.

Other nations have also seen disaster. There have been many other victims of neo-Teutonic barbarity, but those losses were peripheral only. These nations had lost branches, but the tree itself had remained undamaged and unimpaired in its ability to weather the storm. But in the European Jewish community, the entire tree was uprooted, and only a few leaves were left to be scattered across the seas. The enemy had struck at the very heart of the people.

The countries ravaged by the Second World War eventually managed to rebuild their ruins. The wounds of battle were healed, the people recovered; indeed, some nations grew even more prosperous than they had been before. But who can heal our gaping wounds? Who can restore the ruins of our soul? When a country is ravaged by war, its sons rise up and rebuild it. But when a people is shattered—who can bring it back to life?

I stand before the Western Wall where generations had been weeping over the destruction of the Temple, and I ponder the uncanny timeliness of the ancient, well-rehearsed lament: "Oh that one would render my head into water and my eyes into a fountain of tears, that I might weep day and night for the slain of the daughter of my people!" (Jeremiah 8:23).

For here were gathered up all the sighs, the wails, the curses and the outcries of the millions who were tortured and done to death; all the tears of their slaughtered children and infants; all the gasps of the dying that hovered in the endless void; all the hopes and dreams left unfulfilled; all the prayers that went unanswered; all the joys that were not realized—all of these rise up now before me and cry out for revenge.

It was for these sainted martyrs that the State had been envisioned and planned. It was for their deliverance that the Homeland was redeemed. But now, when the wonderful dream of centuries finally came true—where are they?

This is the question to which those who had perished in the German mass murder seek an answer. But, alas, no answer is forthcoming.

Before World War I, Jews living in Jerusalem banded together into "communities" by country of origin. These communities enjoyed a considerable measure of religious and administrative autonomy. Shown here is the seal of the Ashkenazic Jewish community of Jerusalem with a picture of the Western Wall.

208

The second picture that rises before my mind is altogether different from the first. It is the Jewish community of Warsaw at its heyday—prospering, flourishing, creating, during the golden age of its history, like a candle-flame that briefly flares up before going out . . . What would have happened had the glad tidings of the restoration of Israel's Statehood reached this great Jewry at the height of its glory, with all its societies and organizations, its sects and factions, its houses of prayer and study, its humming activity, its bustling masses on the crowded, lively streets of Nalewki, Grzybowska, Franciszkanska and Twarda? How would this community have received the news of the miraculous triumph, of the liberation and unification of the beloved City of David for which countless generations of Jews had hoped and yearned, wept and prayed, and which they had always "set above their highest joy"? . . . All their lives they had mourned for their vanquished Jerusalem but, alas, they did not live to see the shining hour of its redemption . . .

Suddenly my thoughts return to the first scene, the deportation, of the wretched human cargo bound for slaughter. The burning eyes of the innocent, defenseless victims of a mad world silently ask: "Inquire, you who went up in flames" . . .* Their agonized, piercing glance cries out for vengeance for the wrong done those who had perished in their prime, as well as to generations yet unborn . . . vengeance for the futility of their yearnings and aspirations that have gone up in flames unfulfilled, turned into dust and ashes. The blood of these sainted martyrs, spilled like water, should have turned the light of day into the blackest night, and their cries should have risen out of that abysmal darkness to cleave the heavens asunder . . .

"Inquire, you who went up in flames," how is it that the earth did not tremble? How is it that the world was not shattered by the sight of such horror and atrocity?

Just as the decimation of our people in Europe had its beginning in the destruction of our ancient Sanctuary and in the loss of our nationhood, so, too, all the perils that hang like a threatening cloud over the reborn State where our saving remnant has found refuge but not, as yet, tranquility, can be traced back directly to the mass murder perpetrated upon us by the German people. The poison of hatred for our people is now brewing among the assorted heirs of the Nazi madness; it may well continue to plague us for generations. But now, thank God, we are no longer defenseless: we have a proud, independent State that has thrice demonstrated to the world its fighting power and its will to live.

I observe the throngs assembled at the Wall, celebrating restoration even as they mourn destruction, and through the mist of my tears I per-

Seal of community of Hungarian, Moravian, Bohemian and Austrian Jews in Jerusalem, with picture of Wailing Wall.

* From the *Kinot* (Lamentations) for Tisha B'Av: "Inquire, you (Jerusalem) who went up in flames, concerning the welfare of those who mourn for you . . ."

209

ceive the endless, spectral rows of those who deserved most to be comforted by the solace of Zion, but for whom, alas, the comfort came too late. I have seen them in their sorrow and mortification as the German maniac tortured them with sadistic delight before death mercifully put an end to their suffering. The day of the destruction of Jerusalem, and all the dates of subsequent misfortunes of the Jewish people prior to the Nazi holocaust, pale into insignificance before that infamous Tisha B'Av, in the year 1942, which marked the start of the total annihilation of the Jewish community of Warsaw.

When the Jew experiences a happy event, he recites the benediction that is also ordained for festivals: "Blessed art Thou, O Lord our God, King of the Universe, Who hast kept us in life, preserved us, and enabled us to reach this season." Logically, this blessing should have been framed in the singular ("Who hast kept *me* in life," etc.) since, after all, it refers to happy occasions in the personal life of an individual. Instead, it is in the plural form. This is because no matter what life may bring, the Jewish individual never ceases to identify with his people. Regrettably, many, alas, too many of our brethren have not lived to reach seasons of rejoicing. But our people as such lives on, and we survive through our people.

Here we have the answer to the much-debated question whether or not one should perform *Kri'ah** when standing before the Wailing Wall in reunited Jerusalem. Though the relevance of *Kri'ah* in mourning for the destruction of the Temple is open to debate today, there can be no doubt whatsoever that this gesture of mourning is very much in order to express our grief at the catastrophe—far more shocking than even the destruction of the Temple—whose millions of victims cannot behold Jerusalem reborn. *Kri'ah* means "to tear," "to rend." Remembering the holocaust, we recall the prophet's pathetic outcry: "Rend your hearts, and not your garments" (Joel 2:13). And indeed, as I stood by the Western Wall on Tisha B'Av of 1967, I knew that our hearts were rent asunder between exultation over the rebirth of Zion and our grief over those of our brethren who had been dreaming of this glorious redemption but, alas, did not live to see it.

"Inquire, you who went up in flames . . ."

---

* The rending of one's garment, a traditional gesture of mourning for the loss of a close relative, also traditionally performed when visiting the Wailing Wall.

THE LAST DAYS OF JERUSALEM
By Samson Raphael Hirsch

LET US VENTURE A GLANCE at Jerusalem as she was in the days of the Prophets.

Jerusalem, the ancient royal city, was bright and gay, with towering palaces and stately mansions. The homes of her prominent citizens had spacious rooms with huge windows, cedar paneling and wall paintings. They also had winter chambers where open fireplaces provided the heat so welcome during the chilly month of Kislev. New moneyed classes had arisen which took pride in amassing wealth, acquiring property after property and field after field until they forced the unpropertied into the shadow of virtual non-existence. The rich surrounded themselves with luxury even in death, having taken care to provide themselves with high-vaulted rock tombs well in advance. But the wealthy Jerusalemites knew also how to live well.

The Maggid, by Chaim Gross. The Maggid (itinerant preacher) addressing an audience at a synagogue in Jerusalem's Mea Shearim quarter.

Wailing Wall and Temple Area. This drawing (1844) was used for the title pages of a number of religious texts published in Jerusalem during that period.

They arranged balls, concerts and banquets, wine parties with music supplied by harps, kettledrums and flutes; they gave luncheons, dinners and suppers, filling their days and nights with feasting and carousing at the expense of the sheep and the cattle and to the detriment of the wine-cellars, as if they knew that they would die on the morrow. They were bon-vivants, whose greatest concern each morning was to round up the best liquors, rising early lest someone else steal a march upon them in this most important business, and remaining up until late at night when the wine had inflamed them. There were social circles where spirit was defined in terms of the ability to hold one's liquor and talent in terms of the art of preparing the best punch.* Nor was there a lack of tittle-tattle, and the younger set considered it smart to pepper their conversations with obscenities.

Such were the good, solid citizens of Zion who were of a piece with their Samarian counterparts, men for whom bad times were far away, who lolled on ivory couches, stretched out upon their beds, feasted only on the choicest rams and the best calves; dilettantes who fancied themselves the equals of David because they could pluck their harps a little, who drank their wine only from the finest goblets, who anointed themselves with none but the most delicate oils, and to whom it never occurred that someday this whole structure might come crashing down about their heads. Each home had its store of gold, silver, precious stones, choice ointments and spices, and musical instruments and bibelots were considered as much a part of the furnishings of a proper household as the kitchenware. The dress and accessories of the well-turned-out gentleman included hammered silver from Tartessus, finely wrought gold, and blue and red purple robes of foreign cut, while the women adorned themselves with little bells, coifs, snoods, necklaces, bracelets, veils, headdresses, anklets, laces and brooches. The women wore rings on their fingers, in their ears and in their noses, shawls, mantelets, kerchiefs, handkerchiefs, mirrors, bangles, perfumes, girdles and eye shadow. The well-dressed lady of Jerusalem was richly anointed, bedecked with embroideries, shod in the choicest leather, clad in byssus, swathed in silks, and adorned with trinkets. There were bracelets on her hands, necklaces around her neck, nose rings, earrings in her ears, and a tiara on her head.**

No wonder the city of Zion was called "the perfection of beauty." (Jer. 2:15). But Jerusalem was also a bustling, gay and noisy metropolis. Horses, carriages, coaches, mules and dromedaries criss-crossed the city. There were beasts of burden and carriages of state, wedding dances and funeral processions, exuberant carousers, princes on horseback, and old men and women sitting in front of their dwellings, leaning on their staffs because of their age, with little boys and girls playing in the streets around them.

And in the midst of all this there was the hustle and bustle of industry. There were medicine-men, metallists, and forgers of swords, scythes, lances, knives, armors, helmets, bows and arrows; there

* Isaiah, Chapter 5
** Isaiah, Chapter 4

were breeders of cattle and horses, cartwrights and builders who reared turrets, walls, and castles; there were canal builders, launderers, calligraphers, professors of the occult sciences, carpenters with their hatchets and saws, landscape artists, farmers, wine-growers, masons with plumblines and plummets, scholars, scribes, mariners, interpreters, weavers, musicians, surveyors, goldsmiths, silversmiths, burnishers, blacksmiths, cabinetmakers, bladesmiths, sculptors, shepherds, peasants, vine-dressers, potters, bakers, butchers, chefs, tailors, cobblers, fancy-goods workers, ladies' outfitters and merchants.

Such, approximately, was the picture Jerusalem must have presented to the visitor's eye shortly before her fall.

Firmly entrenched at the head of this pleasure-loving, bustling city was a government complete with all the trappings of royalty, administration, justice, police, armed force and politics. There was a Court with princes and courtiers, palace governors and uniformed chamberlains with full-dress sashes, bearing the king's keys. There was a bureaucracy, complete with counselors of state, department heads, senators and notables, legislators, chancery counselors, clerks and scribes, statisticians, a mint, a bureau of weights and standards, officials, advisors to industry, physicists and, last but not least, prophets and orators retained by the government, who constituted the "tail" of the administrative corpus, wagging or lashing out as it pleased those at the head of the establishment. There was a judiciary system with judges, witnesses, records and clerks; a police force with executors, lock-ups, penitentiaries and prisons of every sort; a military machine with heroes, warriors, horses, chariots, engineers, fortification experts, arsenals and depots; and a foreign service with diplomats, embassies and alliances. And then there were just plain people, too, who provided subject matter for the mystery plays of Jerusalem; widows and orphans who suffered because they had been deprived of their basic human rights; debtors, victims of oppression, expropriation and poverty, and the starving masses who "when their hunger grew too strong, waxed angry, strove with their king and their God and looked to heaven above for help."

The Site of the Holy Temple. Artist's conception (1850) of the Mosque of Omar (left) and the Holy Temple (right).

213

FOR CENTURIES BEFORE THE Russian Revolution in 1917 the Jews who dwelt in the vast region that made up the Russian Empire were a vital force in the development of Jewish life the world over. Russian Jewry produced Talmudic scholars who brought their erudition to bear on the interpretation of the Law, poets and writers who revived the Hebrew language and dedicated men and women who laid the groundwork for the rebirth of the Jewish State.

For the past five decades, the Soviet Government has effectively suppressed every form of Jewish education. Any effort to disseminate or transmit Jewish values is a crime in Russia today, subject to punishment subtle or direct, depending on the whims of the authorities.

Still, it seems that no force on earth can root out from the Jews of Soviet Russia their fundamental sense of solidarity with their people in the rest of the world. This unconquerable emotion comes to the fore on the Jewish festivals and on other occasions when Jews feel the impulse to gather and demonstrate their membership in the House of Israel.

Golda Meir, Israel's first ambassador to the Soviet Union, recalls the following incident:

"On the Sabbath, we went to the Synagogue (in Moscow). The Jews did not know that we were coming, but several hundred of them had already assembled there. When they recognized me, their excitement ran high. I sat, of course, in the women's section, upstairs. The rabbi motioned to me to come down. As I made my way toward the rabbi, a red-headed Jew began jumping from bench to bench. He was hopping around and shouting, as if with his last breath: *Am Yisrael Hai! Am Yisrael Hai!** I had the feeling that he had gotten off his chest something that had been bothering him for years."

Mordehai Namir, who was once Israel's ambassador to Soviet Russia, tells the pathetic story of one *etrog* in Moscow:

One year it was utterly impossible to import *etrogim* into Russia for Sukkot. The Soviet government, of course, was none too cooperative. Chief Rabbi Shlomo Schleifer, of blessed memory, was deeply concerned over the gloomy prospect of having to celebrate Sukkot without an *etrog.* The Israeli Embassy in Moscow therefore tried to secure two or three *etrogim,* or at least one *etrog,* for the entire Jewish community of Moscow. Unfortunately, however, the plan to fly in one single *etrog* direct from Israel hit upon a snag. Mr. Namir contacted several European sources by telephone, with an urgent request to find one single "citron" for the Jews of Moscow. Some of the non-Jewish diplomats he

* "The people of Israel lives."

approached could not understand what the Jews could possibly want with a citron. The official of one European embassy curtly said: "Never even heard of such a fruit." A woman in Stockholm promptly reported that she had been lucky enough to obtain a citron, "with a whole branch of some sub-tropical tree thrown in free," but that she had found no way to dispatch it to Moscow in a hurry. Finally, one precious *etrog*, along with a *lulav,* was flown in on a Soviet plane from Prague. Thus, what would seen a simple transaction turned out to be a project of international magnitude.

The agricultural inspection of the *etrog* at the Moscow airport was another hurdle. The Israeli Embassy telephoned the authorities to release the "dry lemon" at once. "In what quantities?" the official inquired. "Only one!" was the reply. "Only one?" The voice at the other end betrayed incredulity and suspicion. Finally, on the evening following the first day of Sukkot, the *etrog* was in the possession of the Israeli Embassy. The end of the story, in Mr. Namir's own words, follows:

"When we arrived at the synagogue the next morning for morning services, we did not find Rabbi Schleifer at his customary place on the *bimah.* He was sitting in his tiny chamber adjoining the platform, alone and visibly perturbed. When we entered with the *etrog* wrapped in a newspaper, we could see that, for a moment, the rabbi was unable to believe his eyes. Then he touched the *etrog* gently, lovingly. And then he gave a deep sigh: '*Oi vei is mir*!' After a while, he calmed down a little and said: 'Now I can put on my holiday clothes and go before my congregation.'

"As he strode out of the room, the sexton told us that on the eve of the holiday and throughout the first day, the rabbi had refused to put on his Sabbath clothes and to take his seat on the *bimah* out of sorrow and shame because his congregation had had no *etrog* and had been unable to observe the precept of reciting the blessings over that hallowed symbol of the Sukkot festival.

"The news of the *etrog's* arrival spread rapidly. Soon a long line of people had formed all the way from the rear of the sanctuary to the rabbi's chamber. At first, it was all very orderly and dignified. One by one the worshippers entered, took the *etrog* tenderly in their hands, pronounced the blessings, shook the *lulav* and filed out, eyes sparkling and faces glowing. But half an hour later, it had become impossible to control the crowd. Hundreds of worshippers started pushing and elbowing their way to the rabbi's chamber to enjoy the unexpected privilege of holding and blessing the *lulav* and *etrog.* Finally, the rabbi came out into the sanctuary and, before a reverently hushed congregation, began

Six-branch candelabrum to honor the memory of the six million Jewish martyrs, designed and executed by Ludwig Y. Wolpert for Congregation Adath Israel, Cincinnati, Ohio.

215

to intone the benedictions over the *etrog*. Suddenly his voice broke. He burst into tears and many of those present wept with him.

"Several days later we saw the *etrog* again, the one and only *etrog* in Russia that year. It was black, almost as black as coal, after having been caressed by thousands of hands and kissed by thousands of reverent lips."

General Yosef Avidar, another Israeli ambassador to the Soviet Union, also has a story to tell:

"One Hanukka evening, I kindled my *menora* and placed it, as is customary, on my window sill. When I looked out to see whether it had stopped snowing, I saw an old Jew, with a long white beard, holding a small boy, probably his grandson, by the hand. Both were gazing up intently at the burning Hanukka candles. The old man and the boy stood there, as if in a trance, watching the tiny lights until they flickered out. The next night the two were there again. In fact, they came on each of the eight nights of Hanukka that year.

"Several days later, as I was getting into the embassy car, the old man with the boy suddenly appeared. After looking on all sides to make sure that no one noticed them, they quietly, stealthily, made their way to the car. The old man tenderly touched one of the small Israeli flags installed upon the fenders and then kissed his fingers, as a pious Jew might do in the synagogue after touching a Scroll of the Law. The boy did the same. Then they hurriedly left the scene, but I distinctly saw that the eyes of the old man were filled with tears."

A poignant account of Jewish holidays spent in Soviet Russia is given by Elie Wiesel in his recently published book on Soviet Jewry.* He tells of the Moscow synagogue on Yom Kippur Eve, filled with worshippers—not only elderly people, but also the middle-aged and even a good number between the ages of twenty and thirty. He describes the awe and devotion that pervaded the congregation as Rabbi Yehuda Leib Levin chanted the opening verse of the service: "Light is sown for the righteous, and gladness for the pure of heart." Forgotten was the dismal reality that held neither light nor gladness. And when the cantor intoned the stirring *Kol Nidre*, religious fervor reached the height of intensity. Soon, however, the presence of a stranger—the author—was discovered, and the worshippers cast furtive looks of fear and suspicion on the unknown newcomer. To allay their misgivings, Wiesel began to pray aloud. When the people realized that he was a fellow Jew, a visitor from abroad, they crowded around him, plying him with questions about Israel and about the Jews of America and Western Europe. As for their own situation, they were afraid to speak "because it's dangerous," they said. Finally, one Jew, obviously upset, whispered into the

* Elie Wiesel, *The Jews of Silence*, Holt, Rinehart & Winston. New York, 1966.

216

stranger's ear: "Don't say anything. Just pray. It's good to know there are young Jews who still know how to pray."

One Sukkot in Leningrad, Wiesel visited a small *sukka* into which about a hundred *hassidim* had crowded to celebrate the holiday with singing, dancing and a "banquet" of bread, fish and homemade wine. An old Jew, with typically *hassidic* ecstasy, exhorted a reluctant friend to sing. After much urging, the latter finally started a romantic Yiddish melody. He had to repeat the song again and again while the old man listened and wept. Others picked up the tune. After a while, the singing stopped. The old Jew indignantly cried out: "Why the silence? What's the matter with you? I tell you we must not give in. I order you to rejoice. I command you to create a disturbance! Well, what are you waiting for? We have a guest, a messenger from across the sea! Is this our gift to our brothers? No, I tell you, no! A song of gladness for our guest! Let him tell of the gladness in our hearts! Do you hear?"

During the modest repast that followed, the Jews began to sing louder and louder. Then, some, despite the narrow quarters, led off a lively dance and the old *hassid,* proud and jubilant, shouted to Wiesel: "Tell the Jews outside that you saw the Jews of Moscow dancing!"

Wiesel's description of the Simhat Torah festivities in Moscow is at once moving and heartening. The Great Synagogue was filled to capacity, and the worshippers, forgetting for once the sad realities of life in a godless world, were drunk with joy. But outside the Synagogue, masses of youth—some thirty thousand, Wiesel says—had assembled openly and without fear, to express their solidarity with the Jewish people and with the State of Israel. Spiritedly they sang Israeli songs and danced one hora after another until late into the night. This "festival of youth" on Simhat Torah night has become a tradition among the young generation of Jews in Moscow. These boys and girls "come to the synagogue to be among Jews, in defiance of all efforts to make of Judaism an object worthy of their hatred ... it is a sign that they wish to live as Jews—at least one evening a year."

After addressing a Jewish audience in a city deep in the interior of Russia, Yosef Tekoah, then Israel's ambassador to the Soviet Union, bade his listeners farewell with the Hebrew words *L'Shana Ha'Baa*— "Next Year!" He did not add the last part of this age-old prayerful wish—*Bi-Y'rushalayim.* But there was no need for him to say it. The audience understood and repeated the first two words with a fervor and enthusiasm that left no doubt as to the place Jerusalem still held in their hearts.

Obviously, a spark of Jewishness still glimmers in the hearts of many Russian Jews and is passed on from one generation to the next. Once again, history has demonstrated the invincibility of the Jewish spirit.

ROSH HODESH, the "Beginning of the Month," is a humble minor festival. None of the prohibitions of work or any other major precept pertaining to the major festivals apply to Rosh Hodesh. Nevertheless, we are commanded to regard it as a holiday: "Also in the day of your gladness, and in your appointed seasons, *and in your new moons, shall you blow the trumpets*" (Num. 10:10).

The Bible thus mentions Rosh Hodesh in one verse with the "appointed seasons," that is, the festivals, the days of our rejoicing.

In the days of the Temple, the first day of the month was a day of joy and gladness. At the same time, Rosh Hodesh was designated as "a day of remembrance" like Rosh HaShana, the festive, solemn beginning of the year, for, like Rosh HaShana, Rosh Hodesh is a milestone in the march of time. As such, it is to be observed by a brief pause in the course of human affairs for the purpose of introspection and self-evaluation.

In eighteen passages in the Holy Scriptures, Rosh Hodesh is referred to simply as Hodesh. The very concept of Hodesh implies *renewal*. Aside from the renewal of the moon, Rosh Hodesh also suggests the renewal of man which should take place as each new month begins.

This concept finds expression in the *Birkat Ha-Hodesh,* the "Blessing for the New Moon," recited on *Shabbat Mevarkhin,* the Sabbath preceding the beginning of a new month. As part of this ceremony, the reader, holding a Scroll of the Law in his arms, announces the one or two days during the forthcoming week on which Rosh Hodesh is to be observed. This formal announcement dates from Talmudic times.

Before the Jewish calendar was permanently fixed, the dates of each Rosh Hodesh and festival had to be determined anew each year by the Rabbinical Court in Jerusalem. The Talmud records that after having heard the testimony of witnesses to the effect that they had seen the new moon, the Rabbinical Court would proclaim: "Hallowed! Hallowed!" thus consecrating the New Moon.

Only the Rabbinical Court in Palestine had the authority to fix the date of Rosh Hodesh each month. The Jews of the diaspora had to await word from Palestine to learn the dates on which they were to observe the Holy Days. The Talmud describes the means of communication used to announce the precise time of Rosh Hodesh to the diaspora and the difficulties they entailed. In the beginning, torch signals were lit successively until, according to one description, the entire diaspora looked like one gigantic bonfire. Later apostates and dissidents, such as the Samaritans, would light signals of their own to create confusion in the Jewish communities. As a result, the torch signals were replaced by messengers sent out from Palestine to spread the word of the exact time of the *molad*; i.e. the appearance of the new moon, which marked the inception of the new month.

The hallowing of the New Moon was thus directly dependent on the existence of a Jewish community in Palestine. According to Maimonides, such a community did not necessarily have to include rabbinic authorities. In fact, he said, even if it were to consist only of vinegrowers, peasants or other simple folk, this colony in the Holy Land would be

Mosaic floor of synagogue from Talmudic times excavated in Bet Alpha, near Haifa. This, the largest of three mosaic panels, depicts the twelve signs of the Zodiac. Figures at each of the four corners depict the four seasons of the year. Picture in the center is the sunrise, represented by a youth riding a chariot drawn by four horses.

Blessing of the new moon, by Chenoch Lieberman. (From the collection of Mr. and Mrs. Seymour Propp, New York City).

qualified to consecrate the New Moon on behalf of the world Jewish community. Maimonides went so far as to state that if, God forbid, a time were ever to come when not a single Jew would dwell in the Land of Israel, all Jewish holidays would fall into desuetude and the Jewish people would disintegrate.

Although the one or two days of Rosh Hodesh today are set according to calendar calculations and are no longer dependent on official proclamation by a Rabbinic Court, the announcement of the advent of Rosh Hodesh, made at the synagogue on the preceding Sabbath, is a solemn act and is surrounded by prayers of profound emotional content. In these prayers, the Jew petitions God for long life and, in accordance with the Rabbinic law that one must present one's supplication before the Almighty in clear and specific terms, he enumerates the favors he seeks for the month to come—a life of health, peace, goodness, sustenance, wealth and honor. In addition to these material blessings, he prays also that God may endow him with spiritual qualities such as "the fear of heaven, the dread of sin . . . and love of Torah."

Though these prayers refer to the needs of the individual, they are phrased in the plural form: ("He Who performed miracles for *our* fathers and redeemed them from slavery unto freedom, may He speedily redeem *us* and gather *our exiles* from the four corners of the earth . . .") for, in fact, they are relevant to the life of the entire community.

The first paragraph of the Blessing, which epitomizes the spirit of the Jewish people and its yearning for the ultimate redemption and ingathering of exiles, ends with a solemn declaration of the unity of all of Israel: "All Israel are one fellowship" (literally, "All Israel are comrades") .

The *Birkat Ha-Hodesh* ends on a note of hope for a month of abundant bounties—again not for the individual, but for the entire commu-

The month of Adar. Woodcut from old Jewish calendar, showing Pisces, the sign of the Zodiac for the month of Adar (February-March).

The month of Sh'vat. Woodcut from old Jewish calendar, showing Aquarius, the sign of the Zodiac for the month of Sh'vat (January-February).

nity of Israel:

"May the Holy One, blessed be He, renew [the coming month] unto us and unto all His people, the House of Israel, for life and peace, for gladness and joy, for salvation and consolation, and let us say, Amen."

The Rosh Hodesh liturgy includes certain features of the Festival Service. The *Amidah*, while basically the same as that for an ordinary weekday, includes the *Yaale V'Yavo*, the Festival prayer invoking God's blessing upon the holiday, which is recited on the Three Festivals, though not on Hanukka or Purim. The *Yaale V'Yavo* prayer is included in the *Birkat Ha-Mazon* (Grace after Meals) as well. The *Shaharit* (morning) service is followed by the "Half-Hallel," an abridged version of "Hallel" (the group of psalms of praise recited on the Intermediate Days of the Three Festivals as well as on Hanukka). As on the Three Festivals, *Musaf*, the Supplementary Service, is added, in keeping with the Scriptural portion relating to the appropriate sacrifices (Num. 28:11). Should Rosh Hodesh fall on Monday or Thursday, *Tahanun*, the penitential devotions normally recited on those weekdays, are omitted, as they are on the Festivals. Finally the Rosh Hodesh liturgy includes a special Torah reading. Rosh Hodesh may thus definitely be classed with the joyous holidays.

The custom of visiting prophets or sages on Sabbaths and holidays—a practice of Biblical origin—was also observed on Rosh Hodesh. Thus, the Shunammite's husband inquires of her: "Why do you go to [the prophet] today? It is neither the *New Moon* nor the Sabbath" (II Kings 4:23). According to the Shulhan Arukh, feasts would be arranged on that day. This custom, too, had its origin in Biblical times. We read (I Samuel 2:5):

"And David said to Jonathan: Behold, tomorrow is the new moon, when I should sit with the king and eat."

Notwithstanding these joyful observances, the rejoicing of Rosh Hodesh has had a muted character, due, perhaps, to the fact that the Jewish calendar is based on the lunar cycle. On the first night of the month, the moon is not visible to the naked eye. Therefore, the New Moon is sometimes referred to as *kesse*, i.e., period of concealment (of the moon), and this spirit of reticence has come to mark the entire observance of the day. In our day Rosh Hodesh has become primarily an inner experience, marked without fanfare or spectacular manifestations.

Its greatest significance in Jewish history is that at one time it was instrumental in the establishment of the dates of the major festivals, so that it was a basic factor in the Jewish calendar.

The New Moon. In the days of the Temple, the New Moons would be fixed by the Sanhedrin on the last day of each month on the testimony of two reliable witnesses. This is an artist's conception of one of the witnesses observing the moon. Print from a 16th century Haggada, Prague.

221

Ark Canopy (Kapporet). This wooden canopy, painted in blue and gold, was made in Italy (ca. 1700). The Hebrew quotation is from Psalm 118: "Open to me the gates of righteousness; I will enter into them, I will give thanks to the Lord" (118:19). (The Jewish Museum, New York City).

THE CENTRALITY OF THE SYNAGOGUE
IN HOLIDAY CELEBRATIONS
"THE LITTLE SANCTUARY"

WHILE THE SYNAGOGUE IS the center of Jewish life throughout the year, it is much more so on the Sabbaths and holidays. On these special occasions, when the Jew is disposed to greater spirituality, the synagogue assumes a new significance, and through the synagogue, the essence of the Sabbath and of the holiday takes on real meaning and expression.

For centuries of exile, the house of prayer has served as an extra-territorial enclave for a people deprived of its physical homeland. A nation must have a measure of sovereignty. While other nations had spread their dominion over vast territories and grown into mighty empires, the Jewish people had preserved its spiritual sovereignty over the synagogue. In ancient times, the Holy Temple had symbolized not only the religious, but also the political independence of the Israelite nation; the destruction of the Temple was therefore tantamount to the fall of the Jewish State. In its place, the synagogue had served as the symbol of spiritual independence which the Jews had kept and cherished in their dispersion and which, in turn, had helped preserve the Jewish people.

As early an authority as the Prophet Ezekiel defined the synagogue as "a Little Sanctuary" (Cf. "Yet I will be to them as a little sanctuary" 11:16), and our Rabbis said: "Said the Holy One, Blessed be He, to [the Children of Israel]: 'Wherever you go, build unto Me a house where I can dwell'" (Midrash Rabba, Exodus 33). This rabbinic dictum echoes the Heavenly command: "And they shall make Me a sanctuary, and I will dwell in the midst of them" (Exodus 25:8).

Thus, the synagogue, in a national-spiritual sense, had exercised a quasi-political function. It became a citadel of Judaism, a secure shelter from alien cultural influences that posed a threat to the survival of our people. Its walls served as dikes to stem the tidal waves of assimilation that, more than once, threatened to engulf Jewish communities.

THE SYNAGOGUE—A CEMENTING POWER

EVEN IN THE THOSE JEWISH communities where Jews went to the synagogue to pray three times a day—morning, afternoon and evening—daily worship could not compare to holiday services, and daily assemblies could not rise to the height of Sabbath and festival convocations. Even the smallest congregation made a particular effort to maintain a daily *minyan* of at least ten worshippers. Jews scattered in out-of-the-way rural communities would come to the nearest town or city for the High Holy

Menora sculptured in stone inside catacombs of Bet Shearim, the site of a synagogue believed to date back to the third century C.E.

Ruins of Synagogue, Jerusalem. The synagogue of Rabbi Judah the Pious was one of the many synagogues destroyed by the Arab Legion when it occupied the Old City of Jerusalem in 1948.

Days to join their brethren in synagogue worship. Consequently, on important religious occasions, the synagogue was a center not only for its own congregation but for the surrounding rural communities as well. Today, also, whether in remote villages of Australia, or in sparsely-populated areas of South Africa, South America, the United States and Canada, the synagogue serves as the cementing force in Jewish communal life, frequently encompassing larger geographic areas where scattered settlements are too small to maintain their own houses of worship and assembly.

THE SYNAGOGUE—A HOUSE OF STUDY

THE SYNAGOGUE HAS ALWAYS served as a *Bet Hamidrash*—a House of Study. Within it, rabbis, scholars and preachers, especially on Sabbaths and holidays, have instructed the people through sermons, discourses and lectures on the Bible, Mishna, Talmud, commentaries, Jewish laws and practices. The synagogue has thus become a center of adult Jewish education, a sort of popular, informal college of Jewish studies.

In order to discharge this educational function effectively each synagogue had a library. Prayer and study were considered two interdependent aspects of Divine Service under one roof.

The attitude of the worshipper-students toward these books was one of loving reverence. A book that was accidentally dropped to the floor would be picked up gently and kissed, as if in apology for the lack of care that might have caused injury to it. Jewish law includes special regulations dealing with the proper care of sacred books.

One of the age-old, important institutions attached to the synagogue was the *Hevrat Tikun Sefarim* (Society for the Acquisition and Repair of Holy Books) whose purpose was to purchase new books and to rebind and refurbish old volumes. Naturally not every book was considered fit to be included in the synagogue library. Only those volumes qualifying as "sacred books" were permitted. Books dealing with such cognate subjects as Jewish history, or geography of Jewish communities were placed in separate sections, apart from "sacred" literature.

Prior to the invention of printing, books had to be laboriously copied by hand; accordingly, only extremely wealthy individuals could afford to buy them. In those days books for synagogue libraries would be purchased with communal funds, and remained the property of the synagogue. Since books were rare, many a synagogue held the only library in the entire town.

The hostile rulers of Europe persecuted not only the Jews but their books as well. Many synagogue libraries were burned or confiscated. On a visit to the Vatican Library, I found a number of ancient books with inscriptions indicating that they had originally belonged to synagogues in Italy and elsewhere.

224

The Talmud was the object of the most severe persecution. Several popes ordered all copies of the Talmud to be burned. Thus, in 1239, by edict of Pope Gregory IX, twenty-four wagon loads of Jewish books were publicly committed to huge bonfires in Paris. In France and Italy, monks searched Jewish homes, and especially the synagogues, for books. When the Jews were expelled from Spain in 1492, they were not permitted to take their books with them; these books were confiscated and presumably destroyed. In more recent years, we were witness to the burning not only of many synagogues, but also of vast quantities of Jewish books, by the Nazi hordes.

When, thanks to the invention of printing, books became accessible to the general population, the character of a Jewish home could be judged by the contents of its bookshelf; even poor Jews would own a

Pair of carved painted doors for the Holy Ark, from a 17th century synagogue in Poland. The Hebrew legend reads: "Strong as a leopard, swift as an eagle, [he] leaps like a deer and [is] brave as a lion." Symbols on doors include the deer, the lion and the lulav of Sukkot. (Hechal Shlomo Museum, Jerusalem).

Portable Ark. This is one of the portable Arks of the Law used at services by the Israeli Army. It bears the emblem of the Israeli Defense Forces and is marked "Military Chief Rabbinate."

modest library of *Sefarim* (sacred books). Particularly synagogues and their *Batei Midrash* (houses of study) were evaluated by their collection of books.

THE SEFER TORAH—A UNIFYING FORCE

THE OBJECT WHICH, by its presence, turns a room into a synagogue is the *Sefer Torah*, the Scroll of the Law. The presence of the Scroll in the Holy Temple invested the *Sanhedrin,* meeting within its halls, with the authority to make legal decisions.

After the destruction of the Temple, the Torah continued to serve in the same capacity—as a force welding many individuals into one congregation, and all the congregations into the *K'lal Yisrael,* the world-wide community of Israel.

It is noteworthy that under certain circumstances, the Talmud endows the Scroll of the Law with personal status. Under a ruling in Tractate *Berakhot* (47:72) nine Jews and the Holy Ark containing a Torah Scroll may, together, be considered as constituting a *minyan,* the quorum of ten adult males needed for congregational worship.

Symbolic, too, of this relationship between the Torah and Israel is the fact that the *Sh'liah Tzibur,* the individual chosen to lead the congregation in prayer, must hold the *Sefer Torah* in his arms when proclaiming the New Moon. The fixing of important calendar-dates, especially of Rosh Hodesh, was by authority of the Sanhedrin, and that authority, as pointed out previously, was derived from the people as a whole, united by the power of the Torah. This thought is expressed by the statement which immediately precedes the Rosh Hodesh declaration and which, at first glance, seems to have no connection with it, namely: *Haverim kol Yisrael v'nomar Amen,* "All Israel are united in one. fellowship, and let us say, Amen." This pronouncement publicly proclaims the source from which the Sanhedrin's authority to fix the time of Rosh Hodesh is legally derived: the entire people of Israel, united in one fellowship.

THE SYNAGOGUE AND THE LAND OF ISRAEL

THE SANCTITY OF THE synagogues emanates not only from the Temple which they had replaced, but also from the Holy Land, and particularly from Jerusalem, the Holy City. Consequently, all synagogues gravitate toward that spiritual center.

Dedicating the Holy Temple, King Solomon envisaged the centrality of the Land of Israel for Divine worship: "And they shall pray to you through their land" (I Kings 8:48). Daniel, in Babylonian captivity, also directed his prayer toward Jerusalem: "Now Daniel . . . went up unto his house where he had open windows in the upper chamber in the direction of Jerusalem; and three times every day he knelt and prayed" (David 6:11). Similarly, we read in the Talmud: "He who stands outside of the Land [of Israel] shall direct his heart toward the Land of Israel . . . he who stands in the Land of Israel, shall direct his heart toward Jerusalem. Thus, all Israel will direct their hearts toward one place" (Berakhot 30:1).

Indeed, synagogues in foreign countries were so built as to have the worshippers face the Holy Land. Maimonides rules that the windows of a synagogue should face Jerusalem (*Mishne Torah,* Laws of Prayer, Chapter 9, Halakha 6).

The prayers themselves reflect this attitude of religious reverence toward the Holy Land and the Holy City, as expressed in the *Amidah*: "Sound the great shofar for our freedom . . . and gather us from the four corners of the earth . . . And to Jerusalem, Thy City, return in mercy . . . And may our eyes behold Thy return in mercy to Zion."

Even more pronounced are Eretz Israel-oriented prayers in the liturgy of holidays, particularly in the *Musaf* service of the three major Festivals: "But on account of our sins we were exiled from our land . . . Bring our scattered ones among the nations near unto Thee, and gather our dispersed from the ends of the earth. Lead us with exultation unto Zion Thy city, and unto Jerusalem, the place of Thy sanctuary, with everlasting joy . . . Rebuild Thy house as at the beginning, and establish Thy sanctuary upon its site. Grant that we may see it in its rebuilding, and make us rejoice in its reestablishment."

Through the rebirth of the State of Israel and particularly through the recent liberation of the Holy Places, utterances from Bible, Prophets and Rabbinic literature that formerly seemed remote and unreal have suddenly sprung forth without quotation marks, passing from vision to fulfillment. For generations, we have prayed: "O raise the banner to gather our exiles . . . from the four corners of the earth" —and now, though not all our exiles from the four corners of the earth have returned to the homeland, though the Jews of Soviet Russia are still languishing in distress and captivity, though complete redemption has not yet come, the banner has indeed been raised. During the tense weeks of the early summer of 1967, followed by days of battle and triumph, the synagogue was the focal point of both shock and awakening. Similarly, on holidays and festivals, our identification with the State of Israel has found its faithful expression within the synagogue.

The celebration of Israel's independence, in the diaspora, will likewise be effectively expressed in synagogue festivities, for the synagogue is truly the heart of our collective religious and national experience.

Altneuschul, Prague. The Altneuschul (at left) is the oldest synagogue in Prague. The synagogue was probably built in the 11th century and restored sometime during the middle or late 12th century. Acccording to legend, the foundations of the synagogue were laid with stones from the Temple of Jerusalem brought by emigrants who came to Prague after the destruction of the Temple in the year 70 C.E. This legend has it that the name Altneuschul did not mean "Old New Shul" but was a corruption of the Hebrew al-tenai ("on condition that"), implying that when the Messiah should come, the building would be torn down and the foundation stones taken back to Jerusalem. The building with the clock is the Hebrew Town Hall; the dial has Hebrew letters instead of Arabic numerals.

YOM HA'ATZMAUT—ISRAEL INDEPENDENCE DAY

WITH EACH PASSING YEAR, Yom Ha'Atzmaut—Israel's Independence Day—acquires new meaning and depth. Each development in the history of the new State spreads the impact of the day and all it signifies to ever growing areas of Jewish consciousness and emotional experience. For the rebirth of the Jewish people through the State of Israel is not one single happening, but a historic process that has gone on through two decades and will continue over many years to come.

Thus a new and great glory came to Israel in the summer of 1967, when the world witnessed six days of heroic battle and victory on that spot of earth which millions call the Holy Land.

The climax of this miraculous transformation of Yom Ha'Atzmaut into something more than Independence Day was the liberation of the Old City of Jerusalem and the Western Wall. As we have "set Jerusalem above our chiefest joy" (Psalms 137:6) throughout the centuries of her desolation, so shall we now continue to place her above our greatest rejoicing also in her deliverance, particularly on Israel's Independence Day.

On Iyar 5, 5708 (May 15, 1948), the foundations were laid for Israel's independence. The tender sapling planted on that day has put forth firm roots and grown into a magnificent tree, holding promise of fruit to surpass even our fondest dreams. It is not given to mortals to foresee the results of their own works. An arrow shot from a bow may hit a mark for which it was not intended. While man must accept responsibility for all his acts and their consequences, no one can predict the effects of his deeds to their last detail with absolute certainty. Even words are beyond our control once they have slipped from our lips. Obviously, then, deeds, too, once completed, operate independently of the motives from which they sprang, to start chains of reactions that often defy every effort at prediction. This has been true particularly in the history of the Jewish people, beginning with the Biblical era and continuing through our own day, a process which, in essence, is a constant continuation and realization of earlier events, and which is controlled by the hand of God that guides the destinies of our people.

The Biblical canon has been completed but not closed. Despite suggestions to the contrary from men of little faith, both on the left and on the right, Divine revelation has not come to an end. It is from this fact of continuous revelation that Judaism derives its vitality. On Tisha B'Av, the national day of mourning that marks the anniversary of the fall of the Temple, we beseech God to "renew our days as of old" (Lamentations 5:21); that is to say, we express our hope that the glo-

Israel Independence Day Parade, 1968. Israel's leaders review Israel's twentieth anniversary parade in Jerusalem. In center of reviewing stand (wearing hat) is President Zalman Shazar; on his right is Premier Levi Eshkol; on his left is Defense Minister Moshe Dayan.

ries of our past may reappear in our none-too-cheerful present which, we pray, may in turn become the gateway to a brighter future.

Lack of faith, exile and destruction are the negative forces snipping away at the thread of our historical continuity; faith, prophetic vision and renewed independence restore the bonds that link our present, past and future in an unbroken chain.

Amidst the stress and anxiety that preceded the six days of struggle and glory in June, 1967, the Jewish people was gripped by the unspeakable fear that the restoration of the State might have been only a brief interlude of respite. But even as the abject terror that struck at the hearts of the Children of Israel in the days immediately preceding the Exodus from Egypt was the prelude of a glorious manifestation of the Divine Presence at work in the destinies of our people, so, too, the terrible anxiety we all felt in May and early June of 1967 turned out to be the herald of a revelation beyond our expectations.

This time the revelation was two-fold—it was a demonstration not only of the mighty hand of God in our history but also of man in his finest hour. The so-called "human factor" to which the world has ascribed Israel's victory over a formidable foe was the people of Israel welded together by one united will and raised to miraculous strength by God Himself at an hour of infinite grace. The Six-Day War was far more than a military operation. Israel's victory was a phenomenon not of quantity but of quality: it was not a consequence of superior armed might but the work of the best there is in man, expressed in terms of determination, selfless sacrifice, and superhuman effort, culminating in the triumph of justice. Israel's victory was a victory of the spirit, another revelation of Divine might through man, even as a prophet of another age proclaimed: "I will no longer hide My face from them, for I have poured out My spirit upon the household of Israel, said the Lord" (Ezekiel 39:29).

Our prayer "May a new light shine forth upon Zion" has been answered beyond our most cherished hopes. For the new light shone forth not only *upon* Zion, but also *from* Zion. The light that appeared in the hour of Israel's trial and triumph was not of this world, but it served to illumine the realities of the world and of human existence. It was reflected in the valor of Israel's defenders and in the faces of Israel's men, women and children, shining with confidence and dedication.

In contrast to other days of fear and trembling, when we resigned ourselves to our fate, justice in June, 1967 came forth at once to thwart the plans of the foe who had openly declared his intentions toward Israel, as the Psalmist put it thousands of years ago, "Come and let us cut them off from being a nation" (Psalms 83:5). Justice as an abstract concept is nothing but a remote ideal, an empty mirage. But in this our most recent struggle for survival, justice appeared not as a nebulous abstraction but as a concrete force, active, powerful and conquering, through the heroism of our defenders.

Maimonides wrote that "good deeds do not necessarily require good intentions." But good intentions, if they are to have meaning, require action. Prayers not rooted in reality, aspirations unproductive of action, objectives without a sound basis are as futile as a fleeting dream.

This time in the history of our people justice became a reality that brought forth strength, achievement and victory. In the wake of this reality, simple words become hymns of praise, Biblical verses cease to be metaphors and become proclamations of miracles repeated in our own day, commonplace incidents are transformed into legends and casual remarks into historical judgments. The chatter of children inspires valor and sacrifice and journalistic reports are read with the sort of reverence customarily accorded only to Scriptural texts. Prophetic utterances leap from scrolls of parchment into streets and battlefields to stir men to turn them into reality.

The greatness of the hour brought forth great events. As men, women and children stood before the hallowed wall, age-old barriers melted away, and reunited Jerusalem, the "city that is joined together" (Psalms 122:3) welded all of Israel into one indivisible community. Every individual in the land discovered a sense of close kinship not only with his brethren beside him but also with his fellow-Jews of ages past. Jerusalem, the cradle of prophecy, site of the Holy Temple, seat of the Sanhedrin, the chosen city in a chosen land, made all Israel brothers as nothing had ever quite done before.

As Jerusalem became one city again, the continuity of history, so cruelly interrupted by the sword plunged into the nation's flesh by bitter exile and enslavement, was restored. The first hour of liberation of Jerusalem in 1967 was a logical continuation of the final hour of Judah's independence before the destruction of the Temple and of Jewish nationhood in the year 70 C.E.

The heroes of Judea's resistance against Roman tyranny lost the battle, but they did not fight in vain. Now they met in spirit with the soldiers of *Tzahal,* Israel's army of defense, who had carried on the age-old struggle for freedom in the spirit of the long-departed soldiers of Judea. The defenders of our own day lived to receive the reward for their dedication and their sacrifice; they were privileged to behold the liberation of Jerusalem the Eternal and of the sacred remnant of the House of our Glory.

Israel's victory in the Six-Day War may have been swift, but it was not sudden. Its roots went deep and wide not only through the nineteen years of the reborn State, but also through two thousand years of exile made endurable by faith, longing and hope. Moments after the liberation of the Old City of Jerusalem, an Israeli soldier standing at the Western Wall said to a newspaper reporter taking notes nearby: "Write that I, Private Such and Such, have returned to this spot after two thousand years." Surely these simple words of a young soldier echoed the sentiments of the entire Jewish people on that historic day.

When the heroic defenders of Israel went forth to battle, they knew that they fought not only for the existence of the Jewish State, but, in fact, for the Jewish people. Their keen awareness of the awesome burden of responsibility they bore not only imbued them with unbelievable courage but also inspired them to prophetic vision which accompanied them on their mission to preserve their people and its heritage. They personified Ezekiel's vision of the dry bones that took on sinews, flesh and skin and rose to new life (Ezekiel 37) —the transformation of the submissive *galut* Jew into the free and proud citizen of an independent Israel. Borne on the wings of Divine promise, they were sustained by the faith of Jews of generations present and past, all over the world, who prayed each day to the Guardian of Israel to guard the remnant of Israel and not to suffer Israel to perish.

Who can put into words the thrill of the moment when, with the Psalmist of old, our feet were "standing within the gates of Jerusalem" (Psalms 133:2)? Even as, according to tradition, the feet of every Jew, from the dawn of history until the End of Days, stood at Mount Sinai at the hour of Revelation*, and even as every Jew should see himself as if he personally had gone forth from Egypt**, so, too, the entire Jewish people, the world-wide community of Israel, stood within the gates of Jerusalem in spirit together with the valiant men who had liberated the City and the Western Wall.

This hour of grace brought out the best and the noblest hidden deep within the hearts and souls of those who stood before the Wall. The *Or HaGanuz*, the "hidden light" so called because it flickers concealed within the innermost recesses of the human heart, shone forth in all its brightness and was reflected in the faces that looked up to the Wall in silent awe. We can see it in the faces of the three soldiers caught by a newsman's camera at that shining moment in the history of our people.

Thus, together with the work of the mighty hand of God, there was revealed the spiritual strength of the men of Israel, strength nurtured by the spark of the Divine that rests deep within the heart of every human being. This explains the ecstasy which moved seasoned soldiers to weep openly before the ancient symbol of the continuity of our history.

The wall of square-hewn stones which was the repository of a people's sorrows for two thousand years stands before our eyes in its full splendor. It is all ours now, and it has given us of its holiness. As Israel's Moshe Dayan declared at the Wall: "We have returned to our Holy of Holies, never to be parted from it again."

A generation seared by the flames of the Holocaust suddenly beheld a great light. The first call of the shofar, sounded at the liberated Wall, echoed throughout the world. No premeditated signal, no matter how powerful, could have traveled so far. The sound of the shofar found instantaneous response because it rose from the very heart of the Jewish people.

The blasts of the ram's horn in the day of Joshua toppled the walls of Jericho. The momentous call of another shofar from the City of David in our day has brought down other walls—the barriers which

---

* "And Moses called unto all Israel, and said unto them: '. . . You are standing this day, all of you, before the Lord your God . . . Neither with you only do I make this covenant and this oath, but with him that stands here with us this day before the Lord our God, and also with him that is not here with us this day. . . '" (Deut. 29).
** Passover *Haggadah*.

Israel Independence Day Parade, 1968. Israel celebrates its twentieth anniversary by the first parade to be held in reunited Jerusalem. (Israel Office of Information).

separated Jews from one another and the Jewish people from its Promised Land. Here was a nation, firmly united, suddenly brought face to face with its historic destiny.

Israel's triumph brought release not only to the Holy City, along with other parts of the land but also the hidden forces of immeasurable power within ourselves. These forces of inner strength will be vital in the long, hard struggle ahead, against our foes from without as well as against dangers of complacency and business-as-usual that threaten us from within. The sacred everlasting covenant between the people and its Land must be preserved and renewed continually, particularly on Yom Ha'Atzmaut, the day which marks the rebirth of Israel's nationhood.

Our recent triumph was the fruit of age-old prayer and yearning. The solemn vow "If I forget thee, O Jerusalem, let my right hand forget its cunning" (Psalms 137:5) was not an empty phrase. We repeated it over and over again and never allowed it to be forgotten. The tears of our ancestors shed over the destruction of our homeland, and the spirit of sacrifice with which thousands of young men and women gave their lives for its liberation emanate from one and the same source. Our Holy City was mourned much longer and much more deeply than any other fallen city on earth, for Jerusalem is the very heart of the Jewish people, and the heart of every Jew is in Jerusalem.

The exultation of the Jewish people at the liberation of Jerusalem derives from the fact that, throughout the centuries of his exile, the individual Jew has consistently placed Jerusalem "above his chiefest joy." Even in the hour of its greatest personal happiness, he remembers the Holy City and voices the hope that "soon there may be heard in the cities of Judah and in the streets of Jerusalem the voice of joy and gladness."*

These yearnings have not lost their relevance even now. For while our physical Jerusalem (*Yerushalayim shel Matta*) has been liberated, our spiritual Jerusalem (*Yerushalayim shel Ma'ala*) is still far off, the sublime object of our noblest aspirations.

In this sense Israel Independence Day is also Jerusalem Day, not only to celebrate the reunification of the capital of Israel but also to express our anticipation of the spiritual goal we have yet to attain.

We regard our past not only as a subject for study and remembrance, but also as a living thing, to be experienced anew, in affliction as well as in deliverance.

* Jeremiah 7:34. Recited in the Marriage Service.

Synagogue candelabrum, contemporary design, with electric bulbs, by Ludwig Y. Wolpert.

ENCOUNTERS WITH HISTORY

ENCOUNTERS WITH HISTORY are not the rare privilege of the select few. They may come to any mortal whom circumstance happens to have placed at the crossroads of history at the proper moment.

My own encounters with history were bound up with the epic struggle of the Jewish people for a land of their own. The first incident which I am about to relate took place under cruel German domination when a Jewish State seemed very far away indeed, the second occurred at the hour of decision that gave birth to the State of Israel, and the third came to pass in the days of the Ingathering of the Exiles which followed the establishment of the State.

Allow me to share these experiences with you.

I

The time was 1943; the place—the Warsaw ghetto, or, more accurately, the ruins of the ghetto. Some of us had managed to secure passports or other documents from certain South American consulates attesting that the holder was a citizen of the issuing country. I had received such a document from the Paraguayan Consul, certifying to all those whom it might concern that I was a citizen of the Republic of Paraguay. In reality, we had citizenship nowhere, yet these pieces of paper represented the one hope we had of surviving the German inferno.

And lo and behold, we soon found out that citizenship—real or pretended—in the proper country could mean a great deal at the proper time. One day the doors of Warsaw's notorious Pawiak prison swung open to release us. We were taken to the railroad station, put aboard first class coaches and transported westward across Europe to an internment camp in Vittel, France. Formerly a plush summer resort, the camp now housed British and American diplomats and other enemy aliens who had been stranded in Europe by World War II and interned during the year that followed. The treatment the Germans accorded these privileged internees was eminently fair. Despite the armed guards and barbed wire which encircled the camp, the inmates lived in the sort of luxury we had all but forgotten in the Warsaw ghetto.

"Just look what difference one little citizenship certificate can make," I remarked to a fellow-internee. "Here we are, a nation of sixteen million"—little did we know then that we were sixteen million no longer— "a nation of prophets, sages and philosophers, who have certainly made an impressive contribution to human civilization—in religion, in the arts, the sciences, philosophy. Just think how many of us are on the list of Nobel Prize winners. Yet we are hunted down like animals, marked out by the Germans for humiliation and slaughter. After all, how can we ask for human rights? There may be sixteen million of us. But we're not citizens any place—just a lot of Jews deprived of all human rights. Except, that is, for those lucky few of us who got here because some papers in our pockets say we're citizens of Paraguay.

"What's so great about Paraguay? It's a little state with a couple of million souls, mostly people who can't even read and write. And yet a little scrap of paper with a Paraguayan consulate seal on it making us citizens of Paraguay, saves our lives and makes us human beings even in the eyes of the Germans. There you see what being a citizen of a state can mean. The lesson for us Jews is that in spite of all our accomplishments, when it comes down to brass tacks, we don't even have a country of our own to protect us."

For the record, I should add that not long after this conversation we learned that the Paraguayan Government had revoked our citizenships. Eventually all the Jews who had got to Vittel—except for eleven of us, including myself, who managed to escape and go into hiding—were killed in Auschwitz. Only the true-blue Paraguayans, who could prove that they had always been citizens of Paraguay, were allowed to sit out the war, untouched, in Vittel.

II

The time: Friday afternoon, May 14, 1948. The place: Flushing Meadows, Long Island. From the press section, I listened to the General Assembly of the United Nations debate on the countless sections and paragraphs of a proposal to establish a U.N. trusteeship over Palestine after the expiration of the British Mandate. The session at Flushing Meadows had begun at four o'clock that afternoon. At six o'clock New York time it would be twelve midnight in Palestine, the hour at which the British Mandate would come to an end. It was clear to everyone that, at this hour, the Jews of Palestine would proclaim the independence of the Jewish State which had been sanctioned by a U.N. resolution less than six months before. But some of the supporters of that Jewish State had undergone a change of heart. Dr. Phillip Jessup, scholar of international law and American representative to the United Nations, employed all the legal casuistry at his command to block the creation of a Jewish State in Palestine. His aim was to force through a resolution placing Palestine under international trusteeship before the Jews there would be able to proclaim their independence.

Presiding over the Assembly was a representative from Argentina who also opposed the establishment of a Jewish State in Palestine.

Israel Independence Day. Fireworks and a military tattoo on the night of Israel Independence Day.

The speeches ran on, with diplomatic oratory flowing freely as the hands of the clock on the far wall opposite the speakers' rostrum moved ever closer to the zero hour. The delegates and observers were no longer listening to the speakers. Their eyes were on the clock. The lenses of the television and newsreel cameras, too, had made a 180-degree turn, deserting the speakers' rostrum for the clock on the wall.

Tension mounted as the big hand moved to three minutes to six . . . two minutes . . . one. . . . Finally the two hands of the clock stretched out to form one straight vertical line. It was now six o'clock in New York—and midnight in Tel Aviv.

A delegate requested the floor on a point of order. He ambled up to the rostrum. Facing the Assembly, he said: "Mr. Chairman: It was stated that six o'clock would be the deadline for a decision on the Palestine trusteeship. I wish to note officially that it is now six o'clock. . . ." With that, he left the rostrum and walked back to his seat.

The chairman turned to his left for a quick whispered conference with assistant Secretary-General Andrew Cordier. Then he continued the proceedings of the Assembly. But no one was listening to speeches any more. The Assembly was buzzing with excitement. All those in the hall felt that they had come to a crossroad in history. On the rostrum, Dr. Jessup of the United States still droned on, interpreting some fine point of the law in support of his argument for U.N. trusteeship over Palestine. Had *Eretz Yisrael* been freed from the dominion of one nation only to be subjected to the rule of a whole array of other nations?

Suddenly there was a stir in the hall. I. L. Kenen, of the Jewish Agency, had come in. He seemed out of breath. He rushed up to the section where the Jewish representatives sat, and whispered something to Dr. Abba Hillel Silver and Barnett Janner, a prominent Anglo-Jewish leader and member of the British Parliament who was then visiting New York. The American rabbi and the Jewish leader from overseas seemed unable to believe what they had just heard. "It can't be . . .!" they stammered. I left my seat in the press section and dashed out into the corridor. I sensed that the news was there, rather than in the Assembly hall. I was not disappointed. The corridors had come alive with unbelievable news. At 6:11 P.M., New York time, exactly eleven minutes after the proclamation of the State of Israel had gone into effect, President Harry S. Truman, overriding the objections of his own Department of State, had extended the recognition of the United States of America to the new-born Jewish State!

When I returned to the Assembly chamber, Jessup was still on the rostrum, grinding out his empty legalisms on the trusteeship proposal. But the hour of destiny had come and history had been made, not in the Assembly hall at Flushing Meadows, but in the auditorium of a museum in Tel Aviv. The dream of two thousand years had come true. The Jewish people had a land to call their own again—the State of Israel, and with the blessings of the mightiest land on earth—the United States of America.

III

"And I bore you upon the wings of eagles, and I brought you nigh unto Me" (Exodus 19:4). On that May afternoon in 1945 when British and American tanks rolled into the death camps of Bergen-Belsen and Buchenwald, the survivors of unspeakable horror had fallen upon their liberators with kisses and tears of joy. Throughout years of torture they had been sustained by the hope that, if only they would manage to sur-

vive until the end of the war, the victorious Allies would take pity upon them and open wide the gates of Palestine to receive them and give them peace at last.

Back in the Warsaw ghetto, we had heard some distburbing reports. There had been rumors about two boats named "Struma" and "Patria" crammed full with Jewish refugees whom the British were supposed to have turned back from the very shores of Palestine, leaving the passengers to die in the Mediterranean Sea. We had refused to believe those stories. But when the war was over at last, we discovered that this was the bitter truth. Instead of helping rescue the remnants of European Jewry left from the German slaughter, the British had declared war on the helpless men, women and children whom they had labeled as "illegal immigrants" because they had attempted to find a haven in the one land where brothers and sisters had been waiting to receive them.

In 1947 I was working with *Aliya Bet,* the "illegal immigration" apparatus. One dark night, at the pier of Port Du Bouc, a small fishing village in the south of France, I watched a group of "illegals" board the decrepit hulk that was to become famous as the "Exodus," braving the British Mediterranean fleet which was waiting to drive the refugees away. I studied the faces of this "contraband" human cargo that was about to board the *Exodus* 1947. I saw neither fear nor despair in their eyes—only steely resolution and purpose.

I remembered all this two years later, after the British had departed and the State of Israel was born. The week that I myself set sail from Marseilles, over three thousand immigrants arrived in Israel aboard the *Negba, Kedma* and *Transylvania.*

The year that followed, I stood at Lydda Airport watching planes land in close order, discharging hundreds of immigrants from Yemen and other lands in the Orient. To these our brethren, who had never seen an airplane before, much less flown in one, the Biblical promise of the "wings of eagles" had come true in a very real sense. I stood there, entranced, watching the passengers, dressed in their colorful native garb and laden with their few belongings, leave the plane and set their feet on the soil of Israel. Were they thinking of what their fathers had told them of the far-off land which they had now been given to behold with their own eyes? I, for one, could recall only the despair of the Warsaw Ghetto, the worthless promises of Paraguay, the departure of the *Exodus* 1947 from Port Du Bouc, and the historic moment when the leader of a great nation, ignoring the dictates of political expediency, recognized the right of a long-martyred people to a home of its own.

Such were my three encounters with history as it happened.